THE NEW ORLEANS OF GEORGE WASHINGTON CABLE

THE NEW ORLEANS

OF

GEORGE WASHINGTON CABLE

THE 1887 CENSUS OFFICE REPORT

EDITED, WITH AN INTRODUCTION, BY

LAWRENCE N. POWELL

Louisiana State University Press
Baton Rouge

Published by Louisiana State University Press
Copyright © 2008 by Louisiana State University Press
All rights reserved
Manufactured in the United States of America

An LSU Press Paperback Original
First printing

DESIGNER: Michelle A. Neustrom
TYPEFACE: Century Schoolbook
PRINTER AND BINDER: Thomson-Shore, Inc.

LIBRARY OF CONGRESS CATALOGING-IN-PUBLICATION DATA:

Cable, George Washington, 1844–1925.
  The New Orleans of George Washington Cable : the 1887 Census Office report /
edited, with an introduction, by Lawrence N. Powell.
    p. cm.
  Originally written as a special section of the 1880 U.S. Census titled Social statistics of cities; subsequently revised as Creoles of Louisiana, the original text has
never appeared in print again except as a facsimile reprint; it is published here
in its entirety for the first time, including Cable's footnotes and other material
deleted from the census publication by its editors.
  ISBN 978-0-8071-3319-4 (paper : alk. paper) 1. New Orleans (La.)—History.
2. New Orleans (La.)—Description and travel. 3. New Orleans (La.)—Social conditions. 4. Creoles—Louisiana—New Orleans—History 5. French—Louisiana—
New Orleans—History. 6. Spaniards—Louisiana—New Orleans—History. I.
Cable, George Washington, 1844–1925. Creoles of Louisiana. II. United States.
Census Office. III. Title.
  F379.N557C225 2008
  976.3'35—dc22

                                                            2007040391

In memoriam
Steve Powell

CONTENTS

MAPS

THE NEW ORLEANS OF GEORGE WASHINGTON CABLE

INTRODUCTION

A Novelist Turns Historian

It isn't often novelists change their politics while writing history. Most fiction writers mine the past to reinforce their preconceptions. George Washington Cable (1844–1925) may be a rare exception. He approached history writing as seriously as he did writing romance, maybe because historical narrative afforded him greater scope for expressing his newfound reform creed. The importance that Cable assigned to studying the past comes across clearly in this "Historical Sketch" of pre–Civil War (but mainly colonial) New Orleans he wrote for a special section of the 1880 U.S. Census titled *Social Statistics of Cities.* Although subsequently revised as *Creoles of Louisiana,* the original text has never appeared in print again except as a facsimile reprint. It is published here in its entirety for the first time, including Cable's copious footnotes and other material deleted from the census publication by its editors.

Cable was already an overnight literary sensation by the time he undertook this project. By then northern critics had begun comparing him to Nathaniel Hawthorne and Bret Harte. Soon Mark Twain, whom Cable once entertained in his Garden District home, would invite him to team up on a successful lecture tour in which Cable would often emerge as the audience favorite. Cable's rise to prominence owed mainly to his short story collection, *Old Creole Days* (1879), and to two novels—*The Grandissimes* (1880), his masterpiece, and *Madame Delphine* (1881). Those books, which had been serialized in the country's best highbrow magazines, largely depicted the clash between American newcomers and a quaint but prideful French-speaking population in post–Louisiana Purchase New Orleans.

Cable wrote in the local-color style then in vogue, painting vivid word pictures of a French Quarter in luxuriant decay. His ear for Creole dialect, black and white, was almost musical. (He could

The author would like to thank Caryn Cossé Bell, Emily Clark, Steven Hahn, Patrick Maney, Wilbur Meneray, Clarence L. Mohr, Berndt Ostendorf, Jesse Poesch, and Rebecca Scott for their helpful suggestions. Of course, I alone bear responsibility for any errors of judgment and fact that remain.

transcribe birdsong.) His was the kind of fiction that used to be read aloud to family members in Victorian parlors or wielded as guidebooks by tourists beguiled by Cable's descriptions of darkened courtyards perfumed with night-blooming jasmine. To him belongs the credit for popularizing New Orleans's exoticism among northern audiences.[1] Yet Cable's early fiction comprised more than picturesque romanticism. His novels and short stories also contained a strain of politicized realism born of a deepening aversion to the racial injustices of his hometown, where a white supremacist coup d'état in 1877 had overthrown the Reconstruction government. Cable's best fiction derives its power and poignancy from that tension between romance and realism.[2]

Cable initially read history to find raw material for his evocative stories. But because his fiction was essentially political (he once said that *The Grandissimes,* recognized as an allegory for Reconstruction, was "as truly a political work as it has ever been called"),[3] he also sought guidance from the past. He studied it to make sense of the controversies swirling around him and to clarify his own values in relation to those conflicts.

Everything was then in flux, including his personal politics. The devastation of war and tumults of Reconstruction had brought to the surface a raft of social and economic problems too glaring to ignore: the feebleness of the city's civic culture; its hedonism and provincialism; the lethargy of the local economy and the medievalism of its sanitation; and, now, despite the sudden emancipation of four million slaves and amendments to the U.S. Constitution declaring them equal before the law, the stubborn persistence of the racial caste system. From this latter problem—the blight of slavery and the heritage of white supremacy—stemmed everything else. That was the lesson Cable derived from reading and reflecting on local history.

Perhaps he would have arrived at this understanding without delving into the past, but not with the same clarity and conviction. By 1885, with the publication of his article "The Freedmen's Case in Equity" in *The Century* magazine, Cable had drifted far from the racial pieties of his time and place. Appearing at a moment when it was still unclear whether federal intervention in southern affairs had truly ended, the essay was the most forthright defense of black civil and political rights ever penned by a nineteenth-century white southerner.

Cable's controversial article, which challenged the Compromise of 1877's goal of giving white southerners sole custody of African American rights, made him a pariah throughout the region but especially in his hometown. Many of his traducers blamed his startling racial heterodoxy on his northern roots, principally his mother's New England background by way of Indiana, where her parents had moved in 1807. The argument is a glass half empty, however. His father, also named after George Washington, hailed from Virginia, where Cables had lived for generations. George senior moved to New Orleans in 1837. By the time George junior, the fifth of six children, was born, seven years later, his father had accumulated a modest fortune and several household slaves thanks to fortunate steamboat investments.

In pre–Civil War New Orleans fortunes were as quickly lost as won, and by the time of his death in 1859 from chronic diarrhea, George senior had been forced to sell off most of the family's assets and find employment in the uncompleted U.S. Customs House on Canal Street, where his namesake son now had to stamp boxes to support his financially strapped family. Despite her northern birth, Cable's mother remained loyal to the Confederacy when the war came. In 1863 she even accepted banishment to Mississippi rather than sign the oath of allegiance required by New Orleans's Union occupiers. Cable accompanied his family into exile, eventually joining a Confederate cavalry unit. In the saddle he must have resembled a jockey more than a burly cavalryman; at five feet five he weighed slightly more than a hundred pounds. "Great Heavens, Abe Lincoln told the truth—we *are* robbing the cradle and the grave," exclaimed one planter who encountered the former clerk during a cavalry raid. But Cable was intrepid in battle and suffered two nasty wounds, one through the chest and armpit, to prove it.[4]

His critics were on stronger ground when they underscored his religiosity, which he had absorbed from his staunchly Presbyterian mother. You don't have to read far in Cable's early fiction to realize he was a Puritan in Babylon—a sensuous Puritan, to paraphrase literary historian Louis Rubin—one of many writers who found the city's seductive charms simultaneously attractive and repellent.[5] Antebellum New Orleans was a great theater town, equally famed for potation and pleasure. Cable resisted its hedonism. He never drank or smoked, and until late in life, for religious reasons, he refused to attend a staged drama. It was rare for him to miss a prayer meeting, rarer still to find him working or traveling on Sunday.

Mark Twain, during their spectacularly successful lecture tour in the 1880s, confessed to liking Cable but loathing his faith. "In him and his person I have learned to hate all religions," he wrote half in jest to fellow novelist William Dean Howells. "He has taught me to abhor and detest the Sabbath-day and hunt up new and troublesome ways to dishonor it."[6] There was more to Cable's piety than punctiliousness, however. It also thrummed with a fierce determination to live life according to the Sermon on the Mount and make the world a better place. Even his fiction was written with uplift in mind. Cable was convinced that people, if informed and appealed to with reasonableness and logic, would ultimately abandon irrational prejudices and narrow self-interest for the broader arena of progress and fair play. That faith led him to posit the existence of a "Silent South" that he believed, almost to the end of his days, would eventually repudiate the ugly apartheid arising around him.

Cable became a reformer almost from the moment he became a writer. Before pursuing either calling he worked as a bookkeeper for a cotton firm. Accounting was a skill he picked up after his father's death forced him to leave school at age fifteen and become the family breadwinner. After the war he found work surveying rail routes in southwest Louisiana, but a bout with malaria sent him back to the counting room in 1868. Ever since boyhood he had been itching to write. The *New Orleans Picayune* gave him the opportunity in 1870, and he penned a series of occasional columns on literature and local matters.

His stint as a journalist lasted less than two years. It was alleged that the *Picayune* let him go when he refused to review a play. The real explanation is that he wasn't cut out for daily reporting. "I was naturally and emphatically unfit for the work of gathering up and throwing down heterogeneous armloads of daily news," he wrote later. "I wanted to be always writing, and they wanted me to be always reporting."[7] Cable's eighteen months with the *Picayune* showed that he wanted to be always reforming as well. Increasingly his "Drop Shot" columns protested political corruption, filthy streets, and public lethargy. Even after Cable returned to the cotton business, the *Picayune* called on him occasionally to write editorials scourging the privately owned Louisiana State Lottery Company, which had won its lucrative monopoly by lavishing state legislators with bribes.[8]

It is probably not surprising Cable's reform leanings eventually dragged him down unconventional pathways. He had a cast of mind that wanted proof, demanded facts, expected logic. He dismissed as unworthy any argument appealing to instinct. There was an almost Euclidean elegance to his retreat from proslavery teachings. Cable had enlisted in the Confederacy convinced of the constitutional right of secession, but if his postwar reminiscences are to be believed, he was profoundly shaken by assertions in the southern press that the sword had settled the issue once and for all. How could might make right? He couldn't fathom the casual renunciation of a principle for which he had fought and hundreds of thousands of fellow Confederates had wasted their lives. He dove into constitutional history.

Studious by temperament, Cable sifted every word, weighed every sentence. He came away with an answer that seemed obvious. The war wasn't about secession at all, but about slavery; therefore, the rebellion was right only if slavery was right. So he interrogated that subject, turning to the Bible, in particular Paul's epistle to Philemon concerning the return of the latter's runaway slave, Onesimus. He had heard many sermons based on Paul's epistle, but only from the proslavery side. An article in a Scottish magazine exposed a different side, emphasizing Paul's urging Philemon to receive Onesimus no longer as a servant but as a "brother beloved." Cable studied the competing sermons, together with the epistle, wrestled with the meaning, and concluded that the biblical defense of slavery was sheer sophistry. Once the iron logic of principle had demolished that cornerstone of prewar philosophy, the edifice of Cable's inherited belief crumbled to the ground. It must have been nearly rubble when the *Picayune* asked Cable, while still on its payroll, to report on the annual examinations in the city's racially mixed public schools.

From 1870 to 1875 about one-third of the city's schools were integrated, a record unmatched anywhere else in the country, let alone the Reconstruction South. Though Cable had earlier written a snide article on an integrated meeting of the city's teachers, he was beginning to view his world through different eyes. The examination period surprised him as much as his account of it displeased his employer. His epiphany merits quoting at length: "In pursuance of this duty I saw, to my great and rapid edification, white ladies teaching Negro boys; colored women showing the graces and dignity of mental and moral refinement, ladies in everything save society's credentials; children and youth of both races standing in the same classes and giving each other peaceable, friendly, effective competition; and black classes, with black teachers, pushing intelligently up into the intricacies of high-school mathematics."[9]

It is a measure of Cable's tough-mindedness that his ethical transformation occurred even as he fraternized with the city's young elite, most of whom were moving down a different political path. Several of his closest associates—top physicians, rising lawyers, leading editors, clerks on the cusp of commercial prominence—would soon become activists in the Crescent City White League, the silk-stocking movement that toppled Reconstruction in the name of racial purity. Cable had gotten to know them through his clerkship in a leading cotton firm, as well as through his part-time work as secretary to the New Orleans Cotton Exchange, then the country's major cotton spot market. Shared literary interests drew them together. After the war they formed a debating society.

There were tense moments during their nightly meetings. Cable's anger rose at discussions of the South's "black peasantry." "There is no room in America for a peasantry," he retorted. He chafed at self-complacent rhetoric about "masterly inactivity," the euphemism regional leaders used for their boycott of Republican government. To Cable that meant, "in plain English, to withhold the co-operation of society's best wealth, intelligence, and power from all attempts to re-establish order and safety on the basis of the amended Constitution. . . ." Even in the cotton office of his employer, William Black, whom he revered for his sagacity, sound judgment, and public virtue, Cable had to practice self-restraint. "I'll have you understand this is a Democratic counting room, sir!" Black used to erupt when Cable reasoned him into a political cul-de-sac. The young secretary could only bite his tongue, grab his hat, and walk out of the office nursing indignation.[10]

But what leaps out about Cable's odyssey toward a new politics was its grounding in history. Those nightly debating society meetings, held on the second floor of the Price-Current building, home of the business journal that took the pulse of the southern economy, were often spent reading and discussing George Bancroft's monumental *History of the United States.* What his fellow discussants took away from Bancroft's spread-eagle patriotism Cable never said, but he himself absorbed, by his own admission, "good political ethics; and I was fast growing ashamed of my [former] political attitude."[11]

By the summer of 1872, while still employed by the *Picayune,* Cable had become fully immersed in Louisiana's colonial past. "I have read a great deal since last May," he wrote his mother. "I had to be posted in State & City history."[12] He had also taken to jotting down observations of characters and scenes encountered on the street for later use in his fiction. But he probably spent more time in the city archives and newspaper morgues poring over leather-bound volumes of musty journalism, especially during the summer, when the port slowed to a standstill. Soon he was writing fictional sketches based on his historical findings. His choice of subjects says as much about his evolving politics as his literary development.

Early on, Cable became fascinated by the liminal world of New Orleans's francophone free people of color, its near-white *gens de couleur libre,* or, in the misleading argot of that day, its quadroon caste, whose debasement at the hands of a society enthralled by one-drop notions of racial identity dramatized in Cable's mind the basic unfairness of *de jure* discrimination. And he was equally revolted at the brutalities he found codified in the early *Code Noir,* the French laws of slavery, which had been adapted for Louisiana from the slave code of its more prosperous sister colony, Saint Domingue. The code's legalized barbarism inspired Cable to fictionalize the real-life story of the African prince who was marooned for years in the back swamp of eastern New Orleans after his hand was amputated for insubordination. Beginning as an unpublished short story, the saga of Bras Coupé eventually became the centerpiece of *The Grandissimes.*[13]

By 1875 Cable's mining of local history had not only exposed a literary vein he would quarry for years to come; it brought into the open his fundamental dissent from local mores. That year, when it had become obvious that Reconstruction in Louisiana was hanging by a thin thread and racial hysteria had won over even so-called moderate Democrats, Cable published a letter in the New Orleans *Bulletin* criticizing the mob of high school hooligans who forcibly resegregated a racially mixed girls' school on Royal Street in the French Quarter. Edited by Page Baker, the brother of Marion Baker, one of Cable's closest confidants, the Bulletin was the chief propaganda organ of the Crescent City White League. Baker published the letter along with a preface condemning Cable's endorsement of "unnatural hybridity." Cable dropped the matter when neither the *Bulletin* nor the *Picayune* ran his rejoinder.

Another decade would elapse before he enunciated his new racial creed in "The Freedmen's Case in Equity," when he was on the verge of relocating his family permanently to Northampton, Massachusetts. By then he had apparently assimilated, perhaps unwittingly, the political vocabulary of the Afro-Creoles whose tragedies he was beginning to fictionalize with great feeling and insight. His spirited defense of the "*public* rights" of American blacks evoked an artful concept introduced into the Louisiana Constitution of 1868 by the intellectual vanguard of the Afro-Creole community, itself the product of a transatlantic movement of people, commerce, and ideas connecting America's most Caribbean society with the wider world of French revolutionary republicanism. That vanguard had fused a concept imported directly from France with a strain of northern "emancipationism" to try to skirt the bugbear of "social equality." The concept turned up in the third plank of the 1872 National Republican platform, which pledged to defend by appropriate legislation "the enjoyment of all civil, political, and *public rights*" throughout the Union (emphasis added), which appeared again in the 1876 platform. Its insertion into Louisiana's radical constitution of 1868, however, marked the first open accommodations law in the American South, affirming in positive law every person's untrammeled right to enter private establishments that were public in nature. Cable accepted those premises unquestioningly. As he later explained, "the day must come when the Negro must share and enjoy in common with the white race the whole scale of *public* rights and advantages provided under the American government; that *public* society must be reconstructed on this basis; and that the Negro must come under this process. . . ."[14]

II

If historical research and reflection had prompted Cable's political change of heart, still needing explanation is why he wrote a history of pre–Civil War New Orleans. He was hardly the first nineteenth-century fiction writer to plunder local lore for stories and ambience. Nathaniel Hawthorne, Cable's literary role model, also set his morally charged stories in a hazy past drenched in social atmosphere and mined his historical surroundings for literary ore. Yet Hawthorne never melded them into a published history. Nor did Washington Irving, unless one wishes to count his burlesqued chronicle of the New York Knickerbockers. (Irving did write subsequently about Columbus and George Washington as well as the conquest of Granada.)

Then there are the wealthy amateurs, patricians all—George Bancroft, William Prescott, and Francis Parkman—who stumbled into writing romantic history almost as a literary afterthought and never looked back.[15] Cable always returned to fiction, even as he stepped up his advocacy journalism and plunged into reform causes. So why did he alone among nineteenth-century novelists decide to write a book-length history of the place in which he set most of his fiction? A partial answer is he needed the money. In the early 1880s he had a growing family, and he wanted badly to quit his day jobs in the cotton firm and as secretary to the Cotton Exchange for full-time writing. Yet the income generated by his work for the Census Office never justified the time Cable devoted to this project. Nor were his northern publishers happy that he was abandoning fiction for history. Clearly, other motives drove him to write a history of pre–Civil War New Orleans.

Chief among them was a desire to show white Creoles that his fiction was more than fabulation, that he had read widely and thought deeply about their history, especially the colonial period, which to his mind held the key to understanding this distinctive people.[16] Cable had probably caught wind of the grumbling in the Vieux Carré provoked by *Old Creole Days,* a murmuring that grew noticeably louder after the 1880 publication of *The Grandissimes.* Knowing what he did about Creole resentment of unbidden intrusions into their private affairs, he couldn't have been too surprised by the reception his short stories and new novel were receiving in downtown quarters.[17] By then prominent white Creoles were beginning to charge Cable with stabbing them in the back for money and cheap notoriety. They accused him of caricaturing their broken English—their "Gumbo French"— mocking their folkways, and lampooning their get-up-and-go. Cable's barely concealed Puritan self-righteousness had a familiar ring. Anglo-American transplants to their city had been characterizing them as slothful and backward for years.

Cable's most unpardonable sin, however, was his frank treatment of the Creole community's mixed origins. Many of the light-skinned free people of color in Cable's stories were hard to distinguish from the white fathers who had often bequeathed them substantial amounts of property, usually by admitting they were their natural children.[18] It was another American slander—this notion that the native-born Gallic population had been "touched by the tar brush," a phrase still heard in modern-day New Orleans—

and it rankled white Creoles as nothing else could. By 1882 Cable had become, in the words of an artist-illustrator sent to New Orleans by Cable's publisher, the "the most cordially hated little man" in the entire city.[19] But as yet the hatred was mostly confined to downtown areas where the francophone population tended to cluster. The first gust of white Creole animosity blew in with an anonymous pamphlet published in December 1880, while Cable was working on his census history. It came from Adrien-Emmanuel Rouquette, a Catholic priest and nature poet whom Cable had once praised. The attack was so extreme—Rouquette in one place calling him "an unnatural southern growth, a bastard sprout"— that Cable's publishers, fearing for his safety, suggested he move North.[20] More blasts came in 1883 from the pen of the aging Creole playwright Placide Canonge, who used the opportunity of an obituary of chess great and New Orleans native Paul Morphy to shower abuse on the author of *The Grandissimes*. But it wasn't until the January 1885 publication of "The Freedmen's Case in Equity" that the gathering tempest broke over Cable's head. The fiercest pelting came from the septuagenarian Charles Gayarré, the Creole community's foremost historian and writer. An attack from that source was just the kind of controversy Cable no doubt hoped to preempt by writing a history of the city.

Cable knew that he was swimming against powerful cultural currents. His treatment of the history and habits of New Orleans Creoles, black and white, came at a culminating moment in the development of this fascinating community. For three-quarters of a century dating back to the Louisiana Purchase, the *ancienne population,* as the white Creoles identified themselves, had been locked in bitter conflict with aggressive Anglo-American newcomers for political and economic dominance. At its zenith the fight for mastery was nothing less than "a struggle for the soul of Louisiana," to quote Joseph Tregle.[21] Reinforced by repeated waves of French-speaking exiles fleeing revolutionary upheavals in France and Saint Domingue, white Creoles tried to prolong their hegemony by gerrymandering the legislative districts and restricting suffrage.

They used their majorities on the city council and their hammerlock on the mayor's office to choke off street-paving and wharf-building funds above Canal Street, where the Anglophone transplants were building an American city and a world-class cotton port. Why would any sane person "improve suburbs while 'the bosom of the city' withered and decayed?" they asked incredulously.[22] In

1825, the American-Creole rivalry might have erupted in armed conflict between the state's ethnically divided militia but for the intervention of the Marquise de Lafayette, the vastly popular hero of the American Revolution then touring the country. Thereafter intermittent duels kept the ethnic factions constantly on edge.

An uneasy truce finally took hold after 1836 when the state legislature, then domiciled in New Orleans, divided the city into three quasi-autonomous municipalities. The arrangement gave the American faction control of its mushrooming tax base. The newcomers started building an American city and a major banking industry (the country's third largest in 1837). They erected hotels and constructed new wharves and warehouses. They dug the New Basin Canal to compete with the Creoles' Carondelet (or Old Basin) Canal for control of the lake trade. By 1852, after railroad developers succeeded in having the municipalities consolidated in order to repair the city's terrible credit rating, the assessed value of property above Canal Street was more than twice that of the two downtown municipalities combined.[23] City hall now moved out of the Cabildo and across Canal Street into Gallier Hall in Lafayette Square, which had been the seat of government of the now defunct uptown municipality. In 1857, the triumphant Americans asserted control over Mardi Gras by establishing the first carnival krewe, the Mystick Krewe of Comus, which paraded on Mardi Gras evening, the most sacred period of the carnival calendar. Comus's founders were neither Catholic nor francophone. They were, almost to a man, Anglo-American residents of the city's newest high-toned neighborhood, the Garden District.[24]

The white Creoles' response to the decline of their community ranged between acquiescence and despair. A high rate of intermarriage between Americans and Creoles smoothed the path toward assimilation in both directions. So did the pull of profit. Ambitious Creoles gravitated to where money was changing hands the fastest, which was in cotton and uptown real estate.[25]

There was a spirited Creole effort to resuscitate the decaying French Quarter, thanks to the generosity of Baroness Micaela Pontalba, now resident in Paris, who used her vast inheritance to refurbish the center of the Vieux Carré in the late 1840s and 1850s, restoring the cathedral and its bookend buildings, the Cabildo and Presbytere, that her father, Baron Almonester, had constructed with his own funds during Spanish rule. She also financed the flanking apartment-storehouses (so named because of the commercial establishments on the ground floor) that still bear her name. The city chipped in by turning the Place d'Armes, the old parade ground that had become a campsite for drunks and derelicts, into a French formal garden, renaming it Jackson Square. It was all for naught. Business continued to move out of the Quarter into the American sector. Even among native-born French speakers English was beginning to supplant French.[26]

The despair became acute among Creole intellectuals who came of age in the 1830s and 1840s, just when the Americans were consolidating their hegemony—men like Gayarré, the playwright-editor-impresario Canonge, the priest-poet Rouquette, the writer John Casmir Delavigne (another Cable critic in the 1880s), and the distinguished linguist and education reformer Alexander Dimitry.[27] By the 1850s they were feeling like exiles twice over. First the Americans had elbowed them aside in the commercial sphere, and now multitudes of German and Irish immigrants were overtaking the Creole parts of town, including the French Quarter. Despite the anti-Catholicism of the national American party, some Creoles even joined the nativist organization because of its opposition to Irish influence in local politics.[28]

Several Creole intellectuals quixotically viewed the breakup of the Union as an opportunity to reverse antebellum trends. During and shortly after the war they established French language journals to return Louisiana to its original estate as a Gallic community in heart, mind, and soul. But the collapse of the Confederacy and the advent of radical Reconstruction, which prohibited the use of French in the schools and made English the official language (Americanizing pressures that the white Creole majority had been able to fend off during the early post–Louisiana Purchase period), not only further diluted Gallic identity but threatened their status as white men, blurring in law as well as fact the already fuzzy line demarcating them from their Afro-Creole relatives.

The response of men like Canonge and Gayarré, ironically, merely underscored how far they had been Americanized. To burnish their Caucasian credentials, they took refuge in a Gallic variant of Lost Cause romanticism, confecting a myth of Creole nobility and racial purity. Much of this reactionary project hinged on the meaning of *Creole*. It would be hard to exaggerate the energy expended on proving the term was a noun exclusive to native-born white descendants of French and Spanish settlers, but merely an adjective for all others, particularly Louisianans of African descent.

There could be creole blacks but never Creoles who happened to be black.

This was argument from anachronism. The Portugese- and Spanish-derived term actually originated in colonial Latin America as a way of differentiating bond people imported directly from Africa from those born in the Americas. The term became politicized in antebellum Louisiana, as more and more of the Louisiana-born francophone population self-identified as Creole in order to build solidarity in the face of the Anglo-American onslaught. But the term was casually applied to all French-speaking native Louisianans regardless of race, just as it had been to Creoles of Saint Domingue and Cuba. As long as most black people remained enslaved, this lexical inclusiveness posed little threat to white status. As Virginia Dominguez, an especially close student of the subject, explains, "The term had always been used to signify local birth and foreign parentage."[29]

All that changed during Reconstruction, when white Creole intellectuals launched their struggle to prove the gentility of their lineage and the whiteness of their nomenclature. They were encouraged by the climate of opinion. Due to imperialistic adventures abroad, scientific racism was gaining in respectability. The high court lent sanction to hardening segregation at home with its 1896 separate-but-equal ruling in *Plessy v. Ferguson*. By the dawn of the twentieth century white Creoles had succeeded in books, lectures, and journals in winning popular acceptance for their redefinition of Creole as something inherent in the properties of blood. Scores of encyclopedias and dictionaries attested to the completeness of this racial-linguistic achievement.[30]

Charles Gayarré was at the forefront of this rearguard movement. And his conflict with Cable was pivotal in the crystallization of the Creole myth. As he himself admitted, "Everyone seemed to think that I was the only one who could couch a lance against the champion of Africa and the idol of the North."[31] It is true he was the most obvious candidate to joust with Cable. Grandson of Étienne de Boré (former New Orleans mayor and generally considered the father of the Louisiana sugar industry) and great-grandson of an official who arrived with the first Spanish administration in 1766, Gayarré commanded more visibility than any white Creole still living. "To Louisianians, indeed, it seemed that Gayarré was not only the historian of Louisiana but the history of it as well," wrote novelist Grace King.[32]

His relatives encompassed the community's crème de la crème: the Grimas and the Marignys, the Forstalls and the Dimitrys. Baroness Pontalba was a friend. George Bancroft and the Charleston novelist and poet William Gilmore Simms praised his published writings. There was another reason besides his great stature that made Gayarré the Creole choice for answering Cable. His declining personal fortunes seem to symbolize the fate of the *ancienne population* at large. Their fall had been pretty steep. Before the war, even while his community was losing ground to pushy Americans, Gayarré had attained real distinction in politics and letters. He had gone to Philadelphia in the 1820s to study law, learn English, and groom himself to fill the vacuum in Creole leadership created by the success of better-educated American newcomers back home. In 1830, shortly after returning to New Orleans, he was elected as a Jacksonian Democrat to the Louisiana legislature by almost unanimous vote; the following year the Whig governor, a Creole like himself, named him as judge of the city court. He lost an 1834 bid for a congressional seat but was elected by the legislature to the U.S. Senate the following year.

Then began a theme in Gayarré's life that remains cloaked in mystery. An undiagnosed chronic illness contracted in childhood flared up. (One biographer speculates it may have been manic depression, which may account for the mood swings between despair and grandiosity so evident in his correspondence.) Gayarré resigned his Senate seat and moved to Paris for eight years to convalesce and consult French physicians. But he plunged back into politics upon his return to Louisiana in 1844, returning twice to the state legislature before the governor appointed him secretary of state, a position he used to build the State Library.

Throughout his long life—he lived to age ninety—Gayarré was constantly running for office or seeking some federal appointment, regarding himself more as a politician than as a man of letters. But posterity remembers Judge Gayarré mainly for his writing, which comprised seven volumes of history, two novels, a couple of dramas, and a slew of pamphlets and magazine articles. His four-volume *History of Louisiana*—constructed partly from archival material he gathered during his European convalescence but mostly drawn from material copied and collected, by other researchers, from repositories in Paris, Seville, and Madrid—was the major achievement of his life.

All these attainments began unraveling after Fort Sumter. He and his wife, the wealthy widow of a New Orleans cotton merchant, invested heavily in Confederate bonds and were left nearly destitute. In the postwar years his law practice floundered, and his occasional contributions to local papers barely yielded pin money. His novels, whose production and printing costs he had to finance personally, were commercial failures. He frittered away more of his wife's inheritance in a feckless speculation in upriver timber property. In 1873 he ran for Congress as a Democrat and lost. Despite his contempt for "the rule of ignorant and filthy negroes," he accepted a court reporter's appointment to the Republican-dominated state supreme court.

Meanwhile, to keep the wolves from the door, Gayarré began liquidating land and personal property, including fancy parlor furniture brought back from France. Soon his library and paintings went on the auction block, along with a prized dagger. His house north of Lake Pontchartrain was sold for less than he hoped. In the late 1870s, Gayarré and his wife moved back to the city. But the relocation did little to alleviate their financial distress.[33]

So desperate had Gayarré's circumstance become that he turned down an invitation to stand for a seat in the 1879 constitutional convention that had been called to overturn the 1868 Radical Reconstruction—era charter, as he wrote a friend, he would be unable to act conscientiously in that body without antagonizing the monied interests. "This would not suit me," he confessed, "inasmuch as those monied men invite me to come to the Garden District and establish under my special supervision a tip top Parisian institution to teach French, and French *only,* to their girls. . . ." There was one hitch. He needed money to set up the school, and he didn't have it. By now the subject of finances was literally consuming Gayarré's life.[34]

It certainly colored his relationship with Cable, which ranged from complicated to duplicitous. At the start of Cable's writing career, the two men developed a cordial relationship, serving together on the board of the Louisiana Historical Association. The young American used to invite the aging Creole to his home to meet out-of-state authors and critics.[35] Gayarré once solicited the American's advice concerning an early installment of a work in progress titled "Blacks of Louisiana." "The subject grows and expands under my pen more than I had intended at first," he wrote, and he planned to expand it into a book-length history of the black Louisianans reaching to the present time aimed at the African

American reading public. "It might be a textbook in their schools. And why not, since it is our constitutional duty . . . to educate them?"[36]

That writing project never went beyond a series of pedestrian articles in the New Orleans Times-Democrat. The Boston publisher Cable had recommended declined to publish Gayarré's novel unless he covered the production costs. The aging Creole demurred, saying he had to return to New Orleans "to ascertain if I could possibly rake up that sum from the impoverished gutters of our beggarly city."[37]

Gayarré's declining fortunes and personal disappointments darkened his mood about everything—his involvement in public affairs, his literary career, the intellectual torpor of his hometown. "Poor Louisiana! Poor New Orleans! Poor insensate population fit only for Bedlam! The curse of God is upon this benighted and rotten community."[38] He considered emigrating to the North or West and writing dime-store books for money. "Well! I could write trash too."[39] Professional jealousy came naturally to Gayarré. Envy was the worm in his apple. Even as he solicited Cable's advice and assistance, he grumbled about the younger man's national success. A rejection letter from a Baltimore publisher saying his manuscript possessed "rare merit" elicited this outburst: "What a satire on American taste and appreciation! A book said to be of 'rare merit' cannot be published, whilst Cable's galimatias under the patronage of Scribner's deluges the land, and is set above Washington Irving's Addisonian works. Ah! Poor South!"[40]

Still, he confined his criticism of Cable to a few indirect swipes in newspaper articles, which included a backhanded suggestion that Cable had borrowed from his history without attribution (on which, more shortly), and a gossip column intimating an anonymous expert (probably Gayarré) had questioned Cable's historical veracity in a conversation with a visiting northern publisher. Mainly, the aging Creole shared his festering resentments with other Creole intellectuals, who had been urging him for years to take the offensive against the uptown defamer of Creole character and customs.[41]

Glowing coverage in the national media of Cable's entertaining rendition of Creole songs and dialect before crowded northern audiences in the fall and winter of 1884–85 brought the Creoles' simmering anger to the boiling point. Still, Gayarré balked at going after the younger author until *The Century* magazine published Cable's "The Freedmen's Case in Equity" in January 1885. Gayarré offered an anguished explanation for his decision to go public with his complaints. It concerned "private feelings of a sacred character," specifically, burning indignation at Cable's alleged assertion that he had gotten inspiration for his Creole stories from the recently deceased Alexander Dimitry. The implication that the great linguist, a Creole among Creoles, had inspired stories of Creole race-mixing, was more than Gayarré could abide. He was haunted by memories of his last meeting with the nearly blind Dimitry. From his deathbed the linguist lunged for Gayarré, asking, "Charley, is that you?" He scanned Gayarré's forehead with his forefinger, pleading, "Charley, don't forget me!" "Well, I did not forget!" Gayarré wrote Dimitry's son.[42] In his own mind Gayarré's public assault on Cable was a down payment on this deeply felt obligation.

The deathbed scene certainly illuminates the inner turmoil that vivified Gayarré's criticisms of Cable, but it is actually more telling of the exaggerated romanticism to which the old Creole was often prone. There is simply no evidence Cable ever claimed Alexander Dimitry had inspired his stories, only that the linguist had furnished him the "Dirge of St. Malo," a song about a slave insurrectionist that Cable later refashioned into his Bras Coupé character.[43] The more skeptical explanation for Gayarré's decision to break his silence was a hesitancy to go public as long as Cable remained popular in the American part of town.

Nothing Cable had published prior to "The Freedmen's Case in Equity" had appreciably lessened that charmed immunity. The anglophone newspapers still lavished praise on his fiction. They continued to write local-boy-makes-good articles about his reception on the national scene. Lafcadio Hearn, whom Cable befriended after the young Bohemian expatriated to New Orleans, championed him with almost missionary zeal. Once he impulsively read out loud portions of Cable's fiction to female friends who refused to open one of his books, and brought them to tears.[44]

As recently as May 1884 Cable had lectured to a large Crescent City hall "filled with probably the most cultivated audience ever assembled in New Orleans (few Creoles attended)," singing Creole songs and reading excerpts from *The Grandissimes* and other stories.[45] Attacking Cable while his stock remained so high in the American sector would likely be seen as Creole sour grapes, reinforcing the smugness Gayarré and others found so maddening.

With the publication of "The Freedmen's Case in Equity," however, Cable's immunity evaporated overnight. "Your *Century* article has been read and criticized and misconstrued and misunderstood terrifically," Cable's close friend and lawyer wrote immediately after receiving a copy. "You have alienated the affections of many of your friends and done no good that can yet be seen." Worse, he added, "you have given Gayarré and others the opportunity of attacking you where you can't defend yourself."[46] Cable's sin is that he had opened up a battleground on which white New Orleanians regardless of ethnicity could stake out a common identity based on putative racial purity.

Gayarré had already pounced by the time Cable's lawyer friend had made known his misgivings. The *Times-Democrat,* heretofore Cable's chief literary backer in town, had invited the old Creole to attack. The paper was now edited by the same Page Baker who had used the *New Orleans Bulletin* to stir up the armed mobs that overthrew Reconstruction and incited the teenage hooligans that disrupted the integrated girls' school on Royal Street.[47]

Gayarré discharged his first volleys in the Sunday editions of the *Times-Democrat* on January 11 and 18, 1885, following up with a fusillade of formal lectures on January 24, March 8, and April 25. The January talk (delivered in "the most florid French")[48] was at the behest of the Athenée Louisianais, an organization established after the Civil War for the revitalization of French culture in the state, and took place in the Union Française Hall. The March event, presided over by the Creole general, P. G. T. Beauregard, was organized by eighteen Creole ladies eager to improve Gayarré's finances. The climax was his April performance at Tulane University, in the heart of the American city. Pulling from the earlier articles and lectures, the talk was a sustained assault on *The Grandissimes.*[49] The unremitting barrage was a huge personal triumph for Gayarré. Editorialists from around the region proclaimed him "The Champion of the South." The poet Paul Hamilton Hayne, who shared Gayarré's yearning for the chivalric values of the hierarchical Old South, wrote to him that only men of Gayarré's "exalted social, & intellectual position should vindicate the character of the People" against internal traitors.[50]

The most gratifying reception, however, came from the Creole audiences who packed his Athenée Louisianais lectures. He described for John Dimitry, the linguist's son, the atmosphere at the second talk. The description evokes an aura of collective catharsis:

The large room was crowded with ladies and gentlemen. There never was a greater triumph. It is declared by everybody present that no speech ever produced such an excitement in New Orleans. I was continually interrupted by a whirlwind of applause of such duration that it became embarrassing. Men and women, say the newspapers, showed the most vociferous enthusiasm. Tears ran down more than one cheek! An extraordinary fact! I made twice a slight allusion to Cable without naming his name. Good God! I wish the poor fellow had heard the howling of the tempest which arose! It seems that, ever since, my address has not ceased to be the subject of conversation in every club and every household. I never have been so astonished. Alas! Much admiration and no bread![51]

Actually, Gayarré's bold attack did improve his finances, thanks to a three-year lecture series organized by a "Ladies Association" devoted to helping him escape genteel poverty.[52] Cable's friend Marion Baker was less than charitable about "the old fool & beggar. He charges you [Cable] with making money by your picture of the Creoles, & he goes whining around getting women to get up entertainments for him—Creole women, whom he poses before in the light of a knight who has slain the offender."[53]

Baker's scorn is easy to understand. Gayarré's performance was an unedifying spectacle from first to last. "He advanced no new argument," writes Cable scholar Arlin Turner of Gayarré's attacks, "but he set the tone which later writers were to imitate."[54] That tone modulated between abuse and silliness. The aging Creole lashed out at Cable's "predatory excursions into the domain of fiction." He accused him of being "completely ignorant" of Creole society. He called Cable a "romancing libeler" and a "literary dime speculator," adding he had a depraved intellect.[55] Gayarré's tenor didn't change in private conversations. "I also had a very interesting, and I must say, amusing interview with Judge Gayarré," an executive with *The Century* magazine wrote Cable shortly after the judge had delivered a lecture in French attacking the veracity of Cable's stories. "If his talk to me could be considered a sample [of his lecture], I think it must have been rather more entertaining than instructive."[56]

Gayarré's diatribe against Cable made one lasting contribution, but it was not to history. It was to linguistic politics; more than anyone else, the old Creole shifted the very meaning of the term *Creole*. Gayarré's lectures and pamphlets laid the foundation for a Creole myth that still hangs on in some quarters: that they sprouted from noble seed, had lived in aristocratic refinement, spoke perfect French, and, most of all, descended from pureblooded Europeans. The term Creole signified unsullied white ancestry, not, as Cable would have it, the strains of many races. This latter point Gayarré could not emphasize enough. In his Tulane address he affirmed it early and often, thirty times in less than an hour: "From the very beginning to the late war of secession, the strongest line of demarcation—I may say an impassable one—was kept up between what may be called these two halves of the population," white and colored.[57] The statement was not merely false; it was dishonest. Many people in the audience probably knew that Gayarré had fathered a child in 1825 with a free woman of color; the boy's baptism is even documented in the records of St. Louis Cathedral. Whether he maintained contact with his son (probably the Charles Gayarré listed in city directories after 1854 as a clerk, a salesman, and a cabinet-maker) is impossible to say.[58]

In his zeal to revive his flagging fortunes and furnish his community with an emotionally satisfying past, Gayarré forgot that he had once been a historian and opted for propaganda. He failed to note that Cable, for all of his deepening commitment to racial equality, actually accepted the *pur sang* definition of Creolism. Gayarré even revised himself on the rebellion of 1768. In his published history Gayarré had characterized the anti-Spanish instigators as firebrands; now he hailed them as heroes and martyrs.[59] It was a sad capstone to a distinguished career.

There was an alternative, however. Cable was wrong to have attributed the tragic history of Louisiana race relations to the misdeeds of the *ancienne population*. The conversion of the Creole three-caste system into the racial binary of the Anglo South came mainly from American, not Creole, pressure. It was the newcomers who were most uncomfortable with the liberties and attainments of the city's francophone free people of color. Their relatively superior status (the vast majority were artisans and tradesmen) defied the logic of race elsewhere in the South, where free blacks were legally closer to being slaves without masters.

The history of antebellum race relations is a largely unbroken record of efforts to reduce their condition to something closer to bondage than freedom. That same history was repeated in Louisiana within a framework of American-Creole rivalry. Gayarré had to have been familiar with the stubborn effort by an increasingly American-controlled legislature to strip Afro-Creoles of their rights. Some of his own relatives, such as Bernard de Marigny, who had an older half-sister of color, had publicly resisted the American onslaught, even advocating on the floor of the 1845 constitutional convention the right to vote for *hommes de couleur libre*. White Creole resistance to the Americanization of Louisiana race relations shouldn't be romanticized or exaggerated. It was never all that strong, and it completely collapsed as the racial hysteria driving the disunion movement reached its zenith in the 1850s. This is when the Louisiana legislature abrogated the charters of Afro-Creole schools and associations and even passed a law inviting free blacks to find themselves a master.[60]

Even so, Gayarré could have drawn on this history to come back at Cable with a tu quoque, "you're another," riposte, emphasizing the complicity of English-speaking whites in each assault against people of color. He could have added more depth and complexity to the racial tragedy that Cable intrepidly addressed. But that course would have obliged the elderly judge to concede the complicated racial heritage of his own people, with all its boundary-crossings, concealed grandmothers, and semi-acknowledged sons. It would have spoiled the rapprochement between Creoles and Americans made possible by an intensifying white supremacy.

By the end of the nineteenth century Creole and American judges and lawmakers alike were vigorously policing the racial boundaries of Louisiana with a one-drop rigor unimaginable at the time of the Louisiana Purchase.[61]

III

The likelihood of Creole attacks on his credibility must have been weighing on Cable's mind when he accepted an invitation to write a history of New Orleans for the Tenth U.S. Census. An internationally renowned agricultural and sanitary engineer, George E. Waring Jr., made the offer after reading *Old Creole Days* during a train trip from the Northeast to New Orleans in early 1880. Waring was in the midst of compiling the first in-depth study of American urban areas ever undertaken by the federal government. Appearing as the two-volume supplement *Report on the Social Statistics of Cities,* the 1880 study covered hundreds of major towns and cities across the country. Each report followed a standard format. First came a "historical sketch" of the municipalities, followed by statistical and descriptive surveys on subjects ranging from streets to sanitation. The historical overviews were usually brief. Waring sent Cable a copy of the overview prepared for Boston to use as a guide. "It is not asked, nor is it desired (varied conditions requiring varied treatment) that this paper be followed as an exact model," Waring wrote, "but it is especially important that I should receive a somewhat similar sketch of the history of each of our cities."[62] Cable honored Waring's wishes, and then some. Instead of a historical sketch, he sent him 313 pages of meticulously documented history. Cable's footnotes alone numbered in the hundreds—647, to be exact.[63]

Cable used sources in three languages—English, French, and Spanish. He drew on early maps, official surveys, travel accounts, medical journals, sanitation reports, city ordinances, American State Papers, city directories, and the New Orleans-based *DeBow's Review*—a treasure trove of history, journalism, and useful statistics. But mostly he relied on published histories: the ones written before the Louisiana Purchase by Antoine Simon Le Page du Pratz, François-Benjamin Dumont de Montigny, and Pierre-François-Xavier de Charlevoix and those authored during the antebellum period, principally the two-volume history by François-Xavier Martin and the various contributions of Charles Gayarré, notably his four-volume *History of Louisiana* (1851–1866). A revered judge in the Crescent City, Martin had written the first history of colonial and territorial Louisiana based on a careful study of documents (though he failed to cite them). Cable used his work extensively. But he drew even more heavily—much more so—on Gayarré's work. In the handwritten manuscript, Cable never disguised his debt to Gayarré, acknowledging in the text where he introduced Don Estevan Gayarré, the first comptroller of Spanish Louisiana: "The last named was the grandfather [actually, great-grandfather] of the historian of Louisiana, whose laborious researches among the archives of the state, destroyed during the late war [the American Civil War], and among those of the French and Spanish governments at Paris and Madrid, are repeatedly taken advantage of in the present pages."[64]

Cable's reliance on Gayarré for the French and Spanish periods is hard to miss. He followed Gayarré on just about every major point. His evidence for the deplorable conditions under French rule came from the Creole writer. He shared Gayarré's critical assess-

ment of the Creole merchants who were jailed and executed for re-
belling against the Spanish takeover. And like Gayarré, Cable believed the colony's transfer to American control was a major stride
for a backward and lethargic community. Indeed, almost nothing
Cable wrote in disparagement of conditions before the Louisiana
Purchase had not already been adumbrated in Gayarré's volumes.
Their most notable disagreement concerned the administration of
Marquise de Vaudreuil, famed, along with his extravagant wife,
for turning New Orleans into a Paris in the Swamps. Gayarré
wrote approvingly about Vaudreuil's tenure; Cable, the diehard
Puritan, dismissed it as frivolous.[65]

Although Cable generally followed Gayarré's storyline and
privileged his interpretations, he didn't slavishly accept his opinions. The younger man offered fresh takes on old subjects. His
insights were original, his judgments, keen. You won't find anything in Gayarré, as you do in Cable, regarding the importance of
a deep civic tradition of "reciprocal justice and natural rights" to
the successful workings of democracy. Nor does Gayarré dwell on
the evils of slavery and racial caste as Cable does. Although the
two men covered the same ground and agreed on many matters,
their philosophies of history could not have been more different.
That philosophical gulf influenced how they handled documents,
sculpted their narratives, sourced their evidence. It explains the
liberties each took, or refused to take, with the historical record.

Unlike Cable, Gayarré was, to quote one student of his scholarship, "essentially a romanticist."[66] His early literary influences
were Sir Walter Scott and James Fenimore Cooper, along with
Lord Byron. Gayarré admired French and Spanish romantic historians, as well as George Bancroft, the latter for his success at
balancing a career in politics and letters. Gayarré's romantic temperament explains why his history was mostly about personalities
(many of them larger-than-life), politics, and grand events, with
hardly any attention paid to social and economic questions. And it
also explains why, in his early histories, he was unable to decide
whether he wanted to write fact or fiction.[67] He frequently split
the difference by promiscuously mixing the two together. Gayarré
invented scenes and changed names.

In one place, without any likeness to draw from, he painted a
vivid portrait of an early Louisiana governor. His description of
de Soto's arrival on the banks of the Mississippi could have been
lifted from the pages of the Leatherstocking Tales, with the armor-

clad Spaniard crashing through the forest to the cadence of blaring music as Indians lurked in the brush. "What materials for romance!" Gayarré gushed. "Here is chivalry, with all its glittering pomp, its soul-stirring aspirations, in full march, with its iron heels and gilded spurs, toward the unknown and hitherto unexplored soil of Louisiana."[68] One historian calculated that about two-thirds of the first volume of Gayarré's *History of Louisiana* is "rhetoric, fabrication, or digression." Those faults diminished in subsequent volumes, especially volume 3, which covered the period of Spanish domination, widely regarded as his finest work.[69] But Gayarré never mastered the art of sustained analysis. One suspects that the discipline of marshaling and weighing evidence wasn't nearly as interesting to him as letting fancy fly.

Nor did Gayarré learn how to handle documents. He had labored mightily to retrieve them, hauling back from Europe some of the archival materials on which his histories were based. The experience made him "a worshipper of documents," like some neophyte graduate student who can't resist displaying his footnotes. Large blocks of original documents—edicts, ordinances, decrees, letters, executive orders—he quoted ad infinitum, and he went into excruciating detail about matters of slight importance. His methodology was largely cut-and-paste. It imparted a lumpy, almost misshapen feel to his volumes. Even Gayarré's principal biographer has to admit, "He began writing history almost casually, and he seems never to have subjected his work to any very profound analysis."[70]

As much as he worshiped documents, Gayarré was slapdash about citing them. When he did reference sources, page numbers were guesswork. His use of quotations was equally slipshod. (He failed to quote accurately until page 582 of volume 3 of the *History of Louisiana*.) More egregious was Gayarré's cavalier way of using the work of other writers, dropping quotation marks here, failing to attribute there. In reality his first foray into writing history was a gloss on François-Xavier Martin, whose findings he simply restated in more flowery prose. Gayarré continued to draw from Martin in subsequent volumes, mostly without acknowledgment. This sort of petty larceny was prevalent among nineteenth-century romantic historians. Bancroft himself fell into the practice. Gayarré hardly thought twice about following his example.[71]

Gayarré's approach to the practice of history would scarcely merit extended treatment had the aging Creole not assailed Cable's integrity. It happened two years before Gayarré launched his frontal assault against Cable, during an 1883 controversy in the pages of the *Times-Democrat* with a descendant of General James Wilkinson. In an article in *The Century* Cable had accused the former commanding general of the American army of conspiring with Spanish officials prior to the Louisiana Purchase. When the late general's kinsman objected, Cable invoked Gayarré as his authority, drawing the Creole historian into the fray. Gayarré wasn't satisfied with censuring Wilkinson; he also took a swipe at Cable: "Why wait, before taking offense, until Mr. Cable had copied my statements and republished them as his own?"[72]

Gayarré's biographer, and others, too, have uncritically accepted the charge of plagiarism the older Creole lodged against Cable. The accusation clearly cut Cable to the quick. He thought he had been extraordinarily scrupulous about acknowledging the sources he drew on. To Marion Baker, his close friend and editorial page editor of the *Times-Democrat,* he sent the manuscript page where he had praised Gayarré's contributions to the history of the state, and asked him to show it to the aging Creole, that he might "indicate in some subordinate and incidental way that I am not reproached by him as making unjust use of his writing. . . ." Cable added for good measure: "The MS of my original census report is positively loaded with footnote references to authorities in which no other name appears so often as that of 'Gayarré'; but the government editor left all that out as unnecessary, simply charging me to retain them for use in the event of future controversy." The restored footnotes in the text published here bear out his debt to Gayarré.[73]

Their contrast in styles didn't begin or end with footnote usage. Cable wrote with great compression, squeezing into a few hundred pages what Gayarré took two thousand pages to cover. Cable was uninterested in romanticizing the past. He studied it in order to illuminate the present and clarify his evolving politics. That orientation often compelled him to put economic and social questions front and center and think about them analytically. It was an approach that had little use for Gayarré's grandiose prose and digressive panegyrics. Gayarré is generally ranked among the best state historians who wrote during the nineteenth-century; some place him only a notch below George Bancroft and Francis Parkman, the giants of that period. John Spencer Bassett even declared, "As an historian he was among our best; for to the capacity of research and clear composition he added the faculty of graceful expression in a degree which few of our historians have equaled. . . . The South has had no other historian to whom nature was so generous of gifts."[74] That may have been so, but Gayarré seems more alien to the modern temperament than Cable, probably because the historian's history is often more novelistic than that of the novelist.

Despite Cable's ability to abridge large blocks of information, the manuscript he finally submitted threw George Waring into a quandary. The "historical sketch" of New Orleans was almost three times longer than the Boston essay he sent Cable to use as a model. Indeed, it was more than twice as long as the comparable treatment of New York City, four times the length of the Baltimore overview, and nearly eight times the length of the history of Chicago.[75] Though impressed with the quality of Cable's manuscript, Waring realized it had to be pruned, probably substantially. He found the going tough, however. "I started in with the intention of slaughtering it severely," he wrote Cable in July 1881, but was able to lop off only ten or so pages after reading to page 179, and cutting even that amount, he confessed, "has been against my will and my judgment." A few weeks later Waring was reduced to penciling out a word here, a phrase there, writing to Cable, "Your work is first-rate. I like it better and better as I get on with it."[76]

A crisis arose after the manuscript was in press. The Census Office pressured Waring to slash the New Orleans section, and the engineer wrote Cable sheepishly asking if he minded cutting his history by half. By this time, Cable had arranged with his commercial publisher, Century, to serialize parts of a revised history in its magazine and bring out the entirety as a book, which doubtless took the sting out of Waring's request.[77] As it finally happened, the Census Office relented, for reasons Waring never divulged, and published everything Cable had submitted save the fourteen handwritten pages previously excised by Waring. The footnotes, however, didn't survive the final cut. Nor, as we've seen, did that portion of the text where Cable acknowledged his great debt to Gayarré's history.[78]

For Gayarré it hardly mattered that the footnotes had been left out of the published history. Their presence wouldn't have dissuaded him from attacking Cable once the novelist's racial treason made him a convenient regional target. The controversy was less about facts and rational argument than racial anxiety. His closest friends warned that he was swimming against powerful currents of unreason, "because," as Cable's lawyer, W. W. Ellsworth, explained, "when southern people get their prejudices aroused they will not listen patiently any more than they will discuss calmly." Ellsworth himself epitomized the strength of those prejudices. African Americans should be imprisoned in even greater proportions than presently was the case, he lectured Cable. "It seems to me so patent that the negroes are lacking in moral sense."[79]

The supreme irony is that few if any of Cable's New Orleans critics bothered to read his history except for the vastly abridged version that appeared in the *Encyclopedia Britannica.* Perhaps they were offended by the local advertising blitz launched by his publisher, which printed fifteen thousand circulars and posters asking "WHO ARE THE CREOLES?" "If we can get one Creole out of twenty anxious to find out who he is and convinced that the Century will tell him, we shall have done good work," one of his publishers wrote.[80] Cable was bemused by the neglect. "It is odd that although this work has never been out of print a day," he wrote in a posthumously published autobiographical essay, "not one of the writers who have accused me of slandering the Creoles has considered, either in the government report or in the expanded volume, this, my only effort or pretense at a full and historical treatment of the subject."[81]

It is unlikely they would have felt more kindly toward Cable had they taken the time to read his gloss on their history. The *ancienne population* who people Cable's history as opposed to his fiction are not very appealing. In his "Historical Sketch" they come across as even more vain and boastful, more ambitious but unfocused. They act first and think later. Little they do is considered. Their bravery is impulse. In Cable's novels and short stories these foibles are sugarcoated with human charm. Not so in his history. Creoles were unprepared for self-government; they lacked all conception of reciprocal rights and obligations.[82] Tropical slavery killed their ambition, too: "A soil of unlimited fertility, instead of being an inducement to industry, became, through the institution slavery, merely a perpetual assurance of plenty, and, with a luxurious and enervating climate, debased even the Gallic love of pleasure to an unambitious apathy and an unrestrained sensuality" (p. 55 of the present edition). The city's francophone free people of color also lose much of their allure when Cable transfers them to the pages of history. Cable thought they were a drag on the city's development. Waring tried to soften Cable's tone by blue-penciling out the novelist's most biting aspersions, but he could hardly eliminate all of them. Doing so would have left gaping holes in the manuscript. Postbellum New Orleans's slow decline in comparison with competing cities such as Chicago and St. Louis was a subject that vexed Cable quite a bit. He had no doubt the baleful legacy of slavery was a major cause for retarding economic growth. But his close reading of the Creole past also convinced him that the mores of its original French-speaking inhabitants, black and white, also checked the city's prosperity. There is a sense in which Cable's history of New Orleans deserves to be read alongside other important New South critiques. The only difference between his commentary and that of, say, Henry Grady, besides Cable's jettisoning of Grady's commitment to white supremacy, is that the New Orleans novelist filtered his critique through the prism of the Creole past.

Around the time the personal attacks against him were escalating, Cable decided to relocate his family to Northampton, Massachusetts. His wife's poor health was one motive for leaving. Painful memories associated with the yellow fever death of his first-born son were another. Still, the vilification had to have weighed heavily in his decision. Cable could abide the newspaper rants. "It isn't pleasant to be hated," he said, "though I dare say it is safer than praise." But he worried about how the hate-filled abuse unleashed by the publication of "The Freedmen's Case in Equity" might affect his family. Shortly after it appeared, Cable's Eighth Street home in the Garden District was vandalized.[83] Meanwhile, the pull of the North was growing stronger. "Huzzah! I cross into New England in a little while," he wrote his wife a year earlier during a lecture tour train stop. "The South makes me sick, the West makes me tired, the East makes me glad. It is the intellectual treasury of the United States. Here is cultivation & refinement & taste."[84]

However true that may have been, the change of intellectual scenery didn't help his novels. Cable's fiction depended on the way New Orleans's special ambience heightened his conflicted feelings toward the voluptuous decay that suffused his stories. Once removed from those direct influences his fiction turned preachy and prosaic.[85] He had been heading toward didacticism even before moving North and plunging more deeply into reform causes. Almost single-handedly he had led the movement for prison reform in New Orleans—visiting northern prisons and asylums, organizing and directing a Board of Prison and Asylum Commissioners, and using the national platform made possible by his recent literary fame to publicize the abuses of convict leasing then prevalent in the South—all this while keeping up with a demanding writing schedule. After settling in Northampton, Massachusetts, he organized an Open Letter Club to help the "silent South" find its backbone—but it didn't. He formed Home-Culture Clubs "for the educational and social culture of working men and women." It was simply impossible for Cable to remain idle in the face of public ills he thought remediable by pen and principle.[86] But his good works hindered the production of good fiction. Cable's prison-reform novel, *Dr. Sevier,* was not of the same quality as *Old Creole Days* and *The Grandissimes.* As the reformer in him trumped his literary instincts, his relations with Lafcadio Hearn began to cool. Hearn, admittedly a difficult personality, started complaining about the churchlike sanctimony that marred even Cable's better fiction.[87]

In later years Cable made several visits to New Orleans, usually to conduct research, but once by invitation to deliver a lecture. His reception was usually cool but polite. During one trip back to his hometown not long before his death in 1925, however, he was warmly embraced by Grace King, the American novelist who had become a champion of both Charles Gayarré and the Creole myth that he more than anyone had helped to confect. She recounted the incident for the *Boston Transcript:*

> I understand him now. I would say he wrote too clearly about the Creoles. He wanted to read something of his at a meeting of our Historical Club. Some of the members objected, but we finally made arrangements. He captured the audience. Everybody rushed up and shook hands with him. Many of us never dreamed the day would come when we would shake hands with Cable. He told us a little story of a Confederate who served in the war and was wounded. It was beautifully written and really the most compelling little incident I have ever heard. The hall was packed. When he finished everybody stood up, and I never heard such applause. I am glad at last he got that compliment from New Orleans. He deserved it, not only as a tribute to his genius, but as compensation for the way we had treated him. I am glad. He is an old man, very picturesque, very sad, with beautiful manners.[88]

However, few Creoles were in the audience. Their antipathy to Cable remained strong even after his death and after they themselves were beginning to become submerged in the white American majority.

Though Cable never complained, it is obvious that the regret of cultural exile lingered with him always. "I felt that I belonged still, peculiarly to the South," he wrote, a feeling shared by other southern expatriates to the North in these years.[89] But Cable's loss to the region was far greater than theirs. He was the first major southern novelist to write with clarity and courage about race. Louis Rubin sums up his legacy best: "What William Faulkner, Thomas Wolfe, Robert Penn Warren, and the other writers of the twentieth-century South made into literary art of national and even international importance, George Washington Cable had, however imperfectly, first sketched."[90] It remains to say that Cable's moral acuity owes importantly to his historical turn, and the validation it furnished to the reformist convictions forged in the crucible of Reconstruction's fiery racial politics.

Except for minor modifications to punctuation to accord with modern American printing conventions, the addition of the accent to "Gayarre" and correction of that on "Mirò" (to "Miró") throughout, and the silent correction of a few inconsistent spellings, the 1887 Census Office text of Cable's "Historical Sketch" is presented here verbatim. Some maps in the Census Office report are not included here. Passages from Cable's manuscript that were omitted from the census publication are restored in italic. While some foreign phrases are in italic in the Census Office document, it can otherwise be assumed that italics indicate passages restored from Cable's manuscript. Cable's citations, which were in the form of footnotes in his manuscript, have here been converted to endnotes and edited for clarity and consistency; full citations for Cable's abbreviated references are provided in the bibliography. Footnotes in the text are mine, as are bracketed insertions (including the chapter numbers) except where otherwise noted.

NOTES

1. Lafcadio Hearn, "Cable's Creole Romances," in *Critical Essays on George W. Cable,* ed. Arlin Turner (Boston: Hall, 1980), 53–62. S. Frederick Starr more or less makes this claim for Lafcadio Hearn, but Hearn's early mentor on New Orleans was Cable. See Starr's insightful introduction to his edition, *Inventing New Orleans: Writings of Lafcadio Hearn* (Jackson: University Press of Mississippi, 2001). Also see Daniel Usner, "Between Creoles and Yankees: The Discursive Representation of Colonial Louisiana in American History," in *French Colonial Louisiana and the Atlantic World,* ed. Bradley G. Bond (Baton Rouge: Louisiana

State University Press, 2005), 1–21, for a smart analysis of how the vices and weaknesses of French and Spanish Louisiana served as a moral foil in English-language histories of Anglo America. New Orleans's voluptuous decadence figured prominently in that counterpoint.

2. Michael Kreyling perceptively makes this point in his introduction to *The Grandissimes* (New York: Penguin Books, 1988), xviii–xx.

3. George Washington Cable, "My Politics," in *The Negro Question: A Selection of Writings on Civil Rights in the South,* ed. Arlin Turner (New York: Norton, 1958), 14.

4. All biographical information comes from Arlin Turner's indispensable *George W. Cable: A Biography* (1956; repr., Baton Rouge: Louisiana State University Press, 1966), esp. 3–51, hereinafter *GWC.* For the quotation see Kjell Ekstrom, *George Washington Cable: A Study of His Early Life and Work* (Cambridge: Harvard University Press, 1950), 26.

5. Tennessee Williams, the self-described "rebellious Puritan," comes to mind. Looking back on his first sojourn in the city, he said he found in New Orleans "the kind of freedom I had always needed. And the shock of it against the Puritanism of my nature has given me a theme, which I have never ceased exploiting." Quoted in Lyle Leverich, *Tom: The Unknown Tennessee Williams* (New York and London: Norton, 1995), 285. See also Louis D. Rubin Jr., *George W. Cable: The Life and Times of a Southern Heretic* (New York: Pegasus, 1969), 26.

6. Quoted in Turner, *GWC,* 187.

7. Cable, "My Politics," 9. See also Lucy L. C. Bikle, *George W. Cable: His Life and Letters* (New York and London: Scribner's, 1928), 39–40.

8. Turner, *GWC,* 40; idem, "George W. Cable's Beginnings as a Reformer," *Journal of Southern History* 17 (May 1951): 140–41. Cable's hatred of lotteries figures prominently in one of his most celebrated short stories, "'Sieur George," which was reprinted in *Old Creole Days.*

9. Cable, "My Politics," 5–6, 8–9 (quotation on p. 8); Louis Harlan, "Desegregation in New Orleans Public Schools During Reconstruction," *American Historical Review* 67 (April 1962): 663–75.

10. Cable, "My Politics," 7–11 (quotations on pp. 7 and 11).

11. Ibid., 7.

12. Bikle, *George Washington Cable,* 44. See also Jay B. Hubbell, *The South in American Literature, 1607–1900* (Durham, NC: Duke University Press, 1954), 808–9.

13. Turner, *GWC,* 54.

14. Cable, "My Politics," 9. On the philosophy and politics of the Afro-Creole radicals of New Orleans, see Joseph Logsdon and Caryn Cossé Bell, "The Americanization of Black New Orleans, 1850–1900," in *Creole New Orleans: Race and Americanization,* ed. Arnold R. Hirsch and Joseph Logsdon (Baton Rouge and London: Louisiana State University Press, 1992), 201–61. For more on the intellectual networks linking Afro-Creoles with France, and particularly the French origins of the concept of "public rights," see Rebecca Scott, "Public Rights and Private Commerce: A Nineteenth-Century Atlantic Creole Itinerary," *Current Anthropology* 48, no. 2 (April 2007): 237–56.

15. Richard Hofstadter, *The Progressive Historians: Turner, Beard, Parrington* (New York: Knopf, 1969), 3–43; John Higham, *History: Professional Scholarship*

in America (New York, Evanston, San Francisco, and London: Harper and Row, 1965), 6–25; Turner, *GWC*, 56.

16. Cable, "My Politics," 16–17.

17. He spelled this out in a short article he penned a quarter century after he left the city: "Leave the initiative to him, and no one will more openly, affably let you see and know all about himself than the Creole; but any semblance of idle curiosity or thoughtless intrusion he instantly—maybe sometimes too instantly—meets with the rebuff it deserves." George W. Cable, "New Orleans Revisited," *Book News Monthly* 27 (April 1909): 563–64.

18. For more on this, see Virginia R. Dominguez, *White by Definition: Social Classification in Creole Louisiana* (New Brunswick, NJ: Rutgers University Press, 1986), 63–64, 71.

19. Quoted in Ekstrom, *George Washington Cable*, 164.

20. Edward Laroque Tinker, "Cable and the Creoles," *American Literature* 5 (January 1934): 320–21; Turner, *George Washington Cable*, 101–2. The pamphlet was titled *Critical Dialogue between Aboo and Caboo on a New Book; or, A Grandissime Ascension.* Rouquette's biographer calls the intemperateness of the attack unworthy of the poet, who supported the Union during the Civil War and contributed to Republican publications during Reconstruction. Only Creole injured pride can explain Rouquette's clumsy outburst. Dagmar Renshaw LeBreton, *Chahta-Ima: The Life of Adrien-Emmanuel Rouquette* (Baton Rouge: Louisiana State University Press, 1947), 319–23.

21. Joseph G. Tregle Jr., *Louisiana in the Age of Jackson: A Clash of Cultures and Personalities* (Baton Rouge: LSU Press, 1999), 69.

22. Ibid., 89.

23. Leon Cyprian Soulé, *The Know Nothing Party in New Orleans: A Reappraisal* ([Baton Rouge]: Louisiana Historical Association, 1961), 23.

24. Reid Mitchell, *All on a Mardi Gras Day: Episodes in the History of New Orleans Carnival* (Cambridge and London: Harvard University Press, 1995), 23–28.

25. Michel Musson, for example, the uncle of French impressionist painter Edgar Degas, got into the cotton business. It's his office that has been immortalized in Degas's famous painting of a New Orleans cotton firm. After the war he had become the political symbol of a newfound American-Creole unity forged in the crucible of white supremacy. Christopher Benfey, *Degas in New Orleans: Encounters in the Creole World of Kate Chopin and George Washington Cable* (New York: Knopf, 1997), 65, 83, 164, 166, 189.

26. Christina Vella, *Intimate Enemies: The Two Worlds of the Baroness de Pontalba* (Baton Rouge and London: Louisiana State University Press, 1997), 273–300; Robert Reinders, *End of an Era: New Orleans, 1850–1860* (New Orleans: Pelican, 1964), 11–13, 51–53.

27. Joseph G. Tregle Jr., "Creoles and Americans," in Hirsch and Logsdon, *Creole New Orleans,* 157; Donald Devore and Joseph Logsdon, *Crescent City Schools: Public Education in New Orleans, 1841–1941* (Lafayette: Center for Louisiana Studies, 1991), 23, 35.

28. Tregle, "Creoles and Americans," 166–67.

29. Dominguez, *White by Definition,* 121–26 (quotation on 122).

30. Ibid., 141–44. See also Berndt Ostendorf, "Creole Cultures and the Process of Creolization: With Special Attention to Louisiana," in *Louisiana Culture*

from the Colonial Era to Katrina, ed. John Lowe (Baton Rouge: Louisiana State University Press, forthcoming).

31. Charles Gayarré to John Dimitry, Feb. 1, 1885, John Minor Wisdom Collection, Special Collections, Tulane University (hereinafter TU).

32. Grace King, "Charles Gayarré, a Biographical Sketch," *Louisiana Historical Quarterly* 33 (April 1950): 159.

33. Edward M. Socola, "Charles E. A. Gayarré: A Biography" (Ph.D. diss., University of Pennsylvania, 1954), 187–88, 222, 233 (quotation), 254, 262–63; Earl R. Saucier, "Charles Gayarré: The Creole Historian" (Ph.D. diss., George Peabody College for Teachers, 1935), 218–21, 231; John Smith Kendall, "The Last Days of Charles Gayarré," *Louisiana Historical Quarterly* 15 (July 1932): 365.

34. Charles Gayarré to J. C. Delavigne, Feb. 9, 1879, Wisdom Collection, TU.

35. Turner, *GWC,* 116, 200; Gayarré to Cable, Jan. 10, 1882, George Washington Cable Papers, TU.

36. Gayarré to Cable, Oct. 27, 1880, Cable Papers, TU. He promised, "The work is to be strictly historical without any admixture of party politics."

37. Gayarré to Cable, Aug. 6, 1882, Cable Papers, TU.

38. Gayarré to J. C. Delavigne, Feb. 9, 1879, Wisdom Collection, TU.

39. Socola, "Charles Gayarré," 219–22 (quotation on 222).

40. Gayarré to John Dimitry, Nov. 14, 1881, Wisdom Collection, TU. The rejected novel was *Aubert Dubayet,* which Cable had recommended to his Boston publisher.

41. Socola, "Charles Gayarré," 266–67.

42. Gayarré to John Dimitry, Feb. 5, 1883, and Feb. 1, 1885, Wisdom Collection, TU; Tregle, "Creoles and Americans," 179–80; Socola, "Charles Gayarré," 266–67.

43. Ekstrom, *George W. Cable,* 100. Gayarré also claimed that he had declined to review *The Grandissimes* after Cable admitted he was unable to name two Creole families with whom he was on intimate terms. Gayarré's claim should be read with skepticism. Turner, *GWC,* 203; Rubin, *George W. Cable,* 178.

44. Marion Baker to Cable, Oct. 8, 1884, and James Guthrie to Cable, Oct. 14, 1886, Cable Papers, TU.

45. Rosary Vera Nix, "Creoles vs. Cable; or, Creoles of Louisiana and George Washington Cable" (M.A. thesis, Columbia University, 1936), 38; Turner, *GWC,* 153.

46. James B. Guthrie to Cable, Jan. 17, 1885. On American smugness, see Guthrie's letter of Oct. 14, 1886, characterizing a young friend's engagement to a society Creole: "That she is a catholic [*sic*] and a creole and has not any great depth of mind is about all that can be said against her." Cable Papers, TU.

47. Marion Baker, Page's brother and Cable's closest friend in town, headed up the paper's editorial page. He confessed, "I came within an ace of handing in my resignation when the attacks began on you." Marion Baker to Cable, Mar. 9, 1885, Cable Papers, TU.

48. Socola, "Charles Gayarré," 277.

49. The talk was published in pamphlet form as *The Creoles of History and the Creoles of Romance* (New Orleans, 1885).

50. Joel Williamson, *The Crucible of Race: Black-White Relations in the American South since Emancipation* (New York and Oxford: Oxford University Press, 1984), 102–3; Charles Roberts Anderson, "Charles Gayarré and Paul Hayne: The

Last of the Literary Cavaliers," in *American Studies in Honor of W. K. Boyd,* ed. David Kelly Jackson (Durham, NC: Duke University Press, 1940), 226.

51. Gayarré to John Dimitry, Feb. 1, 1885, Wisdom Collection, TU; Turner, *GWC,* 200–204; Tregle, "Creoles and Americans," 179–81; Edward Laroque Tinker, "Cable and the Creoles," *American Literature* 5 (Jan. 1934), 323–24.

52. Saucier, "Charles Gayarré," 239–41.

53. Marion Baker to Cable, Mar. 9, 1885, and June 19, 1885, Cable Papers, TU. All that Gayarré's principal biographer can say in extenuation is that Baker's charges of opportunism have to be weighed against Gayarré's poverty, advancing years, and career disappointments. Socola, "Charles Gayarré," 287.

54. Turner, *GWC,* 202. Louis Rubin shares that judgment: "Gayarré's mode of address was hortatory, satirical, malicious; he made no attempt to answer Cable's argument, but merely responded with abuse and condemnation." Rubin, *George W. Cable,* 177.

55. Gayarré, *The Creoles of History and the Creoles of Romance,* 4, 11, 19.

56. Frank Scott to Cable, May 9, 1885, Cable Papers, TU.

57. Dominguez, *White by Definition,* 142–43; Gayarré, *The Creoles of History and the Creoles of Romance,* 2.

58. Socola, "Charles Gayarré," 320–23; Smith, "Last Days of Charles Gayarré," 365; Tregle, "Creoles and Americans," 181. If his audience was unfamiliar with Gayarré's dalliances, many probably still remembered the widely reported court case in 1853 that had driven Alexander Dimitry's nephew from the assistant board of aldermen on grounds he was of mixed racial ancestry. For more on this, see Hirsch and Logsdon, *Creole New Orleans,* 98; Devore and Logsdon, *Crescent City Schools,* 41; Shirley Elizabeth Thompson, "The Passing of a People: Creoles of Color in Mid-Nineteenth Century New Orleans" (Ph.D. diss., Harvard University, 2001), 149–88.

59. Nix, "Creoles vs. Cable," 41–42.

60. These developments are recounted in Logsdon and Bell, "Americanization of Black New Orleans," 201–9; and Caryn Cossé Bell, *Revolution, Romanticism, and the Afro-Creole Protest Tradition in Louisiana, 1718–1868* (Baton Rouge: Louisiana State University Press, 1997).

61. Virginia Dominguez is helpful here. See her *White by Definition,* esp. 23–55.

62. George E. Waring Jr. to Cable, Aug. 21, 1880, Cable Papers, TU.

63. Kjell Ekstrom is the only biographer to comment on Cables's extensive documentation. *George W. Cable,* 85.

64. George Washington Cable, "History of New Orleans," manuscript, Cable Papers, TU, 57 (p. 62 of the present volume).

65. Rosary Nix compares the commercial edition of Cable's history with Gayarré, but her conclusions are also valid for the version Cable wrote for the Tenth Census. See Nix, "Creoles vs. Cable," 27–28.

66. Ibid., 260.

67. A public lecture he delivered in 1847 set forth his creed for the study of history. It was titled, appropriately, "The Poetry, or Romance of the History of Louisiana." Socola, "Charles Gayarré," 61.

68. Quoted in Wilfred B. Yearns Jr., "Charles Gayarré, Louisiana's Literary Historian," *Louisiana Historical Quarterly* 33 (April 1950): 259. See also Socola, "Charles Gayarré," 58–68.

69. Yearns, "Charles Gayarré," 260–64; Socola, "Charles Gayarré," 88–101.

70. Socola, "Charles Gayarré," 109. Socola's introduction to the 5th edition of Gayarré's four-volume history provides a balanced appraisal of the Creole's scholarship. *History of Louisiana,* by Charles Gayarré, 5th edition, vol. 1 (New Orleans: Pelican, 1965). Socola's introduction is not paginated, however.

71. Yearns, "Charles Gayarré," 267–68. On nineteenth-century footnote and attribution usage, see Peter Charles Hoffer, *Past Imperfect: Facts, Fictions, and Frauds in the Writing of American History* (New York: Public Affairs, 2004), 20–22.

72. Quoted in Rubin, *George W. Cable,* 113.

73. Cable to Marion Baker, May 21, 1883, Cable Papers, TU; Turner, *GWC,* 130. Gayarré did have one cause for complaint. Cable never acknowledged his historiographical debt to Gayarré in public print, a failing noted by Jay Hubbell: "if Cable had really cared to indicate his indebtedness to the historian, he could have expressed it in one or another of his various books and articles." See Hubbell, *The South in American Literature,* 816.

74. Quoted in Yearns, "Charles Gayarré," 268.

75. At two-thirds the length of Cable's contribution, the historical sketch for Philadelphia was the closest in number of pages to that for the Crescent City.

76. Waring to Cable, July 22, 1881, and August 11, 1881, Cable Papers, TU.

77. On Cable's negotiations to have his history published commercially, see Turner, *GWC,* 128–29; and Frank H. Scott to Cable, April 18, 1882, Cable Papers, TU.

78. Cable was clearly bothered that the footnotes had been omitted from the printed version. On a scrap of paper included in the beribboned book file housing the manuscript history Cable penned this note: "The MS should be kept entire; it has the original and only footnotes that authenticate the statements made in 'Creoles of LA' [the title of the commercial edition of his New Orleans history]." "History of New Orleans," Cable Papers, TU.

79. W. W. Ellsworth to Cable, Dec. 16, 1882, Cable Papers, TU.

80. James Guthrie to Cable, Jan. 17, 1885, Cable Papers, TU.

81. Cable, "My Politics," 17. Cable had initially recommended Gayarré to write the encyclopedia article, but it isn't clear whether Gayarré declined or Scribner's wasn't interested. Cable's article appeared in the ninth (1884), tenth (1902, where it is revised), and eleventh (1911) editions. See Turner, *GWC,* 200, 361.

82. Ekstrom does a good job analyzing the historical text. See his *George W. Cable,* 143–52. Waring's elisions restored in the present volume are shown in italic.

83. Bikle, *George W. Cable,* 74 (quotation); Marion Baker to Cable, Mar. 9, 1885; Turner, *GWC,* 223; Rubin, *George W. Cable,* 184–85.

84. Quoted in Rubin, *George W. Cable,* 154.

85. See the appraisals of Kreyling and Rubin.

86. Turner, "Cable's Beginnings as a Reformer," 147–61; Bikle, *George W. Cable,* 186–87.

87. Turner, *GWC,* 233–35; Hubbell, *The South in American Literature,* 819–20.

88. Quoted in Hubbell, *The South in American Literature,* 821.

89. C. Vann Woodward, *Origins of the New South, 1877–1913* (Baton Rouge: Louisiana State University Press, 1951), 163–64 (quotation on 164); Bikle, *George W. Cable,* 289–94.

90. Rubin, *George W. Cable,* 277.

REPORT

ON THE

SOCIAL STATISTICS OF CITIES

PART II.

THE SOUTHERN AND THE WESTERN STATES

LOUISIANA.

NEW ORLEANS.

HISTORICAL SKETCH

[1.] SITE AND ORIGIN

The Mississippi river, between the states of Mississippi and Louisiana, flowing at first southward, touches, on its eastern side, at the city of Vicksburg, a line of high, abrupt hills or bluffs, the eastern boundary of its later alluvial basin. The direction of this bluff-line is southwesterly; and the river, turned from its southward course by it, flows in this new direction, occasionally impinging upon the abrupt barrier, as at Grand Gulf, Natchez, and Fort Adams, and presently turns again, with the bluffs, more directly toward the south, striking their base and swinging off from it, at Tunica, at Bayou Sara, and finally at Baton Rouge.

Just beyond this point the bluff-line swerves rapidly to a due eastward course, and declines gradually until in the parish of St. Tammany, in Louisiana, some 30 miles from the eastern boundary of the state, it sinks entirely down into a broad tract of wet prairie and sea-marsh, the mainland coast of various inlets from the Gulf of Mexico. It is the general belief that this line of elevated land, now some 80 or 90 miles due north of the Louisiana coast, was the pre-historic shore-line of the Gulf.

Close under the Mississippi bluffs, where they make their short turn to the east, the bayou Manchac, once the Iberville river, and a chain of lakes—Maurepas, Pontchartrain, and Borgne—connected by navigable *passes* and *rigolets,* formerly (until the obstruction of bayou Manchac by the military forces of the United States in 1814)

Cable's "Historical Sketch" of New Orleans originally appeared in Department of the Interior, Census Office, *Report on the Social Statistics of Cities,* Part II, *The Southern and Western States* (vol. 19 of the report of the tenth census), compiled by George E. Waring Jr., Expert and Special Agent (Washington: Government Printing Office, 1887), 213–67. To the title "Historical Sketch" in that document the following footnote is appended: "In the preparation of the report on the city of New Orleans, the local assistant, George W. Cable, esq., not only secured and transmitted a very large proportion of the detailed information concerning the present and the past condition of the city, in response to schedules of interrogatories, but to him alone is due the careful and elaborate historical sketch with which the report is introduced."

united the waters of Mississippi river with those of Mississippi sound. Meanwhile the river itself, turning less abruptly and taking a southeasterly course, cuts off between itself and these lakes a portion of its own delta formation.[1] This fragment of half-made country, comprising something over 1,700 square miles of river shore, swamp and marsh lands, was once widely known as Orleans island.

In outline it is extremely irregular. Its most regular boundary, that of the river bank, is very tortuous, while its width varies, even in its older portions, from 57 miles across the parishes of Plaquemines and St. Bernard, to less than 5 miles from the river at English Turn to the margin of lake Borgne. Another narrow region is seen between the river and lake Pontchartrain, where these two waters approach to within 6 miles of each other.

This occurs at a point almost equally distant from the closed entrance of bayou Manchac, the upper end of Orleans island, and its lower end at the mouth of the Mississippi. In other words, it is 107 miles above the point where the waters of the river finally meet the sea at the outer end of Eads' jetties; in latitude 29° 56′ 59″ and longitude 90° 04′ 09″ west from Greenwich;[2] distant 1,242 miles by river[3] or 700 by rail from St. Louis;[4] 1,760 by sea[5] or 1,377 by rail from New York;[6] 4,800 from Liverpool and 4,800 from Havre.[7] On this spot, in February of the year 1718, was founded the city of New Orleans.[8]

The colony of Louisiana, established nineteen years before at Biloxi, some 85 miles to the east, on the shore of Mississippi sound, had not exceeded at any time the number of a few hundred souls; yet, from the first it had been divided into two factions, one bent on the discovery of gold and silver, the development of pearl fisheries, the opening of a fur trade, and a commerce with South America, and therefore in favor of a sea-coast establishment; the other advocating the importation of French agriculturists and their settlement, in large numbers, on the alluvial banks of the Mississippi.

This wiser design, though faithfully urged by its friends, was for years overruled under the commercial policy and monopoly of the merchant, Anthony Crozat; but when his large but unremunerative privileges fell from his hands into those of John Law, director-general of the famed Mississippi Company, Bienville, governor of the colony, was permitted to found New Orleans, with a view to removing to the banks of the Mississippi the handful of French and Canadians who were struggling against starvation in the irrational search after sudden wealth on the sterile beaches of Mississippi sound and Massacre island.*

The site, which Bienville had chosen a year before,[9] offered to a superficial glance but feeble attractions. The land, highest at the river's edge, where it was but 10 feet above sea-level, sank back within the course of a mile to a minimum of a few inches. It was covered, for the most part, with a noisome and almost impenetrable cypress swamp, and was visibly subject to frequent if not annual overflow. One hundred miles and more lay between the spot and the mouth of a river whose current, in the time of its floods, it was maintained no vessel could overcome.

But the sagacity and Canadian pioneer craft of Bienville had seen its advantages. The bayous of St. John and Sauvage, navigable by small sea-going vessels to within a mile of the Mississippi's bank, led by a short course to the open waters of the lakes, and thus to the streams emptying into those lakes on their farther side, to the countries pierced by these streams, and eastward through the same lakes to Mississippi sound and the Gulf of Mexico. On the opposite side of the Mississippi another easy avenue to and from the sea was presented by the bayou Barataria and the net-work of streams and bays of which it forms a part. By the same waters the wide countries of the Atchafalaya, the Attakapas, and the Opelousas were also made accessible; while northward the Mississippi and its great valley stretched beyond known limits.

Here, therefore, M. de Bienville decided to establish the post which later became his capital, and placed a detachment of twenty-five convicts and as many carpenters,[10] who, with some *voyageurs* from the Illinois, made a clearing and erected a few scattered huts along the bank of the river.[11]

[2.] POPULATION AND SOCIAL ORDER

In the following year Bienville advocated the removal of the capital to New Orleans; but while the matter was under discussion, the settlement suffered a total inundation, and the project was for a time abandoned.[1] However, it continued to be a trading post of the Mississippi Company;† in January, 1720, it was the final returning

---

*Now known as Dauphin Island.

†Officially it was known as the Company of the West (Occident) when it was chartered by the Scottish financier John Law in 1717; it was renamed the Company of the Indies after absorbing many of France's trading companies.

point of M. de la Harpe, after his arduous expedition up Red river;[2] in April was put under the military command of M. de Noyan,[3]* and in December was again urgently recommended by Bienville, in colonial council, as the proper place for the seat of government.[4] His wishes were still outvoted; but he sent his chief of engineers, Sieur Le Blond de la Tour, a Knight of St. Louis, to the settlement, with orders "to choose a suitable site for a city worthy to become the capital of Louisiana."[5] Stakes were driven, lines drawn, streets marked off, town lots granted, ditched, and palisaded, a rude levee thrown up along the river front, and the scattered settlers of the neighborhood gathered into the form of a town.[6]

In 1721, warehouses had already been erected,[7] and Bienville, in certain governmental regulations, reserved the right to make his residence in the new city.[8] Finally, in June of the following year (1722), the royal commissioners having at length given orders to transfer the seat of government,[9] a gradual removal of the company's effects and troops from Biloxi to New Orleans[10] was begun. In August Bienville completed the transfer, by moving thither the gubernatorial headquarters.[11] The place, in January preceding these accessions, already contained 100 houses and 300 inhabitants.[12]

The large proportion of a house to every three persons—if, indeed, the quartering of troops in barracks, did not make it still greater—points to the fact that most of these dwellings were not homes in that full significance which includes the family relation. Though a church of some humble sort was not wanting, and a public hospital had been established, and though the presence of a few ships in the river lent one characteristic of a sea-port, yet, in the poverty of its appliances for domestic and for public comfort, in the wildness of the half-cleared ground, in the frailness of its palisade huts, and the rude shelters which took the name of public buildings, and especially in the undue preponderance of adults and males in the population, the place presented more the features of a hunting or a mining camp than of a town.

Its instability had already been brought painfully to view. On the morning of September 11, 1722, a storm fell upon the land with such force that the church, the hospitals, and thirty dwellings were destroyed; crops were prostrated, and the rice, in particular, was rendered worthless.[13]

The next year, 1723, brought no better fortune. The "Mississippi

*Gilles-Augustin Payen, Chevalier de Noyan, one of Bienville's nephews.

bubble"* reached that point in its well-known history, where it was beginning to reveal its embarrassments, and the colonists of Louisiana found themselves participating in the widespread distress which those complications produced.[14]

Resort, even in miniature, to the insane example set them in France, of an absurd system of credits, gave its logical results; the year 1724 brought, for the moment, a satisfactory relation between the suffering planting interest and the company's mercantile representatives in New Orleans; moreover, new industries—notably the raising of indigo and its manufacture—were introduced; debts were paid with paper, and the little city in embryo found herself the metropolis of an agricultural province, the total population of whose far-scattered plantations, missions, and military posts, was approaching 5,000 souls,[15] and giving promise of abundant commercial tribute. When the secondary phase—financial collapse—followed, the colonists were extricated from their mutual obligations by the gross expedient of a scaling process, applied by royal edict and four times repeated; and under this treatment, as under a conflagration, the year 1726 brought in a sounder, though a shorn, prosperity.[16]

But though the population of New Orleans was now approaching the number of 1,600 inhabitants,[17] the restraints of social life continued to be few and weak. A few civil and military officials of high rank had brought their wives from France, and a few Canadians had brought theirs from Canada; but these were rare exceptions, inappreciable in the total population. The male portion of the people, composed principally of soldiers, trappers, miners, galley-slaves, and redemptioners bound for three years' service, was hardly of the disposition spontaneously to assume the responsibilities of citizenship, or to realize the necessity of public order, while the still disproportionately small number of females was almost entirely from the unreformed and forcibly transported inmates of houses of correction, with a few Choctaw squaws and African slave women.[18] Gambling, dueling, and vicious idleness were indulged in to such a degree as to give the authorities grave concern.[19]

But now the company, as required by its charter, addressed its efforts to the improvement of both the architectural and the social features of its provincial capital, and the years 1726 and 1727 are conspicuous for these endeavors. The importation of male vaga-

*An allusion to the collapse of the speculative stock boom created by John Law's company and bank.

bonds and criminals had already ceased. Stringent penalties were laid upon gambling,[20] and steps were taken for the promotion of education and religion.

Though the plan of the town comprised a parallelogram of some 4,000 feet river front, by a depth of 1,800, and was divided into regular squares of 300 feet front and depth,[21] yet its appearance was disorderly and squalid. A few board cabins of split cypress, thatched with cypress bark,[22] were scattered confusedly over the swampy ground, surrounded and isolated from each other by willow brakes and reedy ponds and sloughs, bristling with dwarf palmetto and swarming with reptiles.[23]

Midway of the river front two squares, one behind the other, had been reserved, the front one as a parade ground or *Place d'Armes* (now Jackson square), the other for ecclesiastical uses. The middle of this rear square had, from the first, been occupied by a church,[24] and is at present the site of St. Louis Cathedral.

On the left of and adjoining this church was now (1726) erected a convent for a company of Capuchin priests, and the spiritual care of that portion of the province between the mouths of the Mississippi and the Illinois, assigned to them three years before, was given into their charge.[25] A company of Ursuline nuns, commissioned to open a school for girls and to attend the sick in hospital, arrived the year following from France, and was given temporary quarters in a house at the north corner of Bienville and Chartres streets, while the foundations of a large and commodious nunnery were laid for them in the square bounded by the river front, Chartres street, the Rue de l'Arsenal (now Ursulines), and the unnamed street below, afterward called Hospital street*—the extreme lower limit of the town as then settled.[26] This building, completed in 1730, was occupied by the order for ninety-four years, vacated by them in 1824 to remove to the larger and more retired convent on the river shore near the present lower limits of the city, where they remain at this day; the older house becoming in 1831 the state-house, and in 1834, as at present, the seat of the archbishop of Louisiana.[27] A soldiers' hospital was built close to the convent in the square next above.[28]

The enlightened aid of the Jesuits was at the same time enlisted in behalf of male education and of agriculture. On the 11th of April, 1726, Bienville granted to a company of these a tract of land to which much interest attaches, inasmuch as it afterward

---

*Renamed Governor Nicholls Street, after the Redeemer governor elected in 1877.

became the site of the main "American" commercial quarter of New Orleans. It comprised an area of 20 arpents (3,600 feet) front, by 50 arpents (9,000 feet) depth, within straight lines, and lay within boundaries now indicated by Common, Tchoupitoulas, Annunciation, and Terpsichore streets, and the bayou St. John; for at that time this bayou extended far up into the bend of the river in a depression somewhat beyond the present Hagan avenue,* and not yet entirely extinct, parallel with the almost south-to-north course of the Mississippi, as it flowed along the front of the described grant. To this was added, January 22, 1728, another grant of 5 arpents front by 50 deep, next above the first. On the 3d of December, 1745, the fathers bought a further tract of 7 arpents front adjoining the second, and thus eventually comprised within their title the whole of the present first district from Felicity to Common streets. The space between Common and Canal streets was reserved by the government as a "terre commune" for fortifications and a public road.[29] On this grant the Jesuits settled in 1727. A house and chapel were built for them, slaves were furnished for their projected fields, and valuable privileges were given them. No educational enterprise seems to have had their immediate attention, but a myrtle orchard (myrtle wax being a colonial staple) was planted on their river front,[30] and much encouragement was given to agriculture by the example of their industry and enterprise. The orange, the fig, the sugar-cane, and probably the indigo plant, were introduced by them into the colony.[31]

It was not Bienville's privilege to effect these and other grateful changes in the aspect of the city he had founded. The schemes of official rivals had procured his displacement, and in the preceding October he had been recalled to France and the office of commandant-general filled by his successor, M. [Étienne de] Périer. The new governor was a lieutenant in the French navy, and a man of many excellent qualifications for command, though deserving, far more than the captain-general who filled the same chair fifty years later,† the soubriquet of "cruel," which only the latter received.

Under M. Périer improvements progressed rapidly, though several which, in at least one excellent history of the colony,[32] have been enumerated as of this period, must be attributed to later dates. Drainage, however, and protection from flood, received immediate attention. A levee of 18 feet crown was thrown up along

---

*Now Jefferson Davis parkway.
†Alejandro "Bloody" O'Reilly, further discussed in chapter 4.

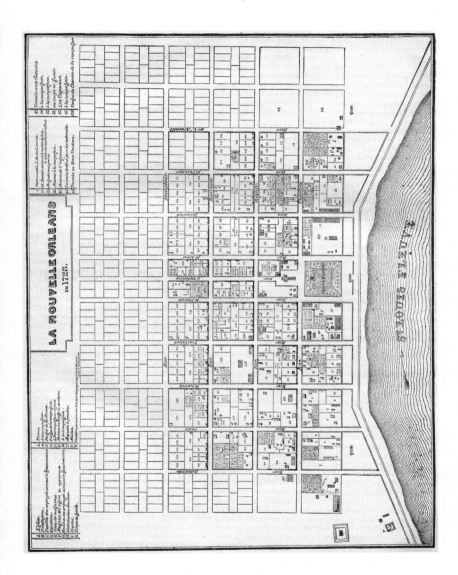

LA NOUVELLE ORLEANS
EN 1728.

the water's edge, exceeding in length the entire front of the town, and was continued, on smaller proportions, 18 miles up, and as many down, the river.[33] But no attempt at fortification was made until three years after.[34] On a well-known official map belonging to the archives of the department of the marine in Paris, the location of every building in New Orleans is shown with undoubted accuracy, as the town presented itself to the eye in 1728. The ancient Place d'Armes, of the same rectangular figure that, as Jackson square, it has to-day, but larger by the width of the present sidewalk, is shown as an open plat of grass crossed by two diagonal paths, and occupying the exact middle of the town front.[35] Behind it stood the parish church, built, like most of the public buildings, of brick,[36] on the site of the present cathedral. On the church's right were a small guard-house and prisons, and on the left was the dwelling of the Capuchins. On the front of the square which flanked the Place d'Armes above, the government-house looked out upon the river. Its ground extended back through the square to Chartres street. In the corresponding square, on the lower side of the Place d'Armes, at the corner of Ste. Anne and Chartres, diagonally opposite the Capuchins, were the quarters of the government employés. The grounds facing the Place d'Armes, in St. Peter and Ste. Anne streets, were still unoccupied, except by cord-wood and intrenching utensils, and a few pieces of parked artillery, on the one side, and a small house for issuing rations, on the other. Just off the river front, in Toulouse street, against the rear grounds of the government-house, were the smithies of the marine, while correspondingly distant on the other hand two long, narrow buildings, lining either side of the street named for the Duc du Maine, and reaching from the river front nearly to Chartres street, were the king's warehouses. The street later known as Ursulines, was called the Street of the Arsenal. On its upper corner, at the river, was the hospital, with its grounds running along the upper side of the street to Chartres, while in the empty square next below, reserved for an arsenal, Charlevoix, in his copy of the map made in 1744, has properly inserted the convent of the Ursulines. The barracks and the company's forges were back in the square bounded by Royal, St. Louis, Bourbon, and Conti streets. In the extreme upper corner of the city, on the river front, at what in late years became the corner of Customhouse and Decatur streets, were the house and grounds of the governor, and in the square immediately behind them the humbler quarters transiently occupied by the

Jesuits. At the north corner of Bienville and Chartres was the temporary dwelling of the nuns. No resident had ventured to build beyond Dauphin street, though twenty-two empty squares were free to choose among, nor had any one settled below the street of the Arsenal or above that of Bienville, except Bienville himself and the Jesuit fathers. Orleans street, cutting the little city transversely in half behind the church, seemed a favorite quarter with inconspicuous citizens, while all along the river front, from Bienville to Arsenal street, and also in Chartres and Royal, rose the homes of the official and commercial potentates of the colony—some small, low, and built of cypress wood; others of brick, or half brick, half frame, broad and high; that is, of two or even two-and-a-half stories.[37] Above the Place d'Armes, between the river front and Chartres street, stood those of Delery, Dalby, St. Martin, Dupuy, Rossard, Duval, Beaulieu-Chauvin, D'Ausseville, Perrigaut, Dreux, Mandeville, Tisseraud, Bonnaud, De Blanc, and Dasfeld: below the square, Villeur, Provenché, Gauvrit, Pellerin, D'Artaguette, Lazon, Raguet, and others; between Chartres and Royal, De Blanc, Fleurieu, Brulé, Lafrenière, Carrière, Caron, Pascal, and others.[38]

Such was the appearance and condition of New Orleans in 1728, as far as maps could be expected to show them. But the crowning benefit, in this period of innovation, was not to be indicated by charts. In the winter of 1727–28, there arrived from France the initial consignment of reputable girls, allotted to the care of the Ursulines, to be disposed of, under their discretion, in marriage. They were supplied by the king, on their departure from France, each with a small chest of clothing,[39] and—with similar importations in subsequent years—were long known in the traditions of their colonial descendants, by the honorable distinction of the "*filles à la cassette*"—the girls with trunks, the casket girls.[40]

Thus, as the first decade in the history of New Orleans drew to a close, it became possible to sum up on her account all the true, though roughly outlined, features of a confirmed civilization: the church, the school, courts, hospital, council hall, virtuous homes, a military arm, and a commerce which, though fettered by the monopoly-rights of the Company of the Occident, comprised in its exports rice, indigo, tobacco, timber, furs, wheat, and flour.

[3.] INDIAN WARS

Hardly had the salutary changes just noted been accomplished, when troubles of the gravest sort threatened to arise from the direction of the Chickasaw and Choctaw Indians. Governor Périer called a council of their village chiefs in New Orleans, and the chiefs responding, met and departed with protestations of friendship and loyalty, which persuaded the governor to believe that he had effected a complete pacification.[1] Suddenly, in the winter of 1729–30, New Orleans was thrown into excitement and consternation by the arrival of a soldier from Fort Rosalie (Natchez),[2] followed in a day or two by a few others, the only survivors escaped to tell of the massacre by the Natchez Indians of over 200 men, and the taking prisoners of 92 women and 155 children.[3] Smaller settlements on the Yazoo river and on Sicily island, in the Washita,* had shared a like fate.[4]

The city became at once the base of military operations, and the governor seized the opportunity to effect some improvements of a defensive character. A broad moat was dug around the town, and, by the end of a year, the place was, for the first time, surrounded with a line of fortifications.[5] Meanwhile, every house in New Orleans, and on the neighboring plantations, was supplied with arms and ammunition. From the town and its surroundings, 300 militia and as many regulars were gathered by the governor, and sent, under one of his captains, to the seat of war.[6]

The community which remained behind soon found itself called upon to bear many of the heaviest burdens of war: terror of attack, days of anxious suspense, sudden alarms, false hopes, industrial stagnation, further militia levies, the issue of colonial paper with its natural result—a financial panic—the reception and care of homeless refugees, and an abiding feeling of insecurity, arising from the restiveness of the African slaves in and near the town, where their number equaled or exceeded that of the master race.[7]

The presence of vagrant bands of professedly friendly Indians also became, said Governor Périer, "a subject of terror," and, with a like fear of the blacks, led to the only acts of bloodshed of which New Orleans was the scene in this war. A band of negro slaves, the property of the company, armed and sent for the purpose by Périer himself, fell upon a small party of Chouachas Indians, dwelling peaceably on the town's lower border, and offending in nothing but their proximity, and indiscriminately massacred the entire village.[8] Emboldened by this show of their strength, these negroes conceived the plan of striking for their own freedom, but

*Variant spelling of Ouachita.

the plot was discovered, and its leaders executed.[9] Nevertheless, the next year after, the same blacks, incited by fugitive slaves sent among them by the Chickasaws, seemed to have maturely planned an insurrection, and fixed a night for a general destruction of the whites. The unguarded speech of an incensed negress, who had been struck by a soldier, again betrayed them, and eight men and the woman, ringleaders, were put to death, the latter on the gallows, the men on the wheel. The heads of the men were stuck upon posts at the upper and the lower ends of the town front, and at the Tchoupitoulas settlement and at the king's plantation, on the opposite side of the Mississippi.[10]

It affords relief to turn from this record to one which displays human nature in a kindlier aspect. The 250 women and children taken by the Natchez, and retaken from them, were received by the people of New Orleans with every demonstration of compassionate sympathy; they were at first lodged in the public hospital, but the Ursulines, probably just moved into their completed convent, adopted the orphan girls among them; the boys found asylums in well-to-do families, and the whole number of refugees was absorbed into the resident population, many of the widows again becoming wives.[11] Thus this generously accepted burden became a blessing.

By the year 1732, every able-bodied citizen of New Orleans had been called into service. The war lasted three years, and resulted in the total dismemberment of the Natchez people, and the incorporation of its small surviving remnant into the Chickasaw nation.[12] The period of comparative peace that followed, was qualified by the depredations of the Chickasaws, or rather by the people that had found harbor among them—the Natchez and Yazoo Indian refugees.

In 1733, another change of administration restored Bienville to the head of affairs, and the confidence and respect he had always inspired among the Indians may well have raised the hope that the colony and its capital were soon to be extricated from their embarrassments. But no such anticipation was realized. In 1735, the Chickasaw aggressions still continuing, Bienville demanded the surrender of the Natchez and Yazoo refugees, and was refused.[13] Upon this he received instructions from France to make war, and the early spring of 1736 found New Orleans again in the excitement and confusion of marshaling a small army, which by and by, in thirty barges and as many large canoes, embarked on the bayou St. John for a war of extermination against the Chickasaws.[14] In the latter part of June of the same year, Bienville, re-entering the bayou

St. John, disembarked the remnant of his forces, sick, wounded, and dispirited, after a short, inglorious, and disastrous campaign.[15]

In September, 1739, another force, consisting of regulars, militia, three companies of marines lately arrived from France, and 1,600 Indians, left New Orleans for the Chickasaw country, this time taking their way up the Mississippi. At a point on the river, near the present site of the city of Memphis, they were joined, according to appointment, by levies from Canada and elsewhere, making a total force of white, red, and black men, numbering upward of 3,600.

Six months passed, the spring of 1740 was at hand, and once more Bienville landed at New Orleans with a sick and starving remnant of the force that had gone out, and with no better result than a discreditable peace.[16] Later, perceiving by the tenor of the French minister's communications to him the severe disfavor with which he was regarded, he wrote to France in January, 1742, asking to be recalled. This was done,[17] and on the arrival of [Pierre de Rigaud,] the Marquis de Vaudreuil as his successor, he bade a last farewell to the city which he had founded, and to that Louisiana of which its people fondly called him "the father."[18]

To one who will observe closely the effects of these wars upon the city of New Orleans, in the light of after-events, two main results will come prominently forward, the one moral, the other commercial.

As to the moral, it is enough here to note these two facts: one, that the first generation native to New Orleans sprang up and grew among the harsh influences of a frontier struggle against savage aggression, and for the maintenance of an arbitrary supremacy over two other races; the other, that this struggle was carried on under the deeply corrupted government of Louis XV of France.

The commercial result was one that marked an era in the history of the city. The Company of the Indies, into which the Company of the Occident, or Mississippi Company, had been absorbed, discouraged by the expense and continuance of the Natchez war, and esteeming their privileges on the Guinea coast and in the East Indies more worthy of their attention, had, in January, 1731, tendered, and in April of the same year had effected, the surrender of its western charter to the French government.[19] Thus New Orleans became for the first time, free from private monopoly rights on its commerce.

In response to the king's establishment, between Louisiana and his subjects elsewhere, of a virtual free trade, a fresh intercourse sprang up with the ports of France and of the West Indies, a moderate but valued immigration set in from these islands and, despite the Chickasaw campaigns and the emission of paper money, increased from year to year, while at the close of these campaigns business still further revived, and the town, as it never had done before, began spontaneously to develop from within outward, by the enterprise of its own people.[20]

[4.] THE FIRST CREOLES

The term Creole is commonly applied in books to the native of a Spanish colony descended from European ancestors, while often the popular acceptation conveys the idea of an origin partly African. In fact, its meaning varies in different times and regions, and in Louisiana alone has, and has had, its broad and its close, its earlier and its later, significance.

For instance, it did not here first belong to the descendants of Spanish, but of French settlers.[1] But such a meaning implied a certain excellence of origin, and so came early to include any native of French or Spanish descent by either parent, whose pure non-mixture with the slave race entitled him to social rank. Much later the term was adopted by, not conceded to, the natives of European-African or Creole-African blood, and is still so used among themselves. At length the spirit of commerce availed itself of the money value of so honored a title, and broadened its meaning to take in any creature or thing, of variety or manufacture peculiar to Louisiana, that might become an object of sale, as Creole ponies, chickens, cows, shoes, eggs, wagons, baskets, cabbages, etc.

And yet the word has its limitations. The Creoles proper will not share their distinction with the native descendants of those worthy Acadian exiles who, in 1756, and later, found refuge in Louisiana. These remain "cadjiens" or "cajuns" in the third person plural, though Creoles by courtesy in the second person singular; and while there are French, Spanish, and even, for convenience, "colored" Creoles, there are no English, Scotch, Irish, Western, or "Yankee" Creoles, these all being included under the distinctive term "Americans."

Neither the subsequent Spanish nor the American domination has given the Creoles any other than the French tongue as a vernacular, and in fine, there seems to be no more serviceable definition of the Creoles of Louisiana or of New Orleans, than to say they are the French-speaking, native, ruling class.

In noticing the origin and development of this people, it does not seem necessary to distinguish narrowly between the upper and lower social ranks of the settlers from whom they sprang. Many lines of descent, it is true, were of such beginnings as are everywhere and always regarded with conventional disfavor,[2] while a few only sprang from progenitors of military rank and social station; yet, in view of the state of society among the French of that day, the misconceptions of civil and personal rights, and the gross oppressions laid upon one rank of society by another, the children of those who held the weapons of tyranny have probably as good reason (but no better) to look with satisfaction upon their origin, as have those whose ancestors suffered the pains and ignominy of strokes that might more justly have fallen on those who inflicted them.

The first forty-six years of the history of New Orleans, between the date of its founding and that of the cession to Spain, divides into two nearly equal periods. The one, 1718 to 1740, includes the origin and struggle for life against neglect, famine, and savages; the other, 1740 to 1764, the formation process of a native community which the first had but brought into existence.

The earlier of these two periods again easily divides into two equal intervals of eleven years each. That from 1718, to the sudden shock of the Natchez outbreak in 1729, was a term of impassive, embryotic accretion in the various parts and functions of the projected town; while the period of Indian wars, beginning in December, 1729, and ending in the peace made with the Chickasaws in 1740, introduced a more active life, evolving as it progressed, a liberation from the trammels of that company to which the city owes its origin, and bringing in, as it drew to a close, the advance-guard of a fresh and native-born generation, and the beginnings of those new sentiments which the succeeding period was to carry to maturity.

As has been seen, New Orleans, at its foundation as throughout its colonial existence, was essentially military. The habits of its population, their moral sentiment, their domestic life, social order and intellectual and spiritual training were at the most only such as could be expected in a military outpost of the French government in the early part of the eighteenth century. The lounging life of the barracks could not but have an unfavorable effect upon all that gathered about it and complaints of general thriftlessness came soon and often from those appointed to govern.[3] The many liberties of the frontier, conferred as they were upon redemptionists and the late occupants of French prisons, combined with the spirit of a French soldiery to promote not only personal valor but an undue readiness for positive strife, so that between the bold, free life of the hunter, Indian-fighter or even marauder, and the dull fatigues of the husbandmen there could be but one popular choice.

Lands were free to any who could assume a grant, but the wants of border life were few, the Company's patronage, or royal succor, was always within reach, at least of hope, and at that turning point when it was decided to make agriculture the leading purpose of the colony the welcome but unfortunate introduction of African slaves by the Western Company[4] cast daily toil—already too lightly esteemed— into permanent contempt.

Such was the intellectual and moral atmosphere in which the first generation of New Orleans Creoles passed the terms of childhood and youth and entered, with ripening years, that period between the close of the Indian wars and the transfer to Spain (1740– 1762) which may be properly considered the field of its career, and in which, under new and unprecedented conditions worthy of careful observation it attained the full breadth and stature of a unique community.

The Natchez war and the company's commercial oppressions—if the statement of the officials who, in 1733, assumed direction of affairs is accepted—had reduced New Orleans almost to starvation.[5] While such a statement, even if accurate, is not proof positive of a state of permanent beggary, it does indicate a non-intercourse with sources of supply and a suffocation of commerce. The comparative freedom offered to trade by the royal government[6] brought, as already noted, a gradual improvement in affairs, which rose, after the close of the Chickasaw campaigns in 1740, into positive commercial life and strength.[7]

Thus private enterprise, the true foundation of material prosperity, was already well established. Indigo, rice, and tobacco were moving in considerable quantities to Europe, and lumber to the West Indies; an import trade especially from St. Domingo,[8] was active, and traffic with the Indians and with the growing white population along the immense length of the Mississippi and its tributaries, was increasing year by year,[9] when, on the 10th day of May, 1743, the Marquis de Vaudreuil landed in New Orleans.[10]

The appointment of the marquis, member of a family of much influence at court, to be governor of Louisiana, inspired in the minds of the colonists bright anticipations of such royal patronage and enterprise as would greatly broaden the prospects of the colony, and, consequently, increase the importance of its capital.[11]

In the whole term of the Natchez and Chickasaw wars but two marked improvements had been added to the town, and but one of these was a government measure: in 1734 barracks had been built in St Peter and St Ann streets opposite either side of the Place d'Armes;[12] and in 1737 a hospital had been founded for the poor, an humble sailor, Jean Louis, having, at death, left his modest fortune of ten thousand livres to this praiseworthy object.[13]

But if the advent of the "Grand Marquis" aroused expectations of municipal adornment and aggrandizement, those expectations were but feebly met. There was an increase in the number of the troops and a great enhancement of military splendor. In 1751 every second man in the population was a soldier in dazzling uniform.[14] But as to material aid or improvement, the very moderate efforts of the government seem to have overreached the town and to have been directed to the encouragement, not to say taxation, of certain agricultural industries, such as the production of tobacco and myrtle wax,[15] the introduction of sugar-cane, and the granting, yearly, to soldiers chosen for good conduct, of tracts of land, and wives from the Casket girls, the last company of which arrived in 1751,[16] honorable source of many of the best Creole families of to-day.

Two exceptional public works were forced upon the superior council, by the stress of events, during the governorship of De Vaudreuil's successor, [Louis Billouart de] Kerlerec, a captain in the royal navy, to whom the marquis gave place February 9, 1753.[17] In the fall of 1758, France and England being at war, the French garrison of Fort Duquesne, on the present site of Pittsburgh, evacuated it, and, taking boats, floated down the Ohio and Mississippi to New Orleans. The barracks flanking the Place d'Armes could not accommodate so many additional occupants, and Governor Kerlerec at once began to build another in the lower part of the city front,[18] at a point afterward indicated by the name Barracks street. Two years later the fortifications about the town, which appear to have fallen into complete dilapidation, were renewed;[19] a line of palisades passed from the river bank below entirely around to the river bank above, with salients at the corners, "a banquette within and a very trifling ditch without."[20] The expected British foe, however, never came to the attack.

Beyond these measures the city was still left to its own spontaneous motion. Drainage, sanitation, fire protection, each a long-felt and urgent need, received no official attention; police regulations, little beyond the strict surveillance of the negro-slave element; and the public credit, alone, a detrimental overshare in further inundations* of paper money.[21]

Yet despite these and other drawbacks, the presence of pirates in the Gulf of Mexico,[22] and of English privateers sometimes at the very mouth of the Mississippi,[23] the disaffection and insolent encroachments of Indian allies,[24] adverse seasons (one winter, 1748, being so cold as to destroy all the orange trees),[25] and a desperate degree of corruption in the government, there was in New Orleans, notwithstanding, a certain amount of material growth and progress hardly to be looked for in the presence of such embarrassments and distractions. Between the autumn of 1749 and 1752, "forty-five brick houses were erected."[26]

The period was also, as on a more extensive scale in France, one of transmutation. The children of the first settlers, coming more and more to the front, were taking their parents' places, and with the ductility characteristic of the Latin race, had adapted themselves to the novel mold of their immediate surroundings. Their fathers and mothers were passing away, or retiring into the inactivity of advanced life, and the new active element of New Orleans and its adjacent delta country, was now that new variety of French-speaking, but not French, people, which is made the subject of the present chapter.

Its variation from the trans-atlantic original was much the difference between France itself and the Louisiana delta. A soil of unlimited fertility, instead of being an inducement to industry, became, through the institution of slavery, merely a perpetual assurance of plenty, and, with a luxurious and enervating climate, debased even the Gallic love of pleasure to an unambitious apathy and an unrestrained sensuality.[27] The courteous manners of France were largely retained; but the habit of commanding a dull and abject slave class, over which the laws of the colony gave every white man full powers of police,[28] induced a certain fierce imperiousness of will and temper; while that proud love of freedom, so pervasive throughout the American wilderness, rose at times to an attitude of arrogant superiority over all constraint, and became the occasion of harsh comment in reports sent to France by the officers of the king.[29]

*A somewhat convoluted reference to price inflation due to the colony's shortage of goods and specie and the surfeit of depreciating paper money.

Faults and virtues alike were the traits of those who commanded, not served, and the distortions of character common in old and crowded communities—penuriousness, avarice, cunning,—all fruits of a servile and sordid spirit—were handed over to their contemned slaves as unworthy a race of masters. A single exception lay in an inordinate worship of military rank; the acquisition of which was the key to power and the universal ambition.[30]

The absence of a necessity to labor and qualities of climate unfavorable to assiduous effort, caused the learned professions and the pursuit of study for its own sake to be neglected. The chase, for which there was an extravagant fondness, was almost the only form of exertion, and woodcraft often the only education.[31]

In such a state of society the sphere of women was necessarily circumscribed. Farther removed from many of the grosser features of negro slavery than the men, she was decidedly superior to them in intellectual and moral aptitude and training and in refinement of manners, although her educational accomplishments were confined to reading, writing and music.[32] The redundancy of vegetation allowed but few out-door recreations, and that French vivacity, which still remained, chose the ball-room as the chief delight of the gentler sex, while the gaming-table was the indoor passion of the other.

To such a people, unrestrained, proud, intrepid, self-reliant, rudely voluptuous, of a highly intellectual order, yet uneducated, unreasoning, impulsive, and inflammable, the royal governors introduced the frivolities and corruptions of the Bourbon camp and palaces.

The Marquis and Marchioness de Vaudreuil held their colonial court with much pomp and dissipation, and it seems fair to impute to their example much of the love of display which, during the twelve years of the "Grand Marquis'" sojourn in Louisiana, began to be developed among the citizens of its humble metropolis.[33]

In the early part of this period of twenty-four years, between 1740 and 1764, New Orleans, itself, contained a comparatively trivial proportion of slaves. In 1744, for example, the census shows but 300 adults of this class, in a total population which, with 800 adult males, "almost all married,"[34] could hardly have been less than 3,000. But these 300 slaves were the servants of that better class of society in which controlling popular sentiments originate, and whose intellectual and moral likeness becomes the conventional pattern. The number of slaves, moreover, rapidly increased, while that of the whites, many, it is likely, being the grantees of lands in the interior, diminished; so that the next census,[35] dating even after the close of this period, shows no perceptible increase in total population, yet gives a proportion of two slaves to every three whites; indicating the general exchange from free white to black slave domestic service and manual labor in New Orleans.

The dwellings of the leading class, built at first principally on the immediate front of the town or the first street behind, seem, later, to have drawn back a square or two. They also spread along toward, and out through, a gate in the palisade wall near its north corner. A road, now one of the streets of the city and still known as Bayou road, issued from this gate and continued its northward course to the village and bayou of St. John.[36] Along this suburban way, surrounded by broad grounds deeply shaded by live-oaks, magnolias, and other evergreen forest trees, and often having behind them plantations of indigo or myrtle, rose the broad, red-roofed, but severely plain and simple frame dwellings of the opulent class, commonly of one or one and a half story height, but generally raised on pillars often 15 feet from the ground, and surrounded by wide verandas.[37]

In the lofty halls and spacious drawing-rooms of these homes, frequently in the heart of the town, in houses of almost squalid exterior, their low, single-story, wooden or brick walls rising from a ground but partially drained even of its storm water, infested with reptile life, and in frequent danger of inundation, was beginning to be seen a splendor of dress and personal adornment,[38] hardly in harmony with the rude simplicity of apartments and furniture, and scarcely to be expected in a town of unpaved, unlighted, and often impassable streets, surrounded by swamps and morasses, on one of the wildest of American frontiers.

To the bad example of ostentatious living, the whole number of colonial officials, with possibly an exception here or there, added that of corruption in office. The governors, the royal commissaries,* post-commandants, the Marchioness de Vaudreuil conspicuously, and many others of less pretension, stood boldly accusing and accused of the grossest and the pettiest frauds; the retention and sale of merchandise destined for friendly Indians, and of breadstuffs imported for the king's troops; the traffic of all manner of government favors; the distribution of cadets' commissions to infants and young children, and the entry of their names on the commissariat

---

*Officially, *commissaire-ordonnateurs,* who functioned, more or less, like intendants in the colonies.

rolls; officers trading, making slaves of their soldiers, and leading idle, dissolute lives.[39]

Doubtless, where all were reciprocally accusers, the degree of corruption was exaggerated; yet the testimony is official, abundant, corroborative, and verified in the ruinous expenses[40] which later drove France to abandon the maintenance and sovereignty of the colony she had misgoverned for sixty-three years.

In the mean time the effect of such widespread official venality on the people was most lamentable. Public morals were debased, idleness and intemperance became general,[41] speculation in the depreciated paper currency which flooded the colony became the principal pursuit, and insolvency the common condition.[42]

The cause of religion and education made little or no headway. Rival ecclesiastical orders quarreled for spiritual dominion. One small chapel, connected with the public hospital, appears to have been the only house of worship founded during the entire period, and finds mention only in connection with the "war of the Jesuits and Capuchins." This strife continued for years, characterized by "acrimonious writings, squibs, pasquinades, and satirical songs" the women in particular taking sides with lively zeal.[43] But in July, 1763, the Capuchins were left masters of the field. Agreeably to a decree of the French parliament of the year previous, ordering the expulsion of the Jesuits from the dominions of France, their plantation adjoining the city was confiscated by the superior council. It was sold for a sum equivalent to $180,000, in the latter part of the same year.[44]

The Jesuit fathers, wherever the fault may lie, seem to have put the people of New Orleans, whose male youth they had engaged to educate, very little in their debt,[45] and from the time of their exile this important work was not again regarded as a public interest, until after Louisiana had become an American state.[46]

Thus have been enumerated the origin, surrounding influences, and resulting character and life of the early Creoles of New Orleans. The few events remaining to complete the record of this formative period are of special value, as explaining the sad episode which followed their change of royal masters.

On the 16th of February, 1763, a treaty of peace between England, Spain, and France was signed at Paris. By this treaty the French king ceded to Great Britain "all that he possessed, or had a right to possess, on the left (east) side of the Mississippi," from its source in lake Itasca, by a line through the middle of the stream, to the mouth of Iberville river (bayou Manchac), and so eastward to the sea through the middle of that line of water already indicated as separating Orleans island from the country north of it. "The town of New Orleans and the island on which it stands," therefore, remained to France and to the still immense French province of Louisiana. The navigation of the Mississippi, "including ingress and egress at its mouth," was made absolutely free to the subjects of both empires alike.[47]

The laws governing the French colonies forbade trade with British vessels; yet the wants of the colonists and the mutual advantages offering, soon gave rise to a lively commerce at a point just above the Jesuits' plantation, afterward the river front of the city of Lafayette, and now the fourth district of New Orleans. Here numerous trading vessels, sailing under the British flag, ascending the river and passing the city on the pretext of visiting the new British ports of Manchac and Baton Rouge, landed and carried on their interlope commerce with the merchants from the neighboring city. The corrupt authorities made no attempt to suppress a traffic so advantageous in its pecuniary bearings to the community, though most unfortunate, in accustoming the highest classes and leading minds of the city to justify and practice the getting of honest rights by disingenuous and dishonest courses, and doubly unfortunate in its stimulation of the slave trade. A large business was done at this so-called "Little Manchac" in Guinea negroes, whom the colonists bought of the British, occasioning an increase in the agricultural laboring force of the surrounding country, and the sudden enriching of many of the community.[48]

Meanwhile the English were taking possession of their newly acquired territory. In February, 1764, a Major Loftus, with 400 British troops, came from Mobile to New Orleans, and embarked up the river in ten barges and two canoes for the new British[49] possessions in the Illinois territory. On attempting to land he was fired upon by Indians in ambush, and was finally compelled to return; whereupon he bitterly, and probably unjustly, charged the French colonists with having treacherously instigated the attack. Thus, even extraneous circumstances seemed unhappily tending to create an excited public feeling, at a time when events were impending that called for the most dispassionate consideration. It might be added, that about this time began that assertion of rights and train of events in the thirteen British colonies on the Atlantic coast, which, a few years later, precipitated the American Revolution.

Even before the treaty of Paris, Kerlerec had received orders to return to France and render account of his conduct in office.[50] In March, 1763, the month after the treaty, the king, under the very plausible pretext of retrenchment, ordered the disbanding of all but 300 of his colonial troops.[51] On the 29th of June M. [Jean-Jacques-Blaise] d'Abbadie landed in New Orleans, commissioned to succeed the governor, under the semi-commercial title of director-general,[52] and Kerlerec a little later sailed for France, where he was cast into the Bastile, and "died of grief shortly after his release."[53] The colony was much agitated by the many observable symptoms of some unrevealed design to make a change in their condition, and by and by rumor of what had been secretly transacted came to take the most repellant shape. Yet M. d'Abbadie himself remained as uninformed as the people, and it was only in October, 1764, twenty-three months after the signing of the secret act at Fontainebleau,* that the official announcement reached New Orleans of her cession, with that of Orleans island and all Louisiana west of the Mississippi, to the king of Spain.[54]

[5.] THE INSURRECTION OF 1768

"As I was finishing this letter," wrote the director-general, M. d'Abbadie, on the 7th of June, 1764, "the merchants of New Orleans presented me with a petition, a copy of which I have the honor to forward. You will find in it those characteristic features of sedition and insubordination of which I complain."[1]

The object of this petition was to point out a condition of affairs[2] which must have appeared to the New Orleans merchants intolerable, as, in the light of the town's commercial progress, it seems incredible, until it is remembered through what a *débris* of public finances the commerce of a city or country may sometimes make a certain progress.

This despised voice bore, unrecognized by the arbitrary steward who so harshly denounced it to his king's minister, a double prophetic value. There was soon to arise, between the material interests of New Orleans and the heartless oppressions of two corrupt governments, a struggle ending, for her citizens, in ignominy and disaster; while in the years yet beyond there was a time to come when commerce, not arms, was to rule the destinies, not of

*Treaty of Fountainbleau.

a French or Spanish military outpost, but of the great southern seaport of a nation yet to be.

The names of those who signed this address are worthy of preservation: Gaillardi, Viviat, Milhet, Braquier amé, Braquier Jr., Caresse, Vienne, Arrivé, Fuselier, Laforcade, Blache, Denis, Rivoire, Duplessy, Lafitte, Saint-Pé, Fournier, Joseph Milhet, Delon, Cousin, Dumas.[3]

Nothing but the extreme disrelish for such an event could have blinded the people to the fact that the cession was genuine. The king's letter made distinct statement of the fact; the official instructions to M. d'Abbadie, as to the manner of evacuating and surrendering the province, were full and precise; they were, moreover, accompanied by copies of the treaty of cession and the Spanish king's letter of acceptance, and they were ordered to be spread upon the minutes of the superior council at New Orleans, in order that the full text might be publicly and universally accessible.[4]

But to the brave and inflammable Creoles, upon whose character no influence in early life had impressed the habit of calm reasoning, facts were of less value than feelings. Nor can they lightly be criticized for the distemper into which they were thrown. The grievances done their sentiments—of nationality, of justice, even of manhood—need no enumeration; while in their pecuniary interests, unless the transfer was a momentary expedient and a political ruse, the commercial revulsion which it threatened, was likely to leave them no better than bankrupt.

When there was no longer any ground for doubt, a hope was still fostered that a prayer to their king might avert the delayed consummation of the treaty. Early in 1765, therefore, a large meeting was held, of planters from all the nearer parts of the province, and of almost all notable persons in New Orleans, including some of the members of the superior council and other officials. Jean Milhet, the wealthiest merchant in the town, and one of those who had signed the address of the previous June, was sent to France with a petition that the king would arrange with Spain a nullification of the late act.[5] A people much more accustomed than the Creoles to the disappointment of their wishes, might have hoped that a request so consistent with natural rights would not be lightly denied.

Milhet met in Paris Bienville, then in his eighty-sixth year, and in company with him sought the royal audience. This the minister, the Duc de Choiseul—in furtherance of whose policy the transfer had been made—adroitly prevented them from obtaining, and their mission was courteously but early brought to naught.[6]

But a hope that never had real foundations could not be undermined, and the Creoles, though in 1766 they received tidings from Milhet announcing the failure of his undertaking, fed their delusion upon the continued non-arrival of any officer from Spain to take possession of the province,[7] and upon the continued stay of Milhet in France.[8]

It would be strange, too, if this error was not further promoted by the contrast between these delays and the promptness with which the British government was taking possession of that part of Louisiana and the Floridas which had fallen to it by the treaty of Paris. For the acting governor, [Charles-Phillippe] Aubry—M. d'Abbadie having died on the 4th of February, 1765—was not a little concerned at the perpetual passage through the harbor of New Orleans of English ships of war and troops, while without ships, ammunition, or money, and only a few soldiers, whose term of enlistment was out, he was compelled to await the slow motions of Spain in receiving a gift which she did not covet, and which had been given to her only for fear it might otherwise fall into the hands of Great Britain.[9]

However, in the summer of this year a rumor came to the colonists that Spain had moved a step forward, and not long afterward the superior council received from Havana a letter of the 10th of July, addressed to them by Don Antonio de Ulloa, a commodore in the Spanish navy, a scientific scholar, an author of renown, and at the date of this letter the royally commissioned Spanish governor of Louisiana. The letter announced his expectation soon to arrive in New Orleans in his official capacity.[10]

And yet this event cast another delusive shadow upon the public mind, and was interpreted as a diplomatic maneuver, when month after month passed by, the year closed, January and February, 1766, came and went, and the new governor had not made his appearance.[11] At length, after nearly eight months of suspense, on the 5th of March, 1766, he landed in New Orleans. He was accompanied by but two companies of Spanish infantry, his government having accepted the assurance of France that no necessity would be found for more than this force: *Loyola, intendant, [Martin] Navarro, treasurer and Don Estevan de Gayarré as comptroller. The last named was the grandfather* of the historian of Louisiana whose laborious researches among the archives of the state, destroyed during the late war, and among those of the French and*

*Actually great-grandfather.

Spanish governments at Paris and Madrid are repeatedly taken advantage of in the present pages.[12]

The new governor was received with a cold and haughty bearing, which was silent only for a moment before it became aggressive. On the very day of his arrival his attention was called, by [Denis-Nicolas] Foucault, the French intendant* commissary, to the 7,000,000 livres of paper money left in the colony by the French government, and at that time depreciated to one-fourth its face value. This vital question was promptly and kindly answered: he would recognize it as the circulating medium at its market value, until instructed from Spain as to its retirement. But the people instantly and clamorously took stand for its redemption at par.[13]

A few days after Ulloa's arrival he was waited on by the merchants, with a memorial comprised of a series of formal questions touching their commercial interests, his answers to which they professed to await in order to know how to order their future actions. An address of so startling a tone could only seem to a Spanish official, what Ulloa termed it in a dispatch to his government, imperious, insolent, and menacing.[14]

The first act of the superior council was quite as hostile and injudicious. It consisted in requesting the governor to exhibit his commission. He replied that he would not take possession of the colony until the arrival of additional Spanish troops, which he was expecting; that at any rate the superior council was a subordinate civil body, and that his dealings would be with Governor Aubry.[15]

Thus the populace, the merchants, and the civil government, which, it will be seen, later included the judiciary, ranged themselves at once in hostile attitude before the untried government, sent them by the king who had unwillingly accepted them as subjects. The military was not long in committing the same error. The three or four companies left in Louisiana, under the command of Aubry, refused point blank to pass, as the French government had promised they should, into the Spanish service.[16] In short, Governor Aubry, almost alone, recognized the cession and Ulloa's powers.

Under these circumstances Ulloa thought it best to postpone publishing the commission he had shown only to Aubry, or taking formal possession of the country. Yet he virtually assumed control of affairs,[17] employing his few Spanish soldiers to build and

---

*Though more exalted in title, intendants under both French and Spanish colonial rule functioned like *commissaire-ordonnateurs* in handling financial and judicial oversight of local affairs.

garrison new forts at important points in various quarters of the province,[18] and, in cooperation with Aubry, endeavored to maintain a conciliatory policy, pending the arrival of troops; a policy of doubtful wisdom in dealing with a people who, but partly conscious of their rights, were smarting under a lively knowledge of their wrongs, and whose impatient and intractable temper could brook any other sort of treatment with better dignity and less resentment, than that sort which trifled with their feelings.[19]

Much ill-will began now to be openly expressed against the really mild and liberal Ulloa. An arrangement by which the French troops remained in service, drawing Spanish pay, while continuing under French colors and the command and order of Aubry, was fiercely denounced by those who had hoped to see the Spanish authority fall into complete contempt.[20]

It seems to have been persistently forced upon Ulloa's recognition, that behind and under all the frivolous criticisms and imperious demands of the New Orleans people, the true object of their most anxious dread and aversion, was the iron tyrannies and extortions of Spanish colonial revenue laws. And for this feeling, notwithstanding the offensive memorial by which it was first made known to him, he appears to have had a kind consideration. As early as the 6th of May, only two months after his arrival, he began a series of commercial concessions, looking to the preservation of that trade with France and the French West Indies which the colonists had believed themselves doomed to lose. Yet neither did these escape the resentment and remonstrance of the citizens, and it clearly shows how supreme the mercantile interest was in this whole movement, that the proposal of Ulloa to fix a schedule of reasonable prices on all imported goods, through the appraisement of a board of disinterested citizens, was the subject of such grievous complaint, even by the mass of consumers whom it was expected to benefit, that the unjust and oppressive, though well-meant, ordinance was verbally revoked.[21]

Quite as active, and not less prevalent, was the influence of those office-holders in the superior council and other civil positions, whom the establishment of a Spanish colonial government might be expected to displace, and it was greatly through the mischievous diligence of these that every incident or mistake, however harmless or trivial, became the subject of vindictive fault-finding against the now incensed and threatening Spaniard, and that even "his manner of living, his tastes, his habits, his conversation, the most trivial occurrences in his household," were construed offensively.[22] The return of Jean Milhet from France in December, 1767, with final word of ill-success, only further increased the hostility of the people.[23]

However, the year passed away and nine months of 1768 followed. Ulloa and Aubry, as between themselves, conducted affairs with almost unbroken harmony, notwithstanding Aubry's poor opinion of the Spanish governor's administrative abilities; and although their repeated innovations in matters of commerce and police, now and then produced painful surprises in the community, yet they were meeting a degree of success which led Aubry to assert, in one of his dispatches to France, and no doubt to believe, that they were "gradually molding Frenchmen to Spanish domination." The Spanish flag had been quietly hoisted over four new military posts, without removing the French ensign from over the older establishments, and the colony was apparently living peacefully under both standards.[24]

But under this superficial disguise, the true condition of the public mind was such as may be inferred from Aubry's own account of the distressing embarrassments that beset the colony; the fate of the 7,000,000 livres of French paper money still remained in doubt; the debts of the colony, assumed by the Spanish government, were unpaid; there were a shrinkage of values amounting to 66 per cent., a specie famine and widespread insolvency, a continued apprehension of disaster to follow the establishment of Spanish power, a governor showing himself daily more and more unable to secure the affections and confidence of the people, and finally, the rumor of a royal decree suppressing the town's commerce with France and the West Indies.[25]

Now it was that a deficiency in habits of mature thought and self-control, and in that study of reciprocal justice and natural rights, which becomes men who would maintain their ground against oppression, became to the people of New Orleans and Louisiana a calamity. With these qualities in them and in their leaders, the insurrection of 1768 might have been a revolution for the overthrow of tyranny, both French and Spanish, and the establishment and maintenance of that right to self-government which belongs to any oppressed people. But the valorous, unreflecting Creoles, though imbued with a certain spirit of freedom, discerned but faintly the profound principles of right which it becomes the duty of revolutionists to assert and to struggle for; they rose merely in passionate revolt against a confused group of real and fancied grievances, sought to be ungoverned rather than self-governed, and, following the lead of a few uneasy office-holders, became a warning in their many-sided shortsightedness, and an example only in their audacious courage.

It was on the 25th of October, 1768, that a secret conspiracy, long and carefully planned, and in which were engaged some of the first officers of the colonial government, and some of the leading merchants of New Orleans, revealed itself in open hostilities. Lafrénière, the attorney-general, was at its head; Foucault, the intendant commissary, was an active spirit; and Jean and Joseph Milhet, brothers, Pierre Caresse, Joseph Petit and Pierre Poupet, prominent merchants, Noyan and Bienville, nephews of the city's founder, Jerome Doucet, a distinguished lawyer, Pierre Marquis, a captain of Swiss troops, and Balthasar de Masan, Hardy de Boisblanc and Joseph Villeré, planters and public men, were leaders in the plot and in its execution.[26]

These men had taken care to create the belief, in the settlement some twenty miles above New Orleans on the Mississippi river, called the German coast, that certain Spanish obligations, some time due the farmers there, would not be paid. On the date mentioned, an agent, intrusted with funds for the payment of these obligations, was arrested by a body of citizens under the orders of Villeré, and deprived of the money.[27]

On the 27th Foucault called a meeting of the superior council for the 28th. "During the night," says the principal historian of this episode,[28] "the guns which were at the Tchoupitoulas gate" (that of the upper river-side corner) "were spiked, and the next morning, on the 28th, the Acadians, headed by Noyan, and the Germans by Villeré entered the town, armed with fowling-pieces, with muskets, and all sorts of weapons." Other gates were forced, other companies entered, stores and dwellings were closed, heavy bodies of insurgents paraded the streets, and, in the words of Aubry, "all was in a state of combustion." A mass meeting was harangued by Lafrénière, Doucet, and the brothers Milhet, and a petition signed by 600 men was sent to the superior council, then in session, asking the official action which the members of that body were ready and waiting to take. With the help of Aubry, whose whole force numbered only 110 men, Ulloa retired with his family on board the Spanish frigate lying in the river. The council met again on the 29th, and, against the warnings and reproaches of Aubry, adopted, as petitioned by the meeting of the day before, a report enjoining Ulloa to "leave the colony in the frigate in which he came, without delay."

Aubry, requested by the leaders of the conspiracy to resume the government, reproached them with rebellion, and predicted their disastrous end. Ulloa, the wisest and kindest well-wisher of Louisiana that had held the gubernatorial commission since Bienville, sailed on the 31st of October, not in the Spanish frigate, which was detained for repairs, but in a French vessel, enduring at the last moment the songs and jeers of a throng of night roysterers, and the menacing presence of sergeants and bailiffs of the council.[29]

The colonists, as well as Aubry, Ulloa, and Foucault, now hurried forward their messengers, with their various declarations, to the courts of France and Spain.[30] That of Aubry, and that of Ulloa, from Havana, may be passed without comment; that of Foucault, with the remark that it was characterized by the shameless double-dealing, which leaves to the intendant commissary alone, of all the participants in those events, a purely infamous memory.

The memorial of the colonists, with its various accompanying depositions, compels a moment's attention. In the midst of a most absurd confusion of truth and misstatement, of admissions fatal to their pleadings, arrogant announcement of unapplied principles, and enumeration of those real wrongs for which France and Spain, but not Ulloa, were to blame, the banished governor was accused on such charges as having a chapel in his own house, absenting himself from the French churches, fencing in a fourth of the public commons to pasture his private horses, sending to Havana for a wet nurse, ordering the abandonment of a brick-yard near the city on account of its pools of putrid water, removing leprous children from the town to the inhospitable settlement at the mouth of the river, forbidding the public whipping of slaves in town, and thereby compelling masters to go six miles to get their slaves whipped, landing at New Orleans during a thunder and rainstorm and under other ill omens, claiming to be king of the colony, offending the people with evidences of "sordid avarice," and (as the text has it) "many others equally just and terrible."[31]

The most unfortunate characteristic of the memorial, however, was the fulsome adulations loaded upon the unworthy king who had betrayed its authors.[32] The chiefs of the insurrection had at first entertained the bold idea of declaring the independence of the colony and establishing a republic. To this end two of their number, Noyan and Bienville,* about three months before the outbreak, had gone secretly to Governor Elliot, at Pensacola, to treat for the aid of British troops. In this they failed; and though their lofty resolution, which might, by wiser leaders, have been communicated to the popular will, was not at once abandoned, it was hidden and finally smothered under a disingenuous pretense of the most ancient and servile fealty to the king and government, whose incapacity and perfidy were the prime cause of all their troubles: "Great king, the best of kings, father and protector of your subjects, deign, sire, to receive into your royal and paternal bosom the children who have no other desire than to die your subjects," etc.[33]

Such was the address which Lesassier, St. Lette, and Milhet, the three delegates representing the superior council, the planters, and the merchants, carried to France.[34] The aged Bienville had at length gone to his final rest, and they were compelled to make their appearance before the Duc de Choiseul unsupported. St. Lette, a former intimate of the duke, was cordially received; but the deputation, as such, was met with frowns, and heard only the ominous intelligence that the king of Spain, already informed, had taken all the steps necessary to a permanent occupation. With these tidings Milhet and Lesassier returned, having effected nothing save the issuing of an order for the refunding of the colonial debt, at three-fifths of its nominal value, in 5 per cent. bonds.[35]

In a letter of the 21st of March, 1769, Foucault cautiously and covertly deserted his associate conspirators, and denounced them to the French cabinet.[36]

On the 20th of April the Spanish frigate sailed from New Orleans, first setting the three Spanish officers, Loyola, Gayarré, and Navarro, ashore in the town, where they remained unmolested.[37]

At length the project of forming a republic was revived and given definite shape and advocacy. But the moment of opportunity had passed, and news of the approach of an overwhelming Spanish military and naval force paralyzed the spirit of the people.[38]

Thus have been shown, in outline, the salient causes and events of this bold but misguided uprising against the injustice and oppression of two royal powers at once, by "the first European colony (in America) that entertained the idea of proclaiming her independence."[39] Its results may be still more cursorily stated.

*Jean-Baptiste Payen de Noyan and Jean-Baptiste Payen de Noyan-Bienville. These two brothers were nephews of Jean-Baptiste Le Moyné, Sieur de Bienville.

On the 18th of August, 1769, Don Alexandro O'Reilly, accompanied by 3,600 chosen "Spanish troops—a force nearly one-half larger than the total number of able-bodied white men in the province—and with fifty pieces of artillery, landed, with unprecedented pomp, at the Place d'Armes, from a fleet of twenty-four vessels.[40]

On the 21st twelve of the principal movers in the insurrection were arrested. Among all the conspirators only one, Villeré, had contemplated flight, and he had later decided to remain.[41] They had even sent three of their number, Lafrénière, Marquis and Milhet, down the river before O'Reilly reached the town, to meet and welcome him with assurances of submission and loyalty. These were among the twelve arrested.[42] On the 23d Foucault was also made a prisoner, in his own house.[43] One other, [Denis] Braud, the printer of the seditious documents, was apprehended, and a proclamation announced that no other arrest would be made.[44]

Foucault, pleading that he had acted throughout in his official capacity was, on the 14th of October, sent, for trial, to France.[45] There he was confined in the Bastile, where he remained about a year, when he was sent as commissary-general and ordonnateur to the island of Bourbon, about four hundred miles east of Madagascar. Braud plead his obligation as government printer to print all public documents, and was liberated.[46] Villeré either "died raving mad on the day of his arrest," as stated in the Spanish official report,[47] or met his end in the act of resisting his guard on board the frigate where he had been placed in confinement.[48] On the 20th of October the remainder were brought to trial and on the 24th were convicted and sentenced. Five, Lafrénière, Noyan, Caresse, Marquis, and Joseph Milhet were condemned to the gallows. The most earnest supplications, even of a number of ladies, as well as of colonists and of Spanish officials, succeeded only in mitigating the sentence so far as to save the condemned from the gallows and on the next day they were shot.[49] The rest of the condemned were sentenced to foreign imprisonment. One, Petit, for life; two, Masan and Doucet, for ten years; and three, Boisblanc, Jean Milhet and Poupet, for six years. The estates of all were sequestered and none of them were to be allowed ever to return to the colony. They were incarcerated in the Moro Castle, Havana, but after a year's confinement were released by order of the Spanish king.[50]

For some cause not discernible the young naval lieutenant, Bienville, seems not have been proceeded against, and his name disap-

pears from the record with his refusal to be the bearer of the confederates' petition to France in October of the previous year.[51]

*The superior council's declaration was burned on the place d'armes.**

On the 21st, twelve of the principal movers in the insurrection were arrested. Two days later Foucault was also made a prisoner. One other, Braud, the printer of the seditious documents, was apprehended, and a proclamation announced that no other arrests would be made. Foucault was taken to France, tried by his own government, and thrown into the Bastile. Braud was set at liberty. Villeré died on the day of his arrest. Lafréniere, Noyan, Caresse, Marquis, and Joseph Milhet, were shot, and the remaining six were sentenced to the Moro castle, Havana, where they remained a year, and were then set at liberty. The declaration of the superior council was burned on the Place d'Armes.[52]

On the 25th of November the official machinery of a new colonial and municipal government replaced the old, and by the year 1770 the authority and laws of Spain were everywhere operating in full force.[53] Aubry refused a high commission in the Spanish army, departed for France, and, after having entered the river Garonne, was shipwrecked and lost.[54]

[6.] THE SUPERIOR COUNCIL AND THE CABILDO

The superior council, the administrative body which, in the struggle of 1768, was the bold advocate and champion of those commercial interests whose preservation was the main motive of the uprising, owed its origin to Louis XV.[†]

In 1712 this monarch had granted to Anthony Crozat his monopoly of the colony's commerce. It had been given in contemplation and consideration of Crozat's intention and pledge to settle the country with Europeans, and there being as yet no officer of justice in the infant colony, it was deemed most convenient to establish, on a sort of probationary tenure of three years, commencing in 1713, a superior council. Jurisdiction was given it in all cases, civil and criminal. It was composed of but two persons at first, the governor and the commissary ordonnateur,[‡] or of three, counting its clerk.[1] The system of laws which this body was to ad-

*The preceding four paragraphs are Cable's longer version of the next paragraph.
†Actually Louis XIV.

‡Under the bicephalous governor structure prevailing in the French colonies, the *commissaire-ordonnateur* was the colony's chief legal and financial officer. He

minister, was the ancient "custom of Paris," with the laws, edicts, and ordinances of the kingdom of France; it being one of the terms of Crozat's charter that the colony should be so governed.[2]

In the month of September, 1716, the provisional three years being about to expire, a perpetual royal edict re-established the council on a permanent footing. Its dignity was raised in accordance with the increasing importance of the colony, and its organization was enlarged to comprise the governor-general of New France, the intendant of the same province, the governor of Louisiana, a senior counselor, the lieutenant-governor, two puisne counselors, and an attorney-general; also, as before, a clerk. Its powers were those of similar bodies in other French colonies, as St. Domingo and Martinique.[3] It held its sessions monthly, dispensing justice for the entire colony as far as called upon, and administering the civil government of the province. Three of its eight members in civil, and five in criminal, cases formed a quorum. A germ of popular government lay in a provision, that in the event of proper or unavoidable absence of members, a quorum could be made by calling in a corresponding number of notable inhabitants.[4]

A peculiar feature of this tribunal was, that though the governor of New France, and, in his absence, the governor of Louisiana, occupied the first seat in the council, yet the intendant of New France, or, if he were not present, the senior counselor, performed the functions of president, collecting the votes and pronouncing judgment. The principle was found still in full play when, in 1768, Foucault ruled the insurgent council and signed its pronouncements, while the protesting but helpless Aubry filled the seat of honor. In all preliminary proceedings, such as the affixing of seals and inventories, the senior counselor officiated and presided as a judge of the first instance.[5]

Crozat, entirely disappointed in his expectation of opening a trade with Spanish America, in August, 1717, surrendered his charter,[6] and, the province being transferred to the Compagnie d'Occident, or Western Company, its directors solicited certain modifications esteemed necessary in the organization and offices of the superior council.[7]

---

shared authority with the governor, who oversaw military and general affairs. See Donald J. Lemieux, "Some Legal and Practical Aspects of the Office of *Commissaire-Ordonnateur* of French Louisiana," in *The French Experience in Louisiana*, ed. Glenn R. Conrad, vol. 1 of *The Louisiana Purchase Bicentennial Series in Louisiana History* (Lafayette: Center for Louisiana Studies, 1995), 395–407.

Consequently, by an edict issued in September, 1719, it was made to consist of such directors of the company as might be in the province, the commandant-general, a senior counselor, the two king's lieutenants or lieutenant-governor, three other counselors, an attorney-general, and a clerk. The quorum, and the arrangements for securing it, remained unchanged; the sessions continued to be monthly; the council was still, as it had been from the first, a court of last resort; but now it was elevated beyond the province of a court of the first instance into a jurisdiction purely appellate, and inferior tribunals were established in various parts of the growing colony.[8]

These lower courts are specially noteworthy, in the fact that they were presided over, not by royal officers, but by agents of the company, one in each, with notables of the neighborhood, two for civil and four for criminal cases.[9] Thus, in various developments, the administration of the colony's civil and judicial affairs was gradually showing more and more the features of a representative rule.

It was this superior council which, in 1722, removed to the new settlement of New Orleans, and thus made it the colony's capital.[10] In 1723 and 1724, it was exercising powers of police,[11] and, in 1726, incurring the searching investigations of the royal commissary, De la Chaise, and the emphatic reprimand of the home government.[12] In 1728, August 10, a decree of the king assigned to the council the supervision of land titles.[13] Special sessions were held once or twice a week as a lower court, by two of its members, chosen, and removable by it, to try causes involving values not exceeding 100 livres ($22).[14]

On surrender of the India Company's charter, in 1732, the superior council was again remodeled. Its membership was increased to twelve and a secretary, beside the governor-general of New France. The twelve were the governor of Louisiana, the commissary, the two lieutenant-governors, the town mayor of New Orleans, six counsellors, and the attorney-general.[15] Two years later, in 1742, the labors of the council were so increased, by litigation arising out of the increase of trade, that four assessors were added, to serve four years, and to sit and rank after the counselors, voting only in cases where the record was referred to them to report on, or where they were needed to complete a quorum, or in the event of a tie vote.[16]

The power over land deeds was, on the 13th of March, 1748, extended, by royal decree, to allow the making of good titles, upon inventories prepared in good faith, and recording them, though unofficial and informal, when such defects were the result of the absence or incompetency of public officers.[17]

Such was the body which, twenty years later, though it could not quite shake off an outward pretense of obeisance to royalty, made bold to demand openly the rights of freemen for the people, of whom it had grown to be a sort of legislature, and to lay plans secretly for free government.

It was through the superior council that, in 1724, was issued that dark enactment which, for so many years, and during three dominations, remained on the statute book—the well-named Black Code.[18] One of its articles forbade the freeing of a slave without reason shown to the council, and by it esteemed good.[19] It was the superior council which, in or about the year 1752, resisted the encroachments of the Jesuits, though these were based on a commission from the bishop of Quebec;[20] and it was this body that, in 1763, anticipated by the space of a year the actual expulsion of the same troublesome order from France, and dispossessed it of its plantations in Louisiana.[21] [Vincent-Gaspard-Pierre de] Rochemore, an intendant commissary sent from France in 1758, found this council, headed by Governor Kerlerec, too strong for him, was rudely jostled by it, and, in 1761, was dismissed from office on its complaint to the king.[22] And it was the superior council which M. d'Abbadie, in a dispatch of the 7th of June, 1764, denounced as a body so filled with what he esteemed the spirit of sedition, that he thought it highly desirable to remove from it the Creole members, and fill their places with imported Frenchmen.[23] It was natural that O'Reilly, invested with special power to establish the civil and military branches of government, in such form as might seem to him best to promote the king's service and the happiness of his subjects,[24] should promptly, and once for all, abolish this exponent of the popular will; and in November, 1769, at his direction, the superior council gave place to the cabildo.[25]

In this passage from French rule to Spanish, the radical nature of the change lay, not in the laws, but in the redistribution of power, the lion's share of which was held in reserve in the hands of the military and ecclesiastical representatives of the crown and the church, while an extremely slender portion was doled out, with much form and pomp, to the cabildo.

This body consisted of ten members, in addition to the governor, who presided at its meetings, and an *escribano,* or minute clerk. Its membership was divided into two main groups, distinguished by the character of their tenure of office: that of the smaller group, of four, being annual and elective, while that of the remaining six was a life tenure acquired by purchase.[26]

The four elected members were chosen on the first of each year, by the whole cabildo, including the votes of those who were about to retire from office. They were required to be householders and residents of the town. Except by a unanimous vote, they could not be re-elected until they had been two years out of office. No officer or attaché of the financial department of the realm, nor any bondsman of such, nor any one under the age of twenty-six, nor any new convert to the Catholic faith, could qualify. Two filled the office of *alcaldes ordinarios,* or common judges, holding each his separate— civil and criminal—daily court in the town hall, and—for causes involving not over $20—an evening court for one hour at his residence, where he rendered unwritten decisions. Their judgments were subject to appeals in all civil cases, and they were without jurisdiction over any who could claim a military or an ecclesiastical connection.[27]

A third elective officer was the *sindico-procurador-general,* or attorney-general-syndic, the official advocate of the people in the deliberations of the cabildo. He was not, as the modern usage of the title might imply, a prosecuting officer, though as the municipal attorney it was his duty to sue for revenues and other debts due the town, and he was present in its interest at all apportionments of land. The last of the four was the *mayordomo-de-proprios,* the municipal treasurer, who made his disbursements upon the cabildo's warrants, and rendered to it annually, on vacating his office, an account of the year's business.[28]

The seats in the cabildo, acquired by purchase, were bought, primarily, at auction from the government. These could be sold again by those leaving them, to their successors, provided that the royal treasury must receive half the price of the first transfer and one-third the price of subsequent transmissions. In these sat the six *regidors* or administrators—literally, rulers. The first held a merely honorary office under the title of *alferez real,* the royal standard-bearer, and was without official functions, unless the death or absence of one of the alcaldes called him to fill the vacancy to the end of the annual term. The second regidor was the *alcalde mayor provincial,* a magistrate with jurisdiction over crimes and misdemeanors committed beyond town or village limits, and with power to overtake and try persons escaped to such regions. The third was the *alguazil mayor,* a civil and criminal sheriff, superintendent of police and prisons; and the other three, ranking according to the seniority of their commissions, were the *depositario-general,* a keeper and dispenser of the government stores, the *recibidor de penas de camara,* a receiver of fines and penalties, and a sixth, to whom no individual official functions were assigned.[29]

Thus constituted, the cabildo met every Friday in the town hall. It heard appeals from the decisions of the *alcaldes ordinarios,* through two of the regidors, chosen by it to sit with the *alcalde,* who had given judgment; but this was only where judgment had been given for not more than $330, larger cases being assigned by the king to such tribunal as he might select.[30] At its discretion it sold or revoked the meat monopoly, and the many other petty municipal privileges which characterized the Spanish rule. The expenditures of town government were made on the cabildo's warrants, but not without consent of the royal governor, except the most paltry sums; while on the other hand the cabildo was required to exact of the governor, before he entered upon the duties of his office, good and sufficient security for its proper conduct, and his pledge to submit to its investigation any or all of his acts.[31]

Full details of the elaborate machinery of administration, with its laborious forms and pomps, would be unprofitable. The underlying design seems to have been not to confer power, but to scatter and neutralize it in the hands of royal officials and of a cabildo which, loaded with titles, and fettered with minute ministerial duties, was, so to speak, the superior council shorn of its locks; or, if not, a body, at least, whose members recognized their standing as *guardians* of the people and *servants* of the king.

Immediately upon organizing the cabildo, O'Reilly announced the appointment of Don Louis de Unzaga, colonel of the regiment of Havana, as governor of Louisiana, and yielded him the presidential chair. Yet, under his own higher commission of captain-general, he continued for a time to govern.[32] The instructions which he had published established in force the laws of Castile and of the Indies, and the use of the Spanish tongue in the courts and public offices,[33] and so far was this carried, that the notarial records of the day show the baptismal names of property-holders of French and Anglo-Saxon origin, changed to a Spanish orthography, and the indices made upon those instead of upon the surnames. The official use of the French language was tolerated only in the judicial and notarial acts of the military commandants, who ruled everywhere outside of New Orleans.[34]

Thus, in all things save the habits and traditions of the people, the town, and the great territory of which it was the capital, became Spanish. The change in the laws was not a violent one; there was a tone of severity and a feature of arbitrary surveillance in the Spanish, that may have carried an unpleasant contrast, but the principles of both the French and the Spanish systems had a common origin, the one remote, the other almost direct, in the Roman code, and their similarity was specially marked in their bearings upon the all-important points of the marital relation and inheritance.[35] The *recopilaciones* of Castile and the Indies went into force, without other friction than resulted from change of tongue, and under these laws, with the Fuero Viejo, Fuero Juzco, Partidas, Autos Accordados, and Royal Schedules, justice continued to be administered up to and through the recession to France, and until the purchase of the province by the United States. And though in 1808, this system gave place in part to a "digest of the civil laws then in force," arranged after the code of Napoleon, yet from it, and especially from the Partidas, are derived many of the features of the code of practice of Louisiana of to-day. For while, by an act of the Louisiana legislature of March 12, 1828, "all the civil laws in force before the promulgation of the civil code" (of 1825) "were declared abrogated," yet the supreme court has decided that they are still the statute laws of the state, and that the legislature did not intend to abrogate those principles of law which had been established or settled by the decision of courts of justice.[36]

After all is said, it is proper to remark the wide difference between the laws themselves and their administration. Spanish rule in Louisiana was better, at least, than French, which scarce deserved the name of government; while as to its laws, the state of Louisiana, in which by reason of its capital these laws were best known and most applied, "is at this time the only state, of the vast territories acquired from France, Spain, and Mexico, in which the civil law has been retained, and forms a large portion of its jurisprudence."[37]

On the 29th of October, 1770,[38] O'Reilly sailed from New Orleans with the greater part of the troops he had brought with him, thus signifying the completion of his commission in the entire and peaceful establishment of the Spanish powers.[39] The force left by him in the colony amounted to 1,200 men.[40] He had himself made several suggestions to the home government, advantageous to the commercial interests of New Orleans,[41] and his departure was the signal for the commencement of active measures intended to induce, if possible, a change in the sentiments of the people consonant with the political changes forced upon them. Such was the kindlier task of the wise and mild Unzaga.

[7.] SPANISH CONCILIATION

While Spain had been delaying to take possession of Louisiana, and temporizing with the mettlesome citizens of her capital, the commercial adventurers of another nation had been more diligent.

"I found the English," says O'Reilly in a dispatch of October, 1769, "in complete possession of the commerce of the colony. They had in this town their merchants and traders, with open stores and shops, and I can safely assert, that they pocketed nine-tenths of the money spent here. . . . I drove off all the English traders and the other individuals of that nation whom I found in this town, and I shall admit here none of their vessels."[1] Thus pointedly did he set forth the despotic relation which the town and province had been, and still were, forced to accept from their European master, whether he were the French Louis or the Spanish Charles.

That the rule of Spain in Louisiana was grossly oppressive in the letter of its laws and regulations, is a fact, however, merely in keeping with the times in which it existed. Colonies had not yet come to be regarded as having inherent rights, but were looked upon in most cases as commercial ventures, projected in the interest of the sovereign's revenues, and upon which monopolies and like restrictions were laid, or indulgences bestowed, simply as that interest seemed to require.

It was on this principle that Crozat, Law, and Louis XV had, each in turn, conducted affairs in Louisiana. In pursuance of the same course, Charles III, after the momentary concessions of May, 1766, in September of the same year, had established those commercial regulations[2] against which the Creoles so boldly protested. It was not alone against the truly Spanish surveillance placed upon the prices of all imported goods, that this protest had been made; by these regulations commerce with France was reduced to the importation of articles of necessity, and that of St. Domingo and Martinique to the exchange of wine and breadstuffs for lumber and grain, in passported ships, on policed bills of lading, and only until such a time as Spain could take measures to supplant these trades by a commerce exclusively her own. Beyond this the port of New Orleans, with the vast province behind it, was shut out from every market in the world, except certain specified ports of Spain; *Seville, Alicant, Carthagena, Malaga, Barcelona, Coruña, etc.,*[3] markets where, her merchants complained, they could neither sell their produce to advantage nor buy the merchandise wanted in the province.[4] They could employ only Spanish bottoms commanded by subjects of Spain. Their vessels could not even put into a Spanish-American port except in distress, and then only under onerous restrictions.[5] The commerce of the port was virtually throttled, merely by an actual application of the principles which had always hung over it, and only by the loose administration of which the colony and town had survived and grown, while Anthony Crozat had become bankrupt, Law's Compagnie d'Occident had been driven to other fields of enterprise, and Louis XV had heaped up a loss of millions more than he could pay.

In fact, the life and growth of the port and of the colony had depended on the double influence of gross disregard of the royal enactments by the officials, and a bold infraction of them by the people.[6] And in 1770 Don Louis de Unzaga, assuming authority, and seeing the extremity to which the people were driven, resumed the accustomed policy, and the same desirable ends began again to be met by the same lamentable expedients. His method, which was also the method of those who came after him, worked in two opposite directions at once, and brought relief to the colony's commerce by procuring, on the one hand, repeated concessions and indulgences from the king, and on the other, by overlooking the evasion by the people of those onerous burdens which the home government still required to be laid on them.

Not that Unzaga began at the beginning. Royal abatements had been made as early as in March, 1768, when an exemption from import duty was decreed on foreign and Spanish merchandise.[7] O'Reilly himself, a year and a half later, had recommended an entirely free trade with Spain and Havana, enumerating the colony's wants—"flour, wine, oil, iron instruments, arms, ammunition, and every sort of manufactured goods for clothing and other domestic purposes"—and its exportable products—"timber, indigo, cotton, furs, and a small quantity of corn and rice,"[8] and recommending that vessels owned in the colony be placed on an equality with Spanish vessels. It was probably due to his efforts that, in 1770 or 1771, permission was given, allowing as many as two vessels a year to enter the port of New Orleans from France.[9]

Upon these followed, from year to year, the concessions procured by Unzaga, the equally effective lenity of his administration, and various other events and conditions of kindred influence. The river trade with British vessels increased. Under cover of trading with the British posts on the eastern bank above Orleans island, they supplied New Orleans and the river "coasts," above and below, with goods and with slaves. Anything offered in exchange was acceptable, revenue laws were mentioned only in jest, profits were large, credit was free and long, and business brisk. Under the river-bank where now stands the suburb of Gretna, opposite the present fourth district of New Orleans, two large floating warehouses, fitted up with counters and shelves, and stocked with assorted merchandise, lay moored, when they were not trading up and down the shores of the stream. The sum of this commerce was some $650,000 a year.[10]

The merchants of New Orleans, shut out from participation in this contraband trade, complained loudly but in vain to Unzaga.[11] In 1773, however, when their complaints were turned against their debtors on the plantations, who, waxing prosperous, were buying additional slaves and broadening their lands with money due the New Orleans merchants for crop advances, the governor's ears were opened, and drawing upon his large reserve of absolute power, he gently but firmly checked and corrected this imposition.[12]

Meanwhile, certain royal concessions, dated August 17, 1772, and made in response to O'Reilly's suggestions, were failing to afford appreciable relief to legitimate commerce, because so narrowed as to be almost neutralized by restrictive provisos.[13] But Unzaga's quiet power worked for the benefit of the people under his rule, not alone in the direction of their commercial relations. While the town was languishing under the infliction of these so-called concessions, his conservative and pacific treatment of a fierce crusade, made by newly imported Spanish Capuchins against their French brethren, and certain customs which these had long permitted to obtain among the laity, averted an exodus of Creoles from New Orleans, which he feared might have even destroyed the colony.[14]

Indeed, the colony had already suffered a grave loss of this character. While O'Reilly was still in the province, so large a proportion of the merchants and mechanics of New Orleans had removed to St. Domingo, that a few days before his own departure he ceased to grant passports.[15] No corresponding influx seems to have offset this depletion,[16] and in 1773 Unzaga wrote to the bishop of Cuba that "there were not in New Orleans and its environs 2,000 souls" (meaning possibly whites) "of all professions and conditions," and that most of these were extremely poor. An imprudent governor might have reduced the town, if not the province also, to a desert. But under Unzaga conciliation soon began to take effect; commissions were eagerly taken in his "regiment of Louisiana" by Creoles—the pay being large and the sword the true symbol of power—while its ranks were filled by soldiers from the late French, as well as from the Spanish troops;[17] and the offices of regidor and alcalde were by and by occupied by the bearers of such ancient Creole names as St. Denis, La Chaise, Fleurieau, Forstall, Duplessis, Bienvenue, Dufossat, Livandais.[18] In 1776 Unzaga was made captain-general of Caracas, and in the following year left in the charge of Don Bernardo de Galvez, then about twenty-one years of age,[19] a people still French in feeling, it is true, yet reconciled, in a measure, to Spanish rule.[20]

At this point a change took place in the Spanish foreign policy, and the French instead of the English merchants commanded the trade of the Mississippi. The British traders found themselves suddenly treated with great rigor, Galvez commencing the new movement by the seizure of eleven of their vessels richly laden, and exceeding the letter of the Franco-Spanish treaty in privileges bestowed upon the French. The prospect for the future of New Orleans brightened rapidly, and the spirit of the people revived.[21]

Under certain restrictions, trade was allowed with Campeachy and the French and Spanish West Indies. The importation of slaves from these islands, because of their spirit of insurrection, had been for a long time forbidden, but the trade in Guinea negroes was now specially encouraged; a little later the prohibition against the former trade was removed. In March, 1777, a 4 per cent. export duty was reduced to 2 per cent. In April, 1778, Galvez, though only governor *ad interim,* by his own proclamation gave the right to trade with any port of France, and a few days later[22] included the ports of the thirteen British colonies then engaged in that struggle for independence, in which the fate of the little captive city at the mouth of the Mississippi was so profoundly though obscurely involved. Furs and peltries shipped to any port of Spain were made free of export duty for ten years. The Spanish government became the buyer of all the tobacco raised in the province, and endeavors were made to induce a French and a French West Indian immigration.[23]

The value of nearly all these privileges was presently reduced to very little, by the issue of British letters of marque against the commerce of Spain, and by the active participation of France in the American revolution.[24] Galvez was looking to his defenses, building gunboats, and awaiting from his king the word which would enable him to try his conscious military talents.[25]

But another trade had sprung up, the direct result of these new conditions. Some eight years before, at the moment when the arrival of 2,600 Spanish troops and the non-appearance of their supply-ships had driven the price of provisions in New Orleans almost to famine rates, one Oliver Pollock entered the port with a brig-load of flour from Baltimore, offered it to O'Reilly on the captain-general's own terms, and finally sold it to him at $15 a barrel, two-thirds the current price. O'Reilly rewarded his liberality with a grant of free trade to Louisiana for his lifetime.[26] Such was the germ of the trade with the United States. In 1776 it appears that Oliver Pollock, at the head of a number of merchants from New York, Philadelphia, and Boston, who had established themselves in New Orleans, had begun, with the countenance of Galvez, to supply, by fleets of large canoes, the agents of the American cause with arms and ammunition delivered at Fort Pitt (Pittsburgh). The same movement was repeated in 1777 and 1778, and Pollock became the avowed agent of the American government.[27]

In this way and in other ways the blockade of the town's West Indian and Transatlantic commerce showed an advantageous side. Immigration became Anglo-Saxon, a valuable increase of population taking place, by an inflow from the Floridas and the United States, of an enterprising element that made its residence in the town itself and took the oath of allegiance.[28] Commercial acquaintance was made with the growing West, as a few years before with Baltimore, Philadelphia, New York, and Boston.[29] To be shut in upon home resources could hardly have been without some lessons of frugality and self-help in the domestic life—the secret of public wealth. This self-sustentation was now practicable; even without the Ohio river. Inside the lines indicated at St. Louis, Natchitoches, New Orleans, and Fort Panmure (Natchez), there was sufficient diversity of products and industries to support an active commercial intercourse;[30] the Attakapas and the Opelousas prairies had been settled by Acadian herdsmen, a long stretch of Mississippi River "coast" by farmers from among the same exiled people;[31] in 1778 immigrants from the Canary islands had founded the settlements of Valenzuela on Lafourche, Galveztown on the Amite, and that of Terre aux Bœufs, just below New Orleans.[32] A paper currency supplied the sometimes urgent call for a circulating medium, and the colonial treasury warrants, or liberanzas, were redeemed by receipts of specie from Vera Cruz sufficiently frequent to keep them in circulation, and at times to give them a moderately fair market value.[33] Such were the sources of a certain prosperity, and to show these is to give the causes of a proportionate degree of public satisfaction.

Whether this feeling had any stronger qualities than that of a passive acquiescence was now to be tested. For in the summer of 1779 Spain had declared war against Great Britain.[34] Galvez discovered that the British were planning the surprise of New Orleans, and under cover of preparations for defense, made haste to take the offensive. Four days before the time he had appointed to move, a hurricane destroyed a large number of houses in the town, and spread ruin to crops and dwellings up and down the "coast," and sunk his gun flotilla. The young commander, nothing dismayed, appeared before the people assembled on the Place d'Armes, and displaying a commission lately received, confirming him as governor of Louisiana, demanded of them to say whether he should appear before the cabildo, as the terms of his commission required, and swear to defend the province from its enemies.[35]

His appeal was responded to with enthusiasm. Repairing his disasters as best he could, and hastening his ostensibly defensive preparations, he marched, on the 22d of August, 1779, against the British forts on the Mississippi. His force, beside the four Spanish officers who ranked in turn below him, consisted of 170 regulars, 330 recruits, 20 carabineers, 60 militiamen, 80 free men of color, 600 men from the coast, "of every condition and color," 160 Indians, 9 American volunteers, and Oliver Pollock.[36]

This little army of 1,434 men was without tents, other military furniture, or a single engineer. The gun fleet followed in the river abreast of their line of march along its shores, carrying one 24-, five 18-, and four 4-pounders. With this force, in the space of about three weeks, Fort Bute on bayou Manchac, Baton Rouge, and Fort Panmure, 8 vessels, 556 regulars, and a number of sailors, militiamen, and free blacks, fell into the hands of the Spaniards.[37] The next year, 1780, re-enforced from Havana, Galvez again left New Orleans by way of the Balize with 2,000 men, regulars, militia, and free blacks, and on the 15th of March took Fort Charlotte on Mobile river.[38]

Galvez next conceived the much larger project of taking Pensacola. Failing to secure re-enforcements from Havana by writing for them, he sailed to that place in October to make his application in person, intending to move with them directly on the enemy. After many delays and disappointments he succeeded, and early in March, 1781, appeared before Pensacola with a ship of the line, two frigates, and transports containing 1,400 soldiers well furnished with artillery and ammunition. Here he was joined by such troops as could be spared from Mobile, and by Don Estevan Miró* from New Orleans, at the head of the Louisiana force, and on the afternoon of the 16th of March, though practically unsupported by the naval fleet, until dishonor was staring its jealous commanders in the face, moved under hot fire, through a passage of great peril, and took up a besieging position. But an account of this engagement and siege is not essential to the history of New Orleans, and it is only necessary to state, that on the 9th of May, 1781, Pensacola, with a garrison of 800 men, and the whole of West Florida, were surrendered to Galvez.[39] Louisiana had heretofore been included under one domination with Cuba,[40] but now one of the several rewards bestowed upon her governor, was the captain-generalship of Louisiana and West Florida. He sailed from St. Domingo to take part in an expedition against the Bahamas, leaving Colonel Miró to govern *ad interim,* and never reassumed the governor's chair in Louisiana.[41]

Such is a brief summary of the achievements of the governor and of the people of Louisiana, operating from New Orleans in aid of the war for American independence; and if the motive of Spain was more conspicuously and exclusively selfish than that shown in the co-operation furnished by France, still a greater credit is due than is popularly accorded to the help afforded in the brilliant exploits of Galvez, discouraged by a timid cabildo, but supported initially, finally, and at the first mainly, by the Creoles of New Orleans and the neighboring coasts. The fact is equally true, though overlooked even in New Orleans, that while Andrew Jackson was yet a child, New Orleans had a deliverer from British conquest in Bernardo de Galvez, by whom the way was kept open for the United States to stretch to the Gulf and to the Pacific.

Spain herself, solicited by Galvez, made practical acknowledgment of her colonists' "zeal and fidelity," tried during the last two

---

*Esteban Miró (1744–95), also know as Estevan Miro and Esteban Miro.

years not only by war but by storms—one of August 24, 1780, being still more destructive than that of the year before—by inundation, contagion, rainy summer, rigorous winter, and an arrested commerce.[42] Galvez, enlightened as young, had asked for them a free trade with all the ports of Europe and America; but in the words of Judge Gayarré, "neither the court of Madrid nor the spirit of the age was disposed to go so far."[43] By a royal schedule published in New Orleans in the spring of 1782, the privileges granted in October, 1778, which the blockade had made valueless, were revived, enlarged, and extended for ten years, to begin from the prospective peace. The reshipment to any Spanish-American colony of goods received from Spain was allowed, but that of goods from other countries was expressly forbidden. Negroes were allowed to be imported duty-free from the colonies of neutral or allied powers, and might even be paid for in specie. Foreign vessels could be bought without duty and registered as Spanish bottoms. An export duty on staves shipped to Spain was removed. But a final article raised the export and import duty on all merchandise to 6 per cent.[44]

By such measures it was that the Spanish king sought "to secure to his vassals the utmost felicity," and to prove to the Creoles of Louisiana "that a change of government had not diminished their happiness." And such was the condition of affairs when, on the 3d of September, 1783, a treaty of peace between Great Britain, the United States, France, and Spain provided, in its eighth article, that the Mississippi, from its source to its mouth, should ever remain free and open to Great Britain and the United States.[45]

[8.] THE CREOLES STILL FRENCH*

The Spanish conquest never became more than a conquest. Those changes of which it originally consisted were almost all that it ever effected. Its customs regulations caused certain transitions in the agriculture of the province and the commerce of the town; and there it stopped—from the beginning to the end a foreign body. The Creole, with a grave and tempered dignity in pathetic contrast with his intemperate fire of 1768,[1] for thirty-five years bore it about in his flesh an unextracted missile, never absorbed, never ejected, but sometimes provocative of slight inflammations that called for wise and gentle handling. The Spanish governors, whatever may

*"The Unbending Creoles" in Cable's manuscript.

be true against them, had the fortunate discretion to treat the people, from first to last, as a wounded and paroled community that might be conciliated, but which it were vain to attempt to proselyte. It was only by such means that the colony was saved to Spain so long as it was. "The people here," wrote Unzaga in 1772, "will remain quiet as long as they are gently treated; but the use of the rod would produce confusion and ruin. Their dispositions are the result of the happy state of liberty to which they have been accustomed from the cradle, and in which they ought to be maintained, so far as is consistent with the laws of the kingdom."[2]

The changes made in the laws and their administration have already been noticed, with the reserve of power in the royal officers, and its comparative absence on the cabildo. [François-Xavier] Martin[3] quotes the United States consul at New Orleans as saying, in 1803: "The auditors of war and assessors of government and intendancy, . . . to them only may be attributed the maladministration of justice, as the governor and other judges, who are unacquainted with the law, seldom dare to act contrary to the opinions they give."

The change of agricultural products was felt or seen in New Orleans, only in so far as it called for a different mode of handling the marketed commodities or brought an increase of trade and profits. The transfer to Spanish domination shut out the indigo of Louisiana from the markets in which its producers had found under French domination protection for it, and forced it into the ports of Spain and into ruinous competition with the superior article made in the older and more southern Spanish colonies.[4] When later this burden was much lightened by wiser commercial regulations, a series of new drawbacks arose in continuously unfavorable seasons, and culminated in the appearance of an insect which, by the years 1793–94, was making such ravages that the planters, despairing of the indigo culture, knew not which way to turn for livelihood.[5]

Cotton had been known in the colony ever since 1713;[6] and as early as 1752 or 1753, M. Debreuil,* a wealthy citizen and landholder, and one of the leading minds in the colony, is said to have invented a cotton-gin sufficiently effective to induce a decided increase in the production of an article to which soil and climate were so favorable.[7] Yet the great importance and commercial value of cotton awaited the discovery of some still more advantageous mode

---

*Claude-Joseph Villars Dubreuil.

of ginning the staple from the seed than any yet known. Those who gave the matter thought had, in 1760, recommended the importation of such apparatus as could be found in India.[8] In 1768, however, with such methods as were known, cotton had already become an article of export from New Orleans, and was mentioned with solicitude in the manifesto of the banishers of Ulloa, as a new and promising source to which they looked for future prosperity.[9]

At the time of the collapse in the indigo culture, the Creoles were still experimenting with it;[10] but the fame of Eli Whitney's newly invented cotton-gin had probably not yet reached them, and the planters—little supposing that in the eighth year from that time the cotton crop of Louisiana and export from New Orleans would be respectively 20,000 and 34,000 300-pound bales[11]—turned their attention in another direction, and renewed their much earlier efforts to produce merchantable sugar.

The sugar-cane, introduced from St. Domingo by the Jesuit fathers in 1751, had been grown in the vicinity of New Orleans ever since. On a portion of the city's wholesale business district, included in the angle of Common and Tchoupitoulas streets, this great staple was first planted in Louisiana.[12] The amount produced, however, was trivial; only in the neighborhood of the town was a limited attention given it.[13] Nothing more than sirup, if even so much, was made from it[14] until M. Debreuil, in 1758, built a sugar mill on his plantation—now that part of the third district adjoining the second on the river front—and endeavored to turn a large crop of cane into sugar.[15]

Accounts of the result vary. It appears, however, that sugar was made, and that for a time the industry grew; but that the sugar was poorly granulated and very wet, and consumed entirely within the province until 1765, when it is said half of the first cargo shipped to France leaked out of the packages before the vessel reached port.[16]

The cession to Spain seems to have quite destroyed this half-developed industry, as might easily have been anticipated, and it was not until the insurrection of the blacks in St. Domingo, in 1791, brought an influx of refugees from that lately prosperous sugar-producing country,[17] that the paralyzed efforts of twenty-five years before came again to life. The connection with Spanish rule may not be as close as would appear, but the coincidence is notable— two Spaniards, Mendez and Solis, erected, the one a distillery and the other a sugar-house, and manufactured rum and sirup.[18]

Thus stood affairs when, in 1794, the people of lower Louisiana despaired of the culture of indigo. At this juncture Étienne de Boré, a Creole of the Illinois district, but a resident of New Orleans, and a son-in-law of [Jean Noel] Destréhan [de Tours], an early colonist, who had himself been one of the last to abandon sugar-culture, bought a quantity of canes from Mendez and Solis, planted on the land where the seventh district (late Carrollton) now stands, erected a mill, and, in 1795, electrified the community by making $12,000 worth of superior sugar.[19] This, the absence of those interdictions which had stifled commerce in the earlier days of Spanish rule, enabled him to market advantageously.[20] The agriculture of the Mississippi delta was revolutionized, and by the year 1802 New Orleans was the market for 200,000 gallons of rum, 250,000 gallons of molasses, and 5,000,000 pounds of sugar. The town contained some twelve distilleries, and a sugar refinery which produced about 200,000 pounds of loaf sugar; while, on the other hand, the production of indigo had declined to a total of 3,000 pounds, and soon after ceased.[21]

The frail character of almost all edifices in New Orleans, at the time of its passage from French hands to Spanish, the long neglect of public works, the readiness of the Spanish to supply this omission, the repeated necessity of repairing the ravages of storm and fire, caused the presence of the Spanish authority to have an effect upon the architecture of the town, which remains conspicuously evident in the ancient quarter at this day.

The census ordered by O'Reilly in 1769, showed the place to contain 468 houses.[22] Undoubtedly the more correct term would be premises, embracing the idea of three separate roofs to each entire household, an arrangement common in New Orleans down to a date almost recent, and occasioned by the general use of slave labor. The total population, 3,190 souls, indicated about seven to a residence, which must, therefore, be assumed to have comprised the family dwelling, a kitchen quite apart from it, and a third roof under which the household slaves were quartered. To these the well-to-do added stables and other buildings, slave-service favoring the multiplication of outhouses quite sufficient to offset the confinement of the poor to narrower limits.

In this light it becomes easy to accept the equally authentic statement, that a conflagration, in 1788, nineteen years after—when the increase of the town was but 67 per cent. over the O'Reilly census—destroyed 856 edifices,[23] nearly twice the number in the entire town according to the literal rendering of the previous census. There were probably as many *roofs* burned, out of about 2,300, or about 285 complete domiciles out of about 770.

This conflagration itself had an odd and accidental connection with the presence of Spanish authority. For it was in the private chapel of Don Vincente José Nuñez, the military treasurer, on Chartres street near St. Louis, that on Good Friday, the 21st of March, 1788, at half-past one in the afternoon, a fire broke out that destroyed nearly half the town. The buildings along the immediate river front escaped; but the central portion of the town, including the entire wholesale commercial quarter, the dwellings of the leading inhabitants, the town hall, the arsenal, the jail, the parish church, and the quarters of the Capuchins, were completely consumed.[24]

Six years later, on the 8th of December, 1794, some children playing in a court in Royal street, too near to an adjoining hay store, set fire to it. A strong north wind was blowing, and in three hours 212 dwellings and stores in the heart of the town were destroyed. The cathedral, lately finished on the site of the church burned in 1788, escaped; but the pecuniary losses exceeded those of the previous conflagration, which had been estimated at nearly $2,600,000. Only two stores were left standing; the levee and the Place d'Armes became, as they had been six years before, the camping ground of hundreds of inhabitants, and the destruction of provisions was such as to threaten a famine.[25]

In consequence of these desolating fires, whose ravages were largely attributed to the inflammable building material in general use, the Baron [Francisco Louis Hector] Carondelet, then governor, recommended to his government to offer a premium on roofs covered with tiles, instead of shingles as heretofore;[26] and whether this premium was ever offered or not, from this time the tile roof came into use, and forms to-day one of the most picturesque features of the old French quarter. As the heart of the town filled up again it was with better structure,[27] displaying many Spanish-American features—adobe or brick walls, arcades, inner courts, ponderous doors and windows, balconies, *porte-cochères,* and white and yellow lime-washed stucco. Two-story dwellings took the place of one-story buildings, and the general appearance, as well as the public safety, was improved.[28]

It is noteworthy, that after these fires the record of disasters wrought upon the town itself by hurricanes, becomes unimportant. The conjecture is common, that in the early days of the city's history

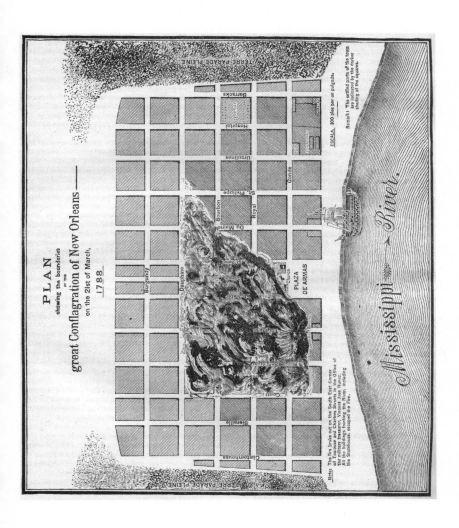

PLAN
showing the boundaries
OF THE
great Conflagration of New Orleans ——
on the 21st of March,
1788

Barracks

Hospital

Ursulines

St. Phillppe

Bourbon

Dry Mano

Royal

Conde

Burgundy

Dauphine

Church

PLAZA
DE ARMAS

St. Louis

Conti

Bienville

Customhouse

ESCALA. 300 pies por un pulgada.

Remark: The settled parts of the town
are indicated by the darker
shading of the squares.

Note: The fire broke out on the South East Corner
of Toulouse and Chartres Streets in the Office of
the military treasurer, Vincent Jose Nunez.
All the buildings fronting the River, including
the Statehouse, escaped the Fire.

TERRE PARADE PLEINE

TERRE PARADE PLEINE

Mississippi → River.

storms were more frequent and violent than in later days. A much simpler explanation lies in the probability, that at first the saturated state of the undrained soil induced the not too energetic colonist to make shift with very defective foundations, scarcely sunk below the surface of the ground. The structures erected under military direction, with an eye to permanence, did not succumb to the wind. One, the convent of the Ursulines, is still standing.

Public municipal improvements under the Spaniards began with O'Reilly. In an ordinance of the 22d of February, 1770, providing a revenue for the city of New Orleans, he first established petty trade-licenses and port-charges, two unfortunate systems of city revenue, which, unchanged in principle and greatly exaggerated in extent, have been perpetuated to the present day. But in the same ordinance the government reservations of 336 feet front by 84 feet depth, on either side of the Place d'Armes, were granted to the town to become to it a perpetual source of revenue, by ground rents.[29]

At this point there appears in the city's history the name of one of the most enterprising and benevolent citizens it has ever counted among its inhabitants. Don Andres Almonaster y Roxas became the buyer, for a perpetual annual rent, of the grounds granted the town,[30] and early erected upon them two rows of stores, built of brick between wooden posts, of a single story's height, and these became, and for a great many years continued to be, the fashionable retail quarters of the town. In 1787 he built in Ursulines street, adjoining the convent, a small chapel of stuccoed brick,[31] for the nuns. The chapel of the Ursulines is well remembered by persons still young, as a quaint and homely relic of the last century.

The charity hospital founded by the sailor Jean Louis, in 1737, seems to have been removed to a wooden building on the west side of Rampart, between Toulouse and St. Peter streets, at that time just outside the town limits, and to have been destroyed by the hurricane of 1779. In 1784, Almonaster began, and in two years completed, at a cost of $114,000, on the same site, a brick edifice, which he called the Charity Hospital of St. Charles, a name the institution still bears.[32]

In 1792, he began the erection, upon the site of the parish church destroyed by fire in 1788, of a brick church, and in 1794, when Louisiana and the Floridas were made a bishopric separate from Havana, this edifice, completed sufficiently for occupation, became the St. Louis cathedral.[33]

Later still, he filled the void made by the burning of the town hall and the jail—which, until the conflagration of 1788, had stood on the south side of the church, facing the Place d'Armes—with the hall of the cabildo, the same that stands there at this time, with the exception of the upper story, added since.[34]

The government itself completed very substantially the barracks begun by the French governor, Kerlerec, on Barracks street. Close by, it build a military hospital and chapel,[35] and near the upper river corner of the town, the square now occupied for the same purpose, but at that time fronting directly on the river, it put up, and then allowed to go into significant dilapidation, a wooden customhouse. The burned jail seems also to have been replaced, likewise the presbytery of the Capuchins. The "old French market," on the river front, just below the Place d'Armes, was erected[36] and known as the Halle de Boucheries.[37]

It was not correct, therefore, for the French colonial prefect, [Pierre Clément de] Laussat, sent to take possession of the receded province, in the spring of 1803, to state "that the Spaniards had not made any solid or permanent constructions."[38]

In January, 1792, the same year in which Almonaster founded the cathedral, Governor Carondelet, on succeeding Miró in office, and issuing his *bando de buen gobierno,* or rule of government, divided the two into four wards, placing an *alcalde de barrio,* or commissary of police, over each, with official control of fire-engines, firemen, and axmen, which have no earlier mention. He also recommended the commissioning of night watchmen and the erection of street lamps, the expense of these improvements to be met by a chimney tax of 9 reales ($1.12½) on each chimney.[39] In 1796 he reported to his government that he had commissioned thirteen *serenos,* night watchmen, and established eighty street lamps.[40] The fire of 1794 had so reduced the income from [the] chimney tax, that another levy was either substituted for or added to it, to wit, a tax on wheat-bread and meat.[41]

With the aid of a large force of slaves, contributed gratuitously by residents and neighboring planters, he began, in 1794, and in the following two years finished, the excavation of the "old basin" and of the Carondelet canal,[42] the former comprising almost its present superficial area of some 10,000 square yards, and the latter connecting it, by a navigable depth of water, with the bayou St. John, and thus with lake Pontchartrain and the maritime world.[43]

This work beyond the rear fortifications of the town, had been undertaken with the double object in view of drainage and navigation. In 1801, as recommended by Carondelet to the cabildo five years before,[44] certain lands contiguous to the basin and canal, which were covered with noisome pools of water, the supposed source of putrid fevers, were divided into garden lots and let out at low ground rents to those who would destroy their insalubrity, by ditching and draining them into the canal.[45]

By such measures as these, which have been described at some length, the government and the laws, the commerce, and the architectural aspect of New Orleans, were made to receive a Spanish impression and acknowledge a Spanish influence. But all that Spain deemed it just or expedient to concede never induced, in the Creole mind, a spontaneous sympathetic response, and not only to the last, but more and more toward the last, their national feeling, their habits of life, their political sentiments, and their language, proclaimed them French Creoles unaltered.

The use of the Spanish tongue, though enforced in the courts and principal public offices, never superseded the French in the mouths of the people, and left but a small proportion of words naturalized in the corrupt French of the negro slaves. *Cocodrie,* from *cocodrilo,* the crocodile, was easier to their African powers of pronunciation than *caiman,* the alligator; the terrors of the famed calaboza, with its chains and whips and branding irons, was condensed into the French trisyllabic *calaboose,* while the pleasant institution of *ñappa,* the petty gratuity added by the retailer to anything bought, grew the pleasanter Gallicized into *lagnappe.* The only newspaper in the town or province, as it was also the first, though published under the auspices of the Baron Carondelet, was *Le Moniteur de la Louisiane,* printed entirely in French. It made its first appearance in 1794.[46] The Spanish Ursulines sent from Havana to teach their own tongue, found themselves compelled to teach in French, and to content themselves with the feeble achievement of hearing the Spanish catechism from girls who recited it with tears rolling down their cheeks.[47] The public mind followed the progress of thought in France. Many Spaniards cast in their lot with the Creoles; Unzaga married a Maxent; Galvez married her sister; Gayarré took for his wife Constance de Grandpré; the intendant, [Cecilio] Odvardo, her sister; Miró wedded a de Macarty.[48] But the Creoles never became Spanish; and in the society balls, when the uncompromising civilian of the one nationality

met the equally unyielding military officials of the other, the cotil-
lion was French or Spanish, according to the superior strength of
the Creole or Spanish party, more than once decided by actual onset and bloodshed.[49] The best that can be said is, that the Spanish
government was least unpopular in New Orleans probably about
the year 1791, when the earlier upheavals of the French revolution
were being contemplated from a safe distance, and before the Republic had arisen to fire the Creole's long-suppressed enthusiasm.[50]

When war broke out between Spain and Great Britain, a power
with whom France was already at war, it was easy enough to
rally the Creoles against their hereditary foes under the Spanish banner; but when, in 1793, his Catholic majesty turned his
arms against republican France, the Spanish governor, Carondelet, found it necessary to take the same precautions against the
people of New Orleans as if he held a town of the enemy. The Marseillaise was wildly called for in the theater, which some French
players from St. Domingo, refugees of 1791, had opened,[51] and in
the drinking shops was sung defiantly the song "*Ça ira—ça ira, les
aristocrates à la lanterne.*" He took the written pledge of the colonists to support the government. He thought it best to make sundry arrests, and, though promising clemency, felt constrained, by
later developments, to send the arrested persons to Havana.[52] He
rebuilt the fortifications around the city, which had again fallen
into ruin,[53] changing their plan[54] and making them stronger than
ever. They were finished in 1794,[55] and consisted as follows: at the
lower river corner, Fort St. Charles, a small pentagonal fortification, with barracks for 150 men, a parapet 18 feet thick faced with
brick, a ditch, and a covered way; at the upper river corner, Fort
St. Louis, similar in all regards, but somewhat smaller. The ar-
mament of these was some twelve 18- and 12-pounders. Between
them, on the river front at the foot of Toulouse street, was a large
battery crossing fires with the forts.[56] In the rear of the town, on
the line imperfectly indicated by Rampart street, were three lesser
forts, one at either corner, and the third a little beyond the straight
line, and midway between the other two. They were mere palisaded
inclosures, with fraises, large enough for a hundred men each, and
armed with eight guns. That which stood at the present corner of
Canal and Rampart streets was Fort Burgundy, that on the present Congo square, Fort St. Joseph, and that at what is now the
corner of Rampart and Esplanade streets, Fort St. Ferdinand. The
wall that passed from fort to fort all around was a parapet of earth

3 feet high, surmounted by a line of 12-foot palisades, and with a moat in front 40 feet wide and 7 feet deep, containing at all times 3 feet of water supplied from Carondelet canal.[57] These fortifications, Carondelet wrote to the Spanish minister, "would not only protect the city against the attack of an enemy, but also keep in check its inhabitants," and added that but for the forts a revolution would have taken place.[58] The enemy looked for from without was the pioneers of Kentucky, Georgia, and so on, instigated by Genet,* the French minister to the United States, and headed by one [George Rogers] Clark and by Auguste de la Chaise, a Creole of powerful family, who had gone to Kentucky to lead a descent upon New Orleans in the name of liberty.[59]

The letters of Unzaga and of Bishop Peñalvert† were written twenty-two years apart, the one in 1773, the other in 1795; but the governor wrote: "I cannot flatter his majesty so much as to say that the people have ceased to be French at heart,"[60] and the bishop echoed: "His majesty possesses their bodies and not their souls."[61]

[9.] THE AMERICAN GRASP

The temper of the Creoles was not the only, or even the principal, source of anxiety to the indulgent governors who held them under the paternal despotism of Spain. Commercially and politically, the province had a destiny alien to Spanish dominion, and kindred to that of the new power, which almost from the beginning of Spanish rule in Louisiana, had begun to make its way down the valley of the Mississippi by its own sheer weight. The restless and intrepid American, therefore, even before he had achieved his independence, or poured his thousands of hardy woodsmen into the district of Kentucky, had become, simply by the distinctness of that destiny, the foremost object of distrust and dread to Spain, in regard to her foothold in the Mississippi valley.

Congress had claimed the free passage of the Mississippi, in the negotiations opened with Spain in 1779 for national recognition, and had failed to obtain either.[1] In 1783, by the eighth article of the treaty of peace, the free navigation of the Mississippi was granted to the subjects of Great Britain and the citizens of the United States forever.[2] But so far was this stipulation from being

*Edmund Charles "Citizen" Genet. President George Washington requested that he be recalled for meddling in American politics.

†Don Luis de Peñalver y Cárdenas.

carried out in good faith, that it became the starting point of a series of Spanish intrigues and American menaces, whose confused
alternations of oppression, concession, aggression, deception, and
corruption, leads the eye of research in hurried review across the
whole remaining term of Spanish occupation. Of all these movements, New Orleans, as the gateway of the Mississippi valley, was
the foremost objective point. Its commercial greatness, in the early
future, had become obvious to all, and while Spain was determined
to retain this key of her possessions, the people of the West, and,
later, Congress, determined to become the holders of the only sea-
port west of the Atlantic then accessible to them.

In the autumn, 1785, the state of Georgia sent commissioners to
New Orleans, where Miró had lately become governor in the room
of Galvez, demanding to be put in possession of the vast territory
between her western boundary and the Mississippi, according to
her understanding of the treaty of peace. Very properly, the matter was referred to the governments of America and of Spain;[3] but
this and similar occurrences aroused the solicitude of the Spaniards, and put them—or probably found them—on their guard. By
1786, if not earlier, the efforts of the settlers on the Ohio and the
Cumberland, to find a port for their flat-boat fleets and a market
for their breadstuffs and provisions, on the Mississippi, were met
with seizure and confiscation.[4]

The instant result of this attitude was excitement, indignation,
and open threats on the part of the Kentuckians, presently taking
the form of distinct proposals and projects for the capture of New
Orleans by force of arms; yet milder counsels presently prevailed,
and Congress was first appealed to to treat with Spain for that
commercial freedom of which they were resolved to be deprived no
longer.[5]

The Spanish officials were in lively and well-grounded alarm, and
saw themselves, in their imagination, already overwhelmed.[6] The
home government was urged to hasten to their relief with certain
proposed measures, if it would save New Orleans, Louisiana, the
Floridas, or even Mexico from early conquest. "*No hay que perder
tiempo,*" wrote the intendant, Navarro. "There is no time to be lost."[7]

Two schemes were projected: the first, so to relax the barri-
ers that had been drawn across the commerce of the river, that
the multitudes hovering so threateningly on their northern and
northeastern borders might be induced to extend their domains,
not as invaders, but as immigrants, ready to yield allegiance to

the authority of Spain;[8] the second, to foster and foment the spirit of insurrection, then rife in the West, against what was deemed the negligence of Congress,[9] as to actually bring about the disruption of the West from the East. These schemes were set on foot; a large American immigration did actually set in, and the small town of New Madrid still remains to commemorate the extravagant schemes of western grantees.[10]

A close observer, he had not let the turn of events escape his notice, and in June, 1787, General James Wilkinson, of the United States service, sent and followed to New Orleans a large fleet of flatboats, loaded with the produce of the West, and, working on the political fears of Miró *and the spirit of intrigue in the court of Spain,* secured many concessions and made way for a trade which began immediately to inure greatly to the pecuniary benefit of New Orleans, not to say of the Spanish officials.[11] *At the same time General Wilkinson entered into a plot* with Spain for that disruption which he had already contemplated,[12] and which he appears to have been, morally and intellectually, capable of doing if it could be done at all.[13]*

But an export trade was only half a commerce, either for the West or for New Orleans. Communication with Philadelphia, however, in a measure, supplied the deficiency, though hampered and qualified by a system of false dealings, than which it would be hard to contrive a group of influences more corrupting to a mercantile community. For a while, on one hand, the colonial officials indulged and promoted this trade. [Diego de] Gardoqui, the Spanish minister at Philadelphia, "finding he did not participate in the profits," moved vigorously against it, and those who were engaged in it were able to persevere only by employing and accepting all the subterfuges of contrabandists, not excepting false arrests and false escapes.[14] The conflagration of 1788 was used as a pretext for the liberation of a number whom the intendant, Navarro, had been driven, by fear of royal displeasure, to imprison, and the return to them of their confiscated goods.[15]

The great scarcity of provisions after the conflagration, gave Miró an opportunity to enlarge the trade with Philadelphia, of which he promptly took advantage, and sent three vessels consigned to Gardoqui—whose opposition was now turned into coöperation—for such miscellaneous cargoes as the general ruin called for. The

*Generally referred to as the "Spanish Conspiracy."

leading item was 3,000 barrels of flour.[16] This exigency met, the trade not only continued but increased,[17] and in August, 1788, Wilkinson received, through his agent in New Orleans, via the Mississippi, a cargo of dry goods and other articles for the Kentucky market, probably the first boat-load of manufactured commodities that ever went up that river to the Ohio.[18]

Others began to follow the example of Wilkinson in matters of commerce, and, under pretense of coming to buy lands and settle, or of returning for their families and property, secured passports and the repeated privilege of buying and selling free of duty. Thus tobacco, flour of a certain poor quality, and the various other crops of the West, were beginning to find a market where they could be profitably exchanged for manufactured goods. As to the communication with Europe, the concessions of 1782 had yielded the transatlantic commerce of New Orleans into the hands of the French traders, and there it still remained. "At this very moment," wrote Miró on the 10th of August, 1790, "France has the real monopoly of the commerce of this colony."[19]

The port of New Orleans, in fact, was neither closed nor open. Commerce was possible, but dangerous, subject to the corrupt caprices of Spanish commandants and customs officers, and full of exasperating uncertainties. While, therefore, Spain was still dealing with Wilkinson and with Dr. [James] O'Fallon, "general agent of the South Carolina Company in Yazoo,"[20] the United States government, through its minister at Madrid, was striving to work upon the Spaniards' new fear of Great Britain, and their knowledge of the feebleness of their foothold in America, to press upon them a cession of Orleans island and the Floridas to the United States.[21] But neither the urgent requests of the United States, the possibility of a British invasion from Canada by way of the Mississippi,[22] nor the proposals of the South Carolina Company, to accept which Miró thought equivalent to "taking a foreign state to board with them,"[23] were sufficient yet to cause any relaxation of the grasp of Spain upon the key of the greatest agricultural valley in the world.

Still the fears of the officials at New Orleans continued. A spirit was responding within the province itself, to the march of events without, and the interdiction of the slave-trade with revolted St. Domingo,[24] the banishment of clocks branded with the Goddess of Liberty,[25] and Carondelet's fortifications, were but symptoms of it, not cures, and in February, 1793, American encroachment won the valuable concession of an open commerce with Europe and America for citizens of the Spanish colonies.[26] "From this period," says Judge Martin, "a number of merchants in Philadelphia established commercial houses in New Orleans."[27]

Francis Louis Hector, Baron de Carondelet, succeeded to the governorship of Louisiana and West Florida on the 30th of December, 1791, and had therefore been in office something more than a year when this broad concession was made. He had not needed it, however, to indicate to him the waning strength of the Spanish tenure, or the growing supremacy of the people whom Navarro had years before described as "a nation restless, poor, ambitious, and capable of the most daring enterprise."[28] "Since my taking possession of the government," wrote Carondelet in May, 1794, "this province . . . has not ceased to be threatened by the ambitious designs of the Americans."[29]

To the vigilance and good faith of President Washington, and not to Carondelet's insignificant defenses, his rigid police, or the counterplots which he carried on through Thomas Power and others, Carondelet owed the deliverance of his capital from the schemes of Genet, La Chaise, Clark, and the Jacobins in Philadelphia; and it was that cause, not these, that maintained the safety of Louisiana as a haven for French royalists.[30] It argues more temerity than wisdom on the part of the baron, that the imminence of these dangers was no sooner removed than he began again to hamper and oppress the trade of the Mississippi, in the hope of yet separating the western people from the union of states, to which they had now become devoted.[31]

Nevertheless, the commercial destiny of New Orleans moved on, and while Power was still conveying Carondelet's overtures to Wilkinson, a treaty was signed at Madrid, October 20, 1795, by which the Mississippi was declared free to the people of the United States, and New Orleans became a port of deposit* for three years, free of duty or any charge on produce or merchandise, beyond "a fair price for the hire of the stores" where they might be deposited. This privilege was to be renewed at the expiration of the three years, or transferred to some "equivalent establishment" on the river bank, according as the king's interest should require.[32] The American was gradually closing in upon the foremost object of his desire. That this was recognized as the true interest of New Or-

*A transshipment center. The treaty is known as Pinkney's Treaty.

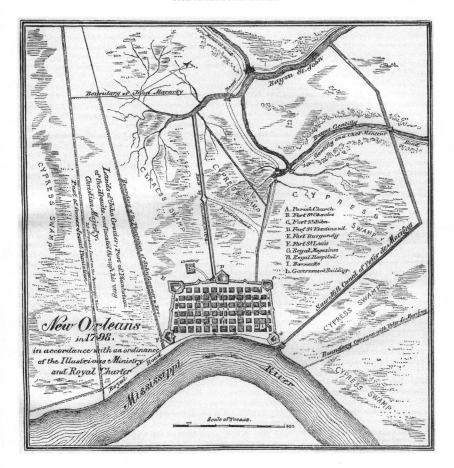

leans is shown in the fact, that though transit shipments were thus made duty free, the revenues of the custom-house aggregated, in 1795, double those of the preceding year.[33]

Still, Carondelet, under various pretexts, continued to hold the territory conceded to the United States on the east bank of the Mississippi,* temporizing with their authorities through the agency of General [Manuel] Gayoso de Lamos, the commissioner for effecting the transfer,[34] spending money freely to procure the treason of unscrupulous Americans,[35] and strengthening his fortifications not only against the federal commanders, but against the

---

*Cable is referring to present-day Mississippi, from the 31st latitude to the mouths of the Yazoo and Chattahoochee rivers.

western settlers who had filled up the country,[36] and the imminent probability of another threatened invasion from Canada.[37]

Yet, even under so troubled a political sky, the commerce of New Orleans steadily increased.[38] War with France had displaced the foreign trade which Bordeaux, Marseilles, and Nantes had so long monopolized,[39] and had thrown it largely into American ports,[40] although not a little harassed by French privateers infesting the Gulf of Mexico.[41] One of these, in October, 1795, seized, and for eight days held, the post at the mouth of the Mississippi, evacuating and destroying it only on the approach of troops from New Orleans;[42] and after hostilities between France and Spain had ceased, a number of American vessels, seized in the Gulf, were taken to New Orleans, the vessels and their cargoes sold, and the crews maltreated.[43]

At length all schemes against the Union having failed, and every pretext for delay being exhausted, Gayoso, who, in August, 1797, had succeeded Carondelet as governor of Louisiana,[44] yielded to the irresistible pressure of United States officers, acting under the orders of Wilkinson, and in March, 1798, abandoned by stealth, rather than surrendered, the territory so long unjustly retained from the states.[45]

But New Orleans still remained a subject of ill-feeling. While the long delays lately terminated had been taxing the patience of the western people, the three years' term, during which New Orleans might be used as a port of deposit, was drawing toward its close, and before the year 1798 could expire, the exasperated Americans found the city again closed against them by the Spanish intendant, [Juan Ventura] Morales. Not only so, but the plain letter of the late treaty was ignored, and no other point on the river was assigned to take the place of the closed port.[46]

The indignation and resentment aroused in the people of the United States, and in the government as well, was energetic and profound, and secret preparations were at once set on foot by President [John] Adams, for an expedition against New Orleans with an overwhelming force.[47] According to an excellent authority, the West could have sent against it between 20,000 and 30,000 men. The two facts that seem to have arrested the movement, were the contemplated retirement of the President from office at the close of his term, then drawing near, and by and by the disavowal of the intendant's action by his government and its restoration of the suspended privilege.[48]

Meanwhile, another eye was turned covetously upon Louisiana, and in the last year of the century it became the settled, secret policy of both the French republic and the American to acquire that vast, but to Spain unremunerative and indefensible, province.[49] The opportunities and the genius of the first consul [Napoleon Bonaparte] enabled him to move with the superior celerity. On the first of October, 1800, the Spanish king privately entered into certain agreements with the French republic by which, on the 21st of March, 1801, Louisiana passed secretly into the hands of Bonaparte, in exchange for the petty Italian kingdom of Etruria.*[50] "France has cut the knot,"[51] wrote Minister [Robert R.] Livingston to Secretary [James] Madison, when in November, 1802, the secret was no longer unknown.

Yet the Spanish domination continued still beyond this date, and it was not until the 26th of March, 1803, that the French colonial prefect, Laussat, landed in New Orleans, specially commissioned to prepare for the expected arrival of General [Claude Perrin] Victor, in command of a large body of troops destined for the occupation of the province, and to arrange for the establishment of a new form of government.[52]

Governor Gayoso had died of yellow fever in 1799. He had been succeeded by the Marquis of Casa Calvo, and he, in June, 1801, by Don Juan Manuel de Salcedo.[53] The intendant, Morales, had used every measure permitted him to discourage American immigration and hamper American commerce in the river, both of which had become objects of dread.[54] Privileges granted when immigration was desired had been withdrawn. In October, 1802, the overzealous intendant had again suspended the right of deposit, and even cut off all commercial intercourse beyond the mere navigation of the river to and from foreign markets, and, six months after, the king again discountenanced the proceeding. *Laussat found the province still in the hands of the aged and weak Salcedo and the quarrelsome Morales.*[55]

On the 18th of May, 1803, Casa Calvo—sent from Havana for the purpose—jointly with Governor Salcedo, proclaimed the coming surrender and its contemplated terms, and they held themselves in readiness for the hourly expected arrival of General Victor. Instead of him came a rumor painful to Laussat and incredible to the Creoles, who had so lately received the news of the cession to

*By the terms of the secret Treaty of San Ildefonso.

France with the liveliest delight, and about the last of July, 1803, a vessel from Bordeaux brought the official announcement that, on the 30th of the preceding April, Louisiana had been purchased by the United States.[56]

On the 31st of October, Congress authorized the President to take possession of the ceded territory. On the 30th of November, with troops drawn up in line on the Place d'Armes, and with discharges of artillery, Salcedo, in the hall of the cabildo, delivered to Laussat the keys of New Orleans, and Casa Calvo declared the people of Louisiana absolved from their allegiance to the king of Spain. From a flagstaff in the square the Spanish colors descended, the French took their place, and the domination of Spain in Louisiana was at an end.[57]

On Monday, the 20th of December, 1803, with similar ceremonies, Laussat turned the province and the keys of its port over to Commissioners Claiborne* and [James] Wilkinson. The French tricolor, which had floated over the Place d'Armes for the short space of twenty days, gave place to the stars and stripes, and New Orleans† was an American town.[58]

[10.] A FRANCO-SPANISH AMERICAN CITY

Within a period of ninety-one years Louisiana had changed hands six times. From the direct authority of Louis XIV it had been handed over, in 1712, to the commercial dominion of Anthony Crozat. From Crozat it passed, in 1717, to the Compagnie de l'Occident; from the company, in 1731, back to the undelegated authority of the government of France; from France, in 1762, to Spain; from Spain, in 1801, back again to France; and at length, in 1803, from France to the United States. Compared with the last of these, the earlier transfers lose even that prominence which is their due, and in the history of the Mississippi valley, the significant transaction which stands at the opening of the present century, indicating the emancipation from the service and bargainings of European masters, needs no other distinctive name than that commonly given it, the Cession.[1]

At the time of this event New Orleans had been under the undisputed sway of Spain for thirty-four years. In the early part of

---

*William C. C. Claiborne, later the first governor of Louisiana.
†Cable refers to New Orleans as "city" in the original manuscript.

this period its interests had languished, and for many years it had made but indifferent progress. During the first four years, according to the statement of Governor Unzaga, and allowing even for careless understatement, the natural increase of its population had been entirely neutralized by emigration.[2]

With concessions to commerce came a certain advance. In 1785, the sixteenth year of Spanish domination, an official census showed a population within the walls of New Orleans of 4,980 persons,[3] an increase of 56 per cent., and another, three years later, in 1788, of 5,338 souls,[4] or a total increase for the nineteen years of 67 per cent.

This seems to have been principally a natural increase. Certain importations had been made of agriculturists from Malaga, the Canary islands, and Nova Scotia; but except a very few, these remained only momentarily in New Orleans, and then passed on into the rural districts.[5] Even that American immigration, which it later became the policy of Spain to foster, though it peopled the province with thousands of new-comers, added to the population of New Orleans only a few scores of mercantile pioneers, sometimes with families, but oftener without. In 1778 and 1779 Count Galvez required all residents of New Orleans, who had come from the British colonies (United Colonies), to swear allegiance to Spain; and the whole number that did so was but 170.[6]

The British traders whom O'Reilly ejected, in 1769, either returned or were succeeded by others.[7] The freedom given in 1782 to trade with France, brought in some French merchants,[8] and a few years later the French revolution drove many royalists to Louisiana, a few of whom no doubt took refuge in New Orleans, with their families, and goods.[9] Some Germans and Italians seem also to have been received into the growing town, straggling in in the fugitive way common in seaports, and finding place according to the commercial and industrial needs of the port.[10] The insurrection in St. Domingo, in 1791, caused some refugees from that island to settle in New Orleans, and in this way came the first theatrical troupe that ever played in Louisiana.[11] But the accession was trivial, by reason of a regulation promptly adopted, prohibiting the importation of slaves from the countries where they had revolted.[12] Toward the close of the Spanish tenure, the inflow of Americans became more considerable, and made its way against all royal obstructions, a matter always possible and often easy, through the laxness or the corruption of the colonial officials.[13]

However—and although in 1803 the population of New Orleans, with its suburbs, had reached the number of 10,000 souls—the great majority of the white inhabitants was still Creole. For even in the province at large, where the proportion of aliens was greater than in the city, a contemporary authority states, that the Creoles were three-fourths of the inhabitants. As to the numbers of the Spanish element, it is a singular, but authentic fact, that outside of government circles there were but few.[14]

The city was fast becoming one of the chief seaports of America. In 1802, 158 American, 104 Spanish, and 3 French merchantmen, in all 265, aggregating a total of 31,241 register tons, sailed from her harbor loaded. The tonnage entering port during the first six months of 1803, indicated an increase over the year before of over 37 per cent. The products of the province alone, exported through its metropolis, exceeded $2,000,000 value. Its imports reached the sum of $2,500,000; 34,000 bales of cotton; 4,500 hogsheads of sugar; 800 casks—equivalent to 2,000 barrels—of molasses; rice, peltries, indigo, lumber, and sundries, to the value of $500,000; 50,000 barrels of flour; 3,000 barrels of beef and pork; 2,000 hogsheads of tobacco, and smaller quantities of corn, butter, hams, meal, lard, beans, hides, staves, and cordage passed, in 1802, across the already famous levee.[15]

Under the river bank, just above the corporation limits of the town, "within ten steps of Tchoupitoulas street," where land has since formed and brick stores now cover the spot to several squares depth, the fleets of barges and flatboats from the West moored, and unloaded, or retailed their contents at the water's edge.[16] Farther down and immediately abreast of the town, between the upper limits and the Place d'Armes, the shipping lay, to the number of twenty or more vessels of from 100 to 200 tons burthen, hauled close up and made fast to the bank, where they received and discharged "with the same ease as from a wharf." Still farther down, beyond the square and the market, and opposite the government warehouse, was the mooring place of the vessels of war.[17]

The town, at this date, had filled and overflowed its original boundaries. From the masthead of a ship at the levee, one looked down upon a gathering of from 1,200 to 1,400 dwellings, or say 4,000 roofs of all kinds and sizes; those near by, generally two, and often three,[18] stories from the ground, covering substantial brick houses, and themselves covered with half-cylindrical or flat tiles or with slates; those further on, behind the first few streets in front, of two or a single story height, of shingles, broad, outstretched at times over spacious dwellings and environing verandahs, and rendered picturesque with dormer windows and square belvederes.[19] Such houses as these were almost always elevated, on pillars, over open or latticed basements of from 8 to 15 feet height above the ground. The homes of the poor, and of many who were well-to-do, were of the humblest exterior, with apartments on the ground, and were scattered indiscriminately among the rest or hovered on the outskirts. Much greenery brightened the tableaux, whether the season was summer or winter, and a line of watery, grass-entangled ruin, surrounding all, marked the line of fortifications which Carondelet's successors had allowed to tumble to wreck.[20]

Immediately before the eye, a street's width beyond the bottom of the Place d'Armes, stood the occupied but unfinished cathedral, lacking those quaint, white Spanish towers and that central belfry which, in 1814 and 1824, were added to it.[21] At the left of it the old hall of the cabildo rose over its heavy half-Moorish arcade, undisfigured then by the French roof which at present distorts its architecture. On either side of the square were the fashionable retail stores, in two long, unbroken, single-story rows. Other structures remained here and there—the government house, the barracks, the hospital, the convent of the Ursulines—unchanged features of the earlier French town.[22]

The straight and fairly spacious streets were unpaved, ill-drained, and filthy, poorly lighted, and often impassable to vehicles by reason of the mire. The unpaved sidewalks were commonly bordered by wooden ways of 4 or 5 feet width, while a few in the heart of the town had narrow walks of brick.[23]

Along these walks and through these streets, the people moved busily to and fro and in and out, with the activity indicating the life of a commercial port. Toulouse, St. Peter, Conti, St. Louis, Royale, Chartres streets, and the levee, were the scenes of brisk negotiations and the receipts and deliveries of merchandise. The restless American was especially conspicuous, and, with the Englishman and the Irishman, composed the great majority of the commercial class.[24] The Frenchmen, except a small number of cultivated people, had subsided into the retail trade, or the mechanical callings. The Spaniards, beyond the military and civil service, were generally humble Catalans, keepers of shops and of numberless low cabarets, which occupied almost every street corner; while the Creoles sought office and military commission, ruled society, lent money, sometimes at 12 per cent. per annum, and sometimes at 1½ or 2 per cent. per month, and took but a secondary part in that commercial life from which was already springing the future greatness of New Orleans.[25]

Nor can this be regarded as strange, when account is taken of one or two relative facts. Their illiteracy, their non-appreciation of toil—a sentiment which had become traditional—and other disadvantageous characteristics, might easily have given way before the change of circumstances and the allurements of wealth; but the Anglo-Saxon occupation of the Mississippi valley, and the superior ability of England and the Atlantic states over France and Spain, to take the products of that entire valley and to supply its wants, gave such overwhelming advantages to the incoming American, English, or Irish merchants, that the ill-equipped and uncommercial Creole was fortunate to secure even a subordinate mercantile rank in the city of his birth.

As they were the holders of the urban and suburban real estate, they had begun, with the vigorous commercial impulse and immigration of the last decade, to figure as the sellers of lots and as *rentiers*. The Jesuits' plantation of 32 arpents front, confiscated in 1763, had been parceled out into five portions. In 1788 an inheritor of 12 arpents front of this tract, a lady who had been a widow [Maria Josefa] Deslondes, and has been married again to Bertrand Gravier, laid out a line of squares along part of this front on the line of Tchoupitoulas road (street), from the upper boundary of the *Terre Commune,* still recognizable in the name of Common street, to the lower boundary of a tract owned by one [Silvestré] Delord[-Sarpy], the line of the present Delord street. She called the prospective settlement Villa Gravier. A few years later she died; her husband extended the partition of streets, squares, and lots to the farther side of St. Charles street, and in her memory gave them the name of Faubourg Ste. Marie. The names of its streets still repeat points in its history, Gravier street perpetuating the memory of the faubourg's founder, Delord, [Pierre] Foucher, and others continuing those of his fellow capitalists. [Julien de Lalande] Poydras had bought the spot which became the corner of Tchoupitoulas and Poydras; Claude Girod another, that of Tchoupitoulas and Girod; another corner became the property of a free woman of color, Julie Fortier, and the street running back from it, Julia street.[26]

The *Terre Commune* was a government reservation, retained on account of the fortifications along which it lay, and also for a public road running back from the river. Its long triangular form, with the apex on the river front, resulted from the upper boundary of the town and the lower line of the plantation having been drawn perpendicular to the changing directions of the river bank. The same explanation applies to the various other fan-shaped sections added, from time to time, to the growing city. *Calle del Almazen,* otherwise the *rue du Magazin,* rendered in English not severely Storehouse street, but Magazine street, took its title from an immense tobacco warehouse—doubtless the place of deposit of the Kentucky tobacco—upon which the street's lower end abutted, very near the site of the present custom-house. Midway between Poydras and Girod streets, behind Magazine, lay a *campo de negroes,* a slave camp, probably of the cargoes of Guinea slaves. The street that cut through it became and has ever since continued to be, the *calle de Campo*—Camp street. Next behind it the Spanish sovereign was remembered in St. Charles street; the next, *Briqueterie,* indicating the road to a brick-yard, and another still beyond called Salcedo, were opened and named later than those in front, most probably by Jean Gravier, the son of Bertrand, and before the cession had changed their names to those which they bear to-day, in honor of Carondelet and his wife, the *Baronne.*[27] •

Maunsell White relates that in August, 1801, when he first arrived in the port of New Orleans and went ashore in Poydras street, the faubourg Ste. Marie consisted of five houses. The whole space between Common and Poydras, from Magazine to Carondelet street, was appropriated for raising vegetables, and the site of St. Charles hotel was the cottage garden of an "old Mr. Percy."[28]

Other faubourgs were springing up, or about to spring up, beyond the various gates and walls. The high roofs of the aristocratic suburb, St. John, could be seen stretching away among its groves of evergreen alongside the bayou road, and by and by clustering into a village near where a bayou still crosses the stream,* some 200 yards below the site of the old one.[29]

Just beyond the parapets of Fort St. Joseph lay the basin and canal Carondelet. They had been allowed to fall into neglect, and had shoaled so that the larger craft had to stop at the village of St. John in the bayou; yet it was still in use by the smaller craft, and in the basin, canal, and bayou together there aggregated, in 1802,

---

*29. Before the city was drained by modern pumps, Bayou St. John branched out into minor streams.

500 arrivals of small half-decked vessels and schooners, of from 8 to 50 tons burden, bringing the cattle and produce of the pine forests from the lake and gulf coasts of East and West Florida.[30]

In this city, in 1803, two dissimilar classes held two distinct dominions. It has been shown that the Anglo-Saxon had easily acquired the leadership in commerce. But in the city's social life this relation was reversed. The incoming aliens had no crusade to wage against the order of society. Coming in for the single purpose of making money, they drew near prepared to accept society as they found it and to make the broadest concessions with the most amiable alacrity if these would but purchase admittance within that circle of invisible defenses against which assault or siege would have been in vain.

The character of that society as described by contemporary observers was exactly that, which, without their evidence, would have been irresistibly inferable from the conditions in which it is known to have been developed; and neither more nor less can be claimed for or against the Creoles than that universal unit of quality which we call human nature was multiplied and divided by the various advantages and drawbacks of inheritance and surrounding forces.

There is, therefore, small room for censure from more fortunate communities when the proper admissions come to be made, although the best that can be said of New Orleans society at the time of the Cession is that its undeniable turpitude did not reach the female portion of white society. To this must at once be added that in the whole course of the Spanish administration there was scarcely a single prominent event, regulation or influence that did not work to the detriment of public morals; and when this immoral tendency of the public administration of affairs combined with the corrupting influence of certain deformities in the earlier structure of this society the effect on the moral tone of the people would not fail to be lamentable.

The errors of government hardly need again to be summarized: Commercial laws so harsh and arbitrary as to invite and promote lawlessness, and so ill adapted to the condition and wants of the people that to break them seemed only the part of patriotism. These laws, moreover, now rigidly enforced and now grossly maladministered or shamelessly set aside[,] and the corruptness of the administration made a source of wealth to the people. Commercial intercourse, as it grew, brought an increasing acquaintance with the semi-barbarous communities of the West Indies and the volca-

nic moral upheavals of France, cargoes of savages from the coast of
Africa, and refugees from the complacent but feeble civilization of
St. Domingo to become the abecedarians and music, dancing and
fencing-masters of the rising generation.

Against such elements of corruption the ineffectual efforts of a
few Capuchin friars and as many Ursuline nuns were the only off-
set in a community entirely destitute of either college, library or
post-office, or of any schools save a few for reading and writing
only, and these but poorly attended.[31]

While the colony's trade was with France—1782, and following—
New Orleans Creoles, without fortune, leaned much to mercantile
life, for which they considered reading and writing in the French
tongue the only education necessary, and toward the end of that
time, in 1788, there were eight schools teaching these two rudi-
ments, attended by some 400 children, about one-fourth or one-
fifth the number that might have enjoyed these limited benefits.[32]
The educational results of Spanish royal patronage were little better than ludicrous. In 1772, there came from Spain Don Andreas
Lopez de Armesto, Don Pedro Aragon, Don Manuel Diaz de Lara,
and Don Francisco de la Calena, to found a school. "No pupil,"
writes Governor Miró, "ever presented himself for the Latin class;
a few came to be taught reading and writing only; these never
exceeded thirty, and frequently dwindled down to six." The fire of
1788 destroyed the school-house and reduced the attendance from
23 to 12, and Don Andreas Almonaster's offer to build another
house, at a cost of $6,000, seems never to have been acted on.[33]

The only other schools were the schools of vice, and the only
other preventive of moral decadence was, toward the close of the
Spanish tenure, a system of police, possessing the questionable
merit of indiscriminate severity. Assemblages of more than eight
persons were not allowed, and every citizen of New Orleans was
required to be and remain indoors by nine o'clock at night, the
hour of shutting the gates; quadroon women were forbidden to
wear jewelry, and were required to keep their hair bound up in a
kerchief. The condition of affairs was none the better, for the fact
that this system was sometimes harshly and sometimes feebly administered.[34]

Under the circumstances and conditions thus sketched forth
the regards for law, education, public integrity, order or morality
was but feeble, and more so in the city than in the outlying prov-
inces. The practice of religion—even of its external observances,

*Lent, saints' days, attendance on mass, etc.,—was confined to a
very small fraction of the people. The only newspaper in the colony
had scarcely a Creole subscriber, a few small private collections of
books were entirely in the hands of Frenchmen; and literature and
learning received no other notice than a complacent contempt. The
contrabandist held, unimpeached, the standing of a merchant alike
in business and in society; fathers and sons met together in the
gambling houses without embarrassment; the keeper of the faro table moved in the community as a "banker"; quarrels were quick and
prompt as they were also easily made up; without a weapon one was
not quite ready to take his ladies to the carnival balls in Orleans
street, and one who could not use it was spurned from the company
of gentlemen; a favorite drink was taffia—rum; with twelve distill-
eries in the town and environs only fourteen thousand gallons were
exported out of two hundred thousand produced; fathers brought
their offspring of mixed blood "to be recorded in the parochial regis-
tries as their natural children," and counted it but proper to provide
for their sons, as they reached the age of manhood, alliances not
convenient to describe, and the quadroons, who graced the crowded
balls of the noted Maison Coquet, began to earn the unbounded
hatred of the mothers and daughters of the dominant race.*[35]

A standard historical writer upon Louisiana, while giving
many of the foregoing and similar facts, yet states that "aggravated crimes were rare in Louisiana," and there is a certain way of
understanding the remark which may make it applicable to New
Orleans. For where so many of the crimes against society went
uncondemned and even approved by the popular voice; where the
dueling-ground was free to all and accepted by all; where license
was almost as broad as the licentiousness that sought it;[36] where
the slave and the quadroon castes were practically powerless for
offense or defense, and where crimes against them were scarce accounted misdeeds, save on some uncut page of the statute-book—
the number of what were set apart in the estimation of society as
"aggravated crimes" could hardly be large, and it need not seem
surprising if the unfortunate people of a city so afflicted with evil
influences and their painful results, were generally unconscious
of a reprehensible state of affairs, and preserved their self-respect
and a proud belief in their moral excellence.[37]

In outward appearance the Creoles had become the handsome,
well-knit race that the freedom of their natural surroundings
would have been expected to produce. Of a complexion lacking

color, yet free from the sallowness of the Indies, there was a much larger proportion of blondes among them than is commonly supposed. Generally their hair was of a chestnut or but little deeper tint, except that in the city a Spanish tincture now and then asserted itself in black hair and eyes. The women were fair, of symmetrical form, with pleasing features, lively, expressive eyes, well-rounded throats, and superb hair; vivacious, yet decorous in manner, and exceedingly tasteful in dress, adorning themselves with beautiful effect in draperies of muslin enriched with embroideries and much garniture of lace, but with the more moderate display of jewels, which indicated a community of limited wealth. They were much superior to the men in quickness of wit, and excelled them in amiability and in many other good qualities.[38] The more pronounced faults of the men were generally those moral provincialisms which travelers recount with undue impatience; they are said to have been coarse, boastful, vain, and they were, also, deficient in energy and application, and without well-directed ambition, unskillful in handicraft, doubtless entirely through negligence, and totally wanting in that community feeling which begets the study of reciprocal rights and obligations, and reveals the individual's advantage in the promotion of the common interest. Hence, the Creoles were fonder of pleasant fictions regarding the salubrity, beauty, and advantages of their town, than of measures to justify their assumptions. Easily inflamed, they were as easily discouraged, thrown into confusion, and subdued, and they expended the best of their energies in trivial pleasures, especially the masque and the dance; yet they were kind parents, affectionate wives, tractable children, and enthusiastic patriots.[39]

[11.] FROM SUBJECTS TO CITIZENS

It is recorded of the Creoles of New Orleans, that as they stood upon the Place d'Armes and saw the standard of a people whose national existence was a mere twenty years' experiment, taking the place of the tricolor on which perched the glory of a regenerated France, they wept.[1]

Doubtless there were men there not too old to be still in active life, who had even participated in the defiant repudiation of the first cession by force of arms. The difference between the two attitudes is strongly indicative of the difference between the two events. The earlier transfer came to the people loaded with disadvantages and tyrannous exactions; the later came freighted with long-coveted benefits, and with some of the most priceless rights of man. This second transition, therefore, while it might arouse the tenderest regrets in hearts that had just rekindled with their old love of France, and although it forced them into civil and political fellowship with the *Américain,* the object of their special antipathy, could not exasperate and inflame the public mind with the sense of outrage which had been produced by the first.[2]

It is true, the revelation that they were "rejected for the second time from the bosom of their mother-country" was received with "extreme bitterness,"[3] yet the silence and tears which was their only greeting to the American flag may be interpreted as the protest of their prejudices and affections far more than of their reason. The emigrant, as well as the exile, has tearful farewells.

Naturally, between these prejudices and affections and the quieter voice of reason, the Creoles did not immediately distinguish, but hoped, as they had done forty years before, that facts might after all turn out to be fictitious, and "could not be persuaded that the convention for the cession of Louisiana was anything but a political trick."[4] Their conviction was openly expressed that, Great Britain, once humbled, the First Consul would "recede from the treaty of cession."[5]

Nor could they long be entirely blind to the contrast between the two periods; O'Reilly had established a government whose only excellence lay in its strength; Claiborne came to set up a power whose only strength lay in its excellence. His task was difficult, principally because it was to be done among a people distempered by the earlier rule and diligently wrought upon by intriguing Frenchmen and Spanish officials.[6]

To such a community, thus excited, the wisest measures, equally with the most obvious mistakes, were the subjects of wordy resentment. The introduction of the English language, and of a not undue proportion of American appointees into the new courts and the public offices, the suppression of disorder in the public balls at the point of the bayonet, a supposed partiality for Americans in cases at law, the personal character of officials, the governor's ignorance of the French tongue, his large official powers, the alleged bad habits of Wilkinson, the scarcity of money, from the cessation of the annual supply of government funds from Vera Cruz, the formation of American militia companies, and their indiscreet parades in the streets—such were the materials with which was soon kindled a serious degree of excitement.[7]

On the 26th of March, 1804, Congress passed an act dividing the province into two parts on the thirty-third parallel of latitude, the present northern boundary of Louisiana, and establishing for the lower portion a distinct territorial government, under the title of the territory of Orleans. The act was to go into effect in the following October. One of its provisions was the interdiction of the slave trade. The Creoles heard of it with the liveliest disrelish. Indignation reigned on every side, insurrectionary sentiments were placarded on the corners of the streets, the crowd copied them, and public officers, in attempting to remove them, were driven away.[8]

But at this point, the power of a government which allowed free speech and free opinion to expend itself unmolested, is seen in the fact that unlawful demonstration went no farther. The benevolent and patient Claiborne recognized in these symptoms an insurrection only of the affections, against a forced alienation from that France which had ever been the source of all inspiration, the mutiny of a haughty people's pride against the unfeeling barter of their fealty.[9] Plainly there was not so much a determination of the will that American domination should not continue, as a simple belief of the heart that it would not, and it was not the government, but only some of the measures, that was causing so much heat.

The inference is strong that in this new commercial city, the merchant who, in 1768, had led the people in revolt against legalized ruin, saw plainly that the unwelcome American rule had brought him out of commercial serfdom, and that as a port of the United States, and only as such, his crescent city could enter upon the great future which was hers in virtue of her geographical position.

Indeed, the majority of merchants, as has been shown, were already Americans. As to other influential branches of the community, it was soon plain that they were not entirely blind to the advantages awaiting them under the new domination. For while they still clung to the delusion of a French or Spanish recession, they presently began to make impatient, if not imperious, demand for the rights of American citizens, as pledged to them in the terms of the treaty. The error made thirty-six years before, of appealing to the country that had cast them off, was not repeated; but when in June and July three public meetings were held, called together by some of the most influential private citizens of the territory and city, it was to memorialize the American Congress, not to rescind the treaty of cession, but for the recall of an action which seemed to them likely to delay their admission into the Union. It is highly characteristic of their provincial short-sightedness, that the committee appointed to bear this important, but vain, appeal to Congress, was composed of MM. [Pierre] Derbigny, [Pierre] Sauvé, and [Jean Noel] Destréhan, two Frenchmen and a Creole.[10]

On the 1st of October the territorial government went into operation. Claiborne was still retained as governor.[11] *Some trouble was found in organizing a legislative council as provided for in the act of Congress, four appointees declining the office and the remainder hesitating for nearly two months to accept their appointment. Yet their roll of thirteen members as finally formed showed a fair proportion of Frenchmen and Creoles.[12] Julien Poydras was one of their number:* "*A beginning must be made," wrote he, "we must be initiated into the sacred duties of freemen and the practices of liberty.*"[13]

The division of the province, the establishment of the legislative council by presidential appointment instead of by the votes of the people,[14] the nullification of certain Spanish land-grants and an official reinspection of all titles,[15] were accepted, if not with patience, at least with a certain characteristic grace, which the Creole is wont to assume before the inevitable; but the lessons of the French and the Spanish rule were not to be unlearned in a day, and his respect was not always forthcoming toward laws that could be opposed or evaded. "This city," wrote Claiborne, "requires a strict police; the inhabitants are of various descriptions—many highly respectable, and some of them very degenerate."[16] The attempt of a sheriff and posse to arrest a Spanish officer was prevented by 200 men; swords were drawn, and the resistance ceased only on the appearance of a detachment of United States troops. Above all, the slave trade, which the protesting delegates had represented to Congress as "all-important to the very existence of their country,"[17] was diligently persisted in through lakes Borgne, Pontchartrain, and Maurepas, the bayou Barataria, and many other inlets in the labyrinthian coast-line of the gulf-marshes.[18]

The labors of the legislative council began on the 4th of December. A charter of incorporation was given by it to the city of New Orleans. *Laussat, the French prefect, during his short term of authority in November and December, 1803, had abolished the cabildo and instituted a government composed of a mayor, two adjuncts and a city council of ten members. Étienne de Boré, the pioneer sugar producer, had been appointed mayor, and Destréhan and Sauvé, adjuncts. Boré was unfavorably disposed toward the American domination and [James] Pitot, after the Cession, seems to have succeeded him. The new charter* constituted "all free white inhabitants of New Orleans a body corporate, by the name of the mayor, aldermen, and inhabitants." There were fourteen aldermen. The city was divided into four wards. The charter went into operation early in March, 1805, and in the election of these aldermen the people of New Orleans, for the first time in her history, exercised the right of suffrage.[19]

The season of amusements was free from the bickerings of the previous winter. The protest of Spain against the cession had long been formally withdrawn, the insinuations and intrigues of her officials, who lingered in Louisiana, were without material effect, and on the last day of the year the governor had reported a gratifying state of order in New Orleans.[20]

The petition to Congress, which had not come before that body until the 4th of January, 1805, was, in the main, as has been intimated, ineffectual. Yet it received some consideration, and on the 2d of March, with many safeguards and limitations unwelcome to the chafing Creoles, the right was accorded them to elect a house of representatives. Thus gradually and guardedly the government began to open before them the wide freedom of American citizenship. The same act empowered them "to form for themselves a constitution and state government as soon as the free population of the territory should reach 60,000 souls, in order to be admitted into the Union."[21]

The course of affairs continued to be marked by a certain feverishness rather than by prominent events. War between Great Britain and Spain, and the opening of Havana to neutral vessels, stimulated the commercial activity of New Orleans;[22] but the pertinacious presence of Casa Calvo, Morales, and other Spaniards (whom Claiborne was finally compelled to force away in February, 1806), the rumors which they kept alive, the apprehension of war with Spain, the doubt as to the resultant attitude of the Creole and European population, the malignant enmity of sundry American malcontents led by the younger Daniel Clark, and a fierce quarrel in the church, between the vicar-general and the pastor of the cathedral, with their respective parties, kept the public mind in a perpetual ferment.[23]

Still, in all this restiveness and discord, there was an absence of revolutionary design. The community, whose planting, springing, and gradual development have been so studiously and minutely followed in the foregoing pages, had at length undergone its last transplanting, and taken root in American privileges and principles. From this point its interesting history, replete with the incidents of war, fire, pestilence, blood, commercial aggrandizement and decay, as it will be shown to be, may often be treated with comparative cursoriness, which could not be indulged in while studying the causes of its existence and the origin and growth of its peculiar people.

Of this people Claiborne, in November, 1806, was able to write, alluding to the seditious plot which is next to be considered: "Were it not for the calumnies of some Frenchmen who are among us, and the intrigues of a few ambitious, unprincipled men, whose native language is English, I do believe that the Louisianians would be very soon the most zealous and faithful members of our republic."[24]

[12.] BURR'S CONSPIRACY

On the 26th day of June, 1805, there arrived in the port of New Orleans from the West "an elegant barge," equipped with "sails, colors, and ten oars," manned by "a sergeant and ten able, faithful hands," and carrying a single passenger. He was the bearer of letters from General Wilkinson, introducing him in the city, and one, specially, to Daniel Clark, stating that "this great and honorable man would communicate to him many things improper to letter, and which he would not say to any other." Governor Claiborne wrote to Secretary Madison, "Colonel [Aaron] Burr arrived in this city on this evening." He remained in New Orleans ten or twelve days, receiving much social attention, and then left for St. Louis, expressing his intention to return in the following October.[1]

During the winter of 1805–06 the seeming imminence of war with Spain induced the governor to make such diligent preparations for defense as his meager resources allowed, and he naturally thought it strange that at such a juncture General Wilkinson should, from only 220 serviceable troops in the city, remove to Mississippi territory an entire company, but, forced to look to his Creole militia as a source of reliance, he was pleased to see them throw off, momentarily, their habitual apathy, and to hear from them expressions of patriotic ardor. The city banks contained at that time some $2,000,000, and with good reason he feared that it would attract the cupidity and arouse the enterprise of its enemies. The real danger, however, lurked where it was little suspected, for as yet he probably knew nothing of the dark plot for the

plunder of New Orleans and the conquest of Mexico, growing in
the mind of the man in whose honor he had himself, a few months
before, spread a public banquet.[2]

The expulsion of Casa Calvo and Morales, on the 1st and 15th
of February, 1806, increased the ill-feeling between the United
States and Spain. On the 15th of March the Spanish governor on
the east of the territory forbade the future transmission of United
States mails through his province, and on the western border, at
the river Sabine, the Spanish-American officials began a show of
armed muster and aggression. The upright young patriot who governed at New Orleans, passed the spring and summer in sad per-
plexity, beset by dangers both outward and manifest and internal
and hidden. The encroachments of the Spaniards, the fierce enmity
of certain influential American residents, the mortifying supine-
ness of the Creoles, for which he was continually making excuses,
the too hastily suspected sedition of Père Antoine,* the pastor of
the cathedral, were not to him more serious cause of alarm and
mortification, than the inactivity of the United States forces under
the orders of Wilkinson.[3]

"My present impression is," he wrote to the acting governor of
Mississippi territory,"that *all is not right*. I know not whom to censure, but it seems to me that there is wrong somewhere."[4]

Even the brighter hopes now and then inspired by the more
generous freaks of an unstable and whimsical public sentiment,
betrayed a touch of pathos. On the 17th of October he wrote to
the Secretary of war: "I hasten to announce to you the patriotism
of the citizens of New Orleans and its vicinity. At a muster this
morning of the first, second, and fourth regiments of militia, every
officer, non-commissioned officer, and private present made a vol-
untary tender of their services for the defense of the territory generally, and more particularly for the defense of the city. This display of patriotism affords me much satisfaction, and has rendered
this [day?][†] among the happiest of my life."[5] Within three months
he wrote: "Their enthusiasm has in a great measure passed away,
and the society here is now generally engaged in what seems to be
a primary object, the acquisition of wealth."[6]

But unknown equally to the preoccupied money-getters of New
Orleans, and to their anxious governor, the principal danger had

*Friar Antonio de Sedella.
†Bracketed in Cable's manuscript and in the census publication.

passed. Late in the previous September Wilkinson had arrived at Natchitoches, and had taken chief command of the troops there confronting the Spanish forces. On the 8th of October Samuel Swartwout, an adherent of the bad cause, brought him a confidential letter from Aaron Burr. He was received with much attention, remained eight days, and departed for New Orleans. On the 21st of October Wilkinson dispatched a messenger to the President of the United States, bearing a letter, in which the nefarious schemes believed to be cherished by Aaron Burr were exposed *by his senior and superior in sordid venality and treason.*[7]

Eight days later he effected an arrangement with the Spaniards for the withdrawal of the troops of both governments from the contested boundary, leaving the question of its final location to be settled by their respective governments, and, dispatching Major Porter in advance of him with a force of artificers and a company of 100 soldiers, hastened to New Orleans.[8]

The arrival of these in the city in November, their early reenforcement, the hurried repairing, mounting, and equipping of every siege gun and field piece in the town, the preparation of shell, grape, and canister, of buckshot cartridges and of harness, and manning of the redoubts, the issue of contracts for palisades and other appointments of defense, and the prevalence of many rumors, threw the city into a state of panic.[9]

Wilkinson, *in the bombastic style of one who plays a part,* demanded of Claiborne the proclamation of martial law: "The dangers which impend over the city and menace the laws and government of the United States, from an unauthorized and formidable association, must be successfully opposed at this point, or the fair fabric of our independence, purchased by the best blood of our country, will be prostrated, and the Goddess of Liberty will take her flight from this globe forever."[10]

To this request the law-honoring Claiborne declined to accede; but the chamber of commerce of the city was called together, the plot laid before them, and the resources and needs of land and naval defense explained. The members at once subscribed several thousand dollars, and recommended a transient embargo of the port for the purpose of procuring sailors.[11] But Wilkinson presently decided to act without Claiborne's co-operation. If Claiborne did not distrust his motives, it was not from want of advice from one who did. The acting governor of Mississippi territory wrote to him in December:[12]

Should he [Burr] pass us, your fate will depend on the general [Wilkinson],* not on the colonel. If I stop Burr, this may hold the general in his allegiance to the United States. But if Burr passes this territory with 2,000 men, I have no doubt but the general will be your worst enemy. Be on your guard against the wily general. He is not much better than Catiline. Consider him a traitor, and act as if certain thereof. You may save yourself by it.[13]

Wilkinson, on his part, wrote: "I believe I have been betrayed, and therefore shall abandon the idea of temporizing or concealment the moment after I have secured two persons now in this city."[14] On Sunday, the 14th of December, Dr. Erick Bollman was arrested by order of Wilkinson. On the 16th, when a writ of *habeas corpus* was obtained from the courts in favor of Bollman and of two others, Swartwout and Ogden,† who had been arrested at Fort Adams and were then confined on board a United States bomb-ketch in the river, opposite the city, Bollman was not to be found; no boat could be hired to carry the officer of the court to the bomb-ketch, and on the following day, when one was procured, Swartwout had been removed. Ogden was set free, but only to be rearrested with one Alexander, and held despite writs of *habeas corpus,* a powerless writ of attachment against Wilkinson, and the vain application of the court to the governor to sustain it with force. The judge resigned, and the power of Wilkinson became supreme.[15]

On the 14th of January, 1807, General [John] Adair, the intimate of Burr, arrived in New Orleans unannounced, stating that Colonel Burr, unattended save by a servant, would be in the city in three days. The same afternoon his hotel was surrounded by 120 regulars, commanded by one of Wilkinson's aids, by whom he was arrested at the dinner table. He was put in confinement and presently sent away. The troops beat to arms, a force of regulars and militia paraded the streets of the terrified city, and Judge [James] Workman, the issuer of the late writs, and two others, Kerr and [William] Bradford, were thrown into confinement. Bradford was at once released, however, and Workman and Kerr were set at liberty the next day on writs from the United States district court.[16] At this inopportune moment a Spanish force of 400 men, from Pensacola, arrived at the mouth of bayou St. John, a few miles from the city, on their way to Baton Rouge. Their commander asked of

*Brackets in Cable's MS and the census publication.
†Peter V. Ogden, the son of Burr's stepbrother.

Claiborne, for himself and suite, the privilege of passing through New Orleans. They were promptly refused.[17]

On the 22d of January the legislative council, which had convened ten days before, addressed the governor, disclaiming for the Creoles all participation and sympathy in the treason which threatened their peace and safety, but boldly expressing their intention to investigate the "extraordinary measures" of Wilkinson "and the motives which had induced them, and to represent the same to the Congress of the United States."[18]

On the 28th of January news was received that Burr, having arrived at a point near Natchez with fourteen boats and 80 or 100 men, had been met by a large detachment of Mississippi militia, arrested, taken to Natchez, and released on bond to appear for trial at the next term of the territorial court. He left the territory, however; the governor of Mississippi offered a reward of $2,000 for his apprehension, and on the 3d of March word came to New Orleans announcing his rearrest at Fort Stoddart, Alabama.[19]

About the middle of May Wilkinson sailed from New Orleans to Virginia, to testify in that noted trial[20] which, though it did not eventuate in the conviction of Aaron Burr, made final wreck of the treasonable designs attributed to him, and restored public tranquillity.

[13.] THE WEST INDIAN IMMIGRATION

Between the suppression of the Burr conspiracy in 1807 and the outbreak of war between the United States and Great Britain in 1812 a term of years passed in the history of New Orleans characterized by events not calculated to attract the special attention of the world without, yet internally of decided and lasting significance.

Among these one that, in the ultimate reach of its effects upon the moral and intellectual character of the people of New Orleans, easily takes rank with the most important is that which is made the subject of this chapter.

The fact, that in the period between the cession and the taking of the United States census of 1810, the city more than doubled its population, has given color to the erroneous impression, that there occurred as early as this a large influx of Americans. This was not the case.[1]

In 1806, the third year after the cession, the whole number of white inhabitants in New Orleans whose language was not French or Spanish, comprised but 350 men capable of bearing arms. If allowance is made for the fact that many of these were most likely newcomers and unmarried, the whole number of souls represented by these 350 able-bodied men can hardly be estimated to have exceeded 1,400. In 1803 the population of New Orleans was over one-fourth that of the whole population of those portions which became the territory of Orleans. A like proportion in the census of 1806, would show a population in the city not less than 12,000, of which about three-fifths, or 7,500, were white. There were, there-fore, only about 14 Americans in each 75 white—18½ per cent., or 12 per cent. of the whole population.[2]

Between 1806 and 1809, the total American immigration to the whole territory was scarcely 2,400 persons, and the American population within the city most likely did not rise above a total of 3,100. Yet the United States census, taken in the following year, showed an entire population in New Orleans and its precincts of 24,552.[3] The American element, therefore, was a very inconsid-erable part of the whole, at least as to numerical value, and the source of increase must be looked for in an opposite direction.

The wars of Napoleon had provoked the descent of hostile ex-peditions upon various islands of the French West Indies, and brought much distress upon their inhabitants. In Cuba large num-bers of white and mulatto refugees, who, on the occasion of the in-surrection in St. Domingo, had escaped across to Cuba with their slaves, were now, by the state of war between France and Spain, forced again to become exiles. Within sixty days, between the 19th of May and the 18th of July, 1809, 34 vessels from Cuba brought to New Orleans over 1,800 whites, nearly as many free persons of color, and about 2,000 slaves; in all, 5,797 souls.[4] Others fol-lowed later from Cuba, Guadeloupe, and other islands, until they amounted in total to 10,000.[5] There is no record of any consider-able number having returned home after the termination of these wars, or of their leaving New Orleans to settle elsewhere.

The ties of a common religion, a common tongue, and a common political sentiment, with what probably seemed to many a similar-ity of misfortunes, naturally made the Creoles of the West Indies welcome to the Creoles of Louisiana. To these they came somewhat in the character of re-enforcements, at a moment when the power of the "*Américains*," few in numbers but potent in energy and in advantages, was looked upon with hot jealousy.[6]

On the other hand, the Americans quite as naturally looked upon these unprofitable raisers of the price of bread and of rent with fierce disfavor. They had themselves done little to improve the state of morals or of order. Some had come to the region to make their permanent residence there; many more had no such intention; both sorts were, alike, simply and only seeking wealth. *But the degraded morality that would be brought in from the West Indies was positively uncommercial and therefore the object of incessant denunciatory protest in the* New Orleans Gazette.[7]

In fact the city was ill prepared to receive a large and sudden accession to its population, unless the increase was to come from some superior source. To re-enforce and fortify the indolent and unyielding Creoles, inflamed and exasperated by the new and untempered national pride and aggressive energies of the Americans, was to postpone the common harmony which it was so desirable to hasten. And yet the native Creole element was one of the best in the community. The Spaniards were very few, being in all probability less in number than in 1806, when the mayor of New Orleans reported their total at 230. But few as they were, fewer would have been better. "They are generally of that description," wrote [Treasury] Secretary [John] Graham to [Secretary of State James] Madison, "who would be ready to seize any moment of disturbance to commit the vilest depredations, and, whether in peace or in war, they are a nuisance to the country."[8] Even the mild Claiborne mentioned them as "for the most part composed of characters well suited for mischievous and wicked enterprises."[9] *In general they seem to have been men without family ties, many of them deserters from the Spanish forces in Florida.*[10]

The free people of color were an unaspiring, corrupted, and feeble class, of which little was feared and nothing hoped. In numbers they were on the increase, and from an official report of those among them able to bear arms in 1806, their whole number in 1809 must be estimated at not under 2,000. The German and Irish elements had begun to come in, but were inappreciable. The floating population was extremely bad. Sailors from all parts of the world took sides, according to the hostile nations from which they came, in bloody street riots and night brawls, and bargemen, flatboatmen, and raftsmen from the wild regions, not then entirely wrested from the Indians, along the banks of the Ohio, Tennessee, and Cumberland rivers, abandoned themselves, at the end of their journey, to the most shameful and reckless excesses.[11]

With such elements within its ruined walls a city so lately and suddenly loosed from the yoke of Spanish police government and

*given the freedom of early American frontier rule could hardly hope
to escape, as a first effect, an eruption of public vice and disorder
calculated to alarm the most sanguine advocate of free institutions.*
A spirit of strife seemed to pervade the whole mass. A newspaper article reflecting upon Napoleon, in 1806, gave rise to a storm
of indignation that had almost ended in a riot, and that led the
governor to suspect the French consul of intriguing with the Creoles. Plays were put upon the theater boards which caused the
Ursulines to appeal to the governor for protection against public
derision. Even the humble Père Antoine, the pastor of the cathedral, was momentarily under suspicion of exercising a seditious
influence among the people of color. In 1807 a public uprising was
hardly prevented, as the consequence of the action of three young
officers of the navy forcibly releasing a slave girl who was being
punished by her master.[12]

In September of the same year occurred the "batture riots," a
fierce contest between the public and some private claimants, represented by the noted jurist, Edward Livingston, for the ownership
of the sandy deposits made by the Mississippi river in front of the
faubourg Ste. Marie. Two distinct outbreaks occurred. In the second, which took place on the 15th of September, 1807, the Creoles,
ignoring the decision of the Supreme Court, rallied by thousands
to the *batture* (as the new deposits of alluvium outside the levee
are called), led by the beat of a drum, and were only quieted and
dispersed by the patient appeals of Governor Claiborne, addressed
to them on the spot, and by the recommittal of the contest to the
United States courts, in whose annals it is so well known a cause.[13]
The month of August, 1808, was rendered conspicuous by collisions between American and European sailors, who met each other
in battle array and actual skirmish on the levee. The condition of
the city became alarming, and Claiborne wrote to the commander
of the United States troops in Mississippi for a re-enforcement of
regulars.[14]

At this time the United States government was preparing for
the war which threatened with transatlantic powers. Claiborne,
though anxious to speak well of his people, was forced to confess
some lack of confidence in the ardor of a populace that—always
ripe for disturbance—furnished no volunteers for war. "You are not
uninformed," he wrote in 1809, "of the very heterogeneous mass of
which the society of New Orleans is composed. England has her
partisans; Ferdinand the Seventh some faithful subjects; Bonaparte

his admirers; and there is a fourth description of men, commonly called Burrites, who would join any standard which would promise rapine and plunder."[15] A paper was published, devoted to the interests of this faction, and known as *La Lanterne Magique,* whose "libelous publications against the government and its officers" gave the executive much anxiety, issued among a people "still for the most part strangers to our government, laws, and language."[16]

Such was the city into which, suddenly—despite the loud hostility of Americans, English, and Spanish, the laws against the importation of slaves, the appeal of Claiborne to the American consuls at Havana and Santiago de Cuba to impede the movement, the point-blank order to the free people of color to depart from the territory, and the actual effort to put it into execution—there began to pour these thousands of West Indian exiles; Creoles, free mulattoes, and slaves, some with goods and chattels, others in absolute destitution, and "many . . . of doubtful character and desperate fortune," until their numbers about equaled the original population upon whose hospitality they were thrown, and the cost of living daily increased the numbers of distressed poor.[17]

The readiness with which the three different classes of this immigration dissolved into the corresponding parts of the New Orleans community, is indicated in the fact, that they never appeared again in the city's history in anything like a separate capacity. And yet it might be much easier to underestimate than to exaggerate the silent results of an event that gave the French-speaking classes twice the numerical power with which they had begun to wage their long battle against American absorption.

But it was not by the force of mere numbers that the American was either to assert his value or to be more than momentarily checked in his peaceful onset. He confronted the Creole with the power of capital and of an active, enterprising, practical mind, a vigorous offshoot of the greatest commercial nation on the earth; with new aims, a new tongue, new modes of thought, new conceptions of the future destiny of New Orleans, and with an ill-disguised contempt for the more dignified sentiments and customs of the ancient Louisianians, he came unasked, proposing to accomplish a commercial conquest of their city and territory.

The year 1811, therefore, may be set forward to mark a turning point in the history of New Orleans. The Creole, attained to the climax of comparative numerical strength, and armed with all the privileges and advantages with which a free government could in-

vest him, stood forth to give to American civilization the only pro-
longed conflict that has ever been maintained against it by a small
and isolated community. The course of events now turned to the
advantage of the new New Orleans and its prospective new master. On the 4th of November, 1811, a convention, elected by the
people of Orleans territory, met in New Orleans, and on the 28th
of the following January adopted a state constitution; and on the
30th of April, 1812, "Louisiana" was admitted into the Union.[18]

In the meantime an incident has occurred of even greater significance. "On the 10th of January, 1812, the inhabitants of New Orleans witnessed the approach of the first vessel propelled by steam"
that navigated the Mississippi,[19] the "Orleans" from Pittsburgh.

[14.] THE WAR OF 1812–15

A magnificent future seemed now to await only a clearer political
sky on and across the Atlantic, to lift and bear New Orleans forward to an imperial position among the great commercial cities of
the world. The Spanish-American colonies encircling the Gulf of
Mexico, were asserting their independence; the triumphs of inven-
tive genius were making cotton one of the world's great staples;
steam navigation promised a secured and a mightier freedom of
the Mississippi; and the boundless valley of which New Orleans
seemed the only gateway for commerce, was bidding fair to become
the provision-house of the world, and the consumer of an untold
wealth of European manufactures. But even the partial realiza-
tion of these expectations was destined to be forerun by a season
in which the very existence of the city was threatened. On the 18th
of June, 1812, Congress declared war against Great Britain.[1]

The persistent effort to make Canada the seat of hostilities, left
New Orleans virtually undefended, though surrounded and infested with dangers. Congress, it is true, authorized the President
to hold and occupy that part of Florida west of the Perdido river. In
1813, Wilkinson marched to the Mobile, drove the Spaniards out of
Fort Charlotte on the 13th of April, and established a small fortification, Fort Bowyer, on a point of land commanding the entrance
to Mobile bay, thus removing as far as Pensacola a neighbor only
less objectionable than the British. But, this done, he was ordered
to the seat of operations on the Canada line, and even a part of the
small force of regulars which was in Louisiana was withdrawn in
the same direction.[2]

The English were already in the Gulf of Mexico; the Creek Indians were growing offensive; in July, 700 of them crossed the Perdido, and, on the 13th of September, 350 whites—men, women, and children—were massacred at Fort Mimms, in Mississippi, and the Creek war set in. Within New Orleans the elements of danger were almost equally great. Bands of drunken Choctaws—a people who, it was constantly feared, would take up the hatchet and join the Creeks—roamed through the streets. [Jean] Lafitte and his men, a numerous band of piratical smugglers, made their rendezvous in the neighboring waters of Barataria bay, and appeared daily in the city's public resorts. A crevasse overflowed a portion of the town, and incendiary fires became so common as to produce a profound sense of unsafety through this cause alone. In the midst of these excitements and alarms, the batture trouble again sprang up, and for a time agitated the public mind.

Under this condition of affairs, Claiborne, in July and September, ordered the state militia to hold itself ready to take the field at a moment's notice, and was much encouraged by the alacrity with which this easy preliminary of a sterner duty was performed. As the autumn wore on the rumors of invasion multiplied, relief continued still to be unfurnished, and the commander of United States forces in Mississippi and Louisiana (the seventh military district), not only assured Governor Claiborne that he could muster at most only 700 regulars, but, under order of the President, made requisition upon the state of Louisiana for 1,000 militia, to be mustered into the service of the general government for six months.

On the 25th of December, 1813, Claiborne ordered the mustering of this quota. Certain rural parishes at once responded; but New Orleans as promptly displayed that perfectly sincere insubordination of the individual's liberty and opinion to the common welfare or the common conviction. Three or four companies only of the city militia answered the call. The rest firmly refused either to volunteer or to be drafted, some at the same time expressing their entire readiness to do service within the state, while others were ready for duty inside the limits of the city and its suburbs, but only by companies, under their own officers, and in such a way as to be relieved at short intervals.

In February, 1814, 400 militia from the rural districts having reported in a body at the Magazine barracks, opposite New Orleans, the governor renewed his order of the previous December, and directed that delinquents be dealt with according to law and

military usage. It was met with clamorous denunciation and refusal to obey. The country militia declined to be mustered in without the city militia, and volunteered their services to enforce obe-
dience; this tender came to the knowledge of the city companies,
and only the discreet refusal of Claiborne to lean upon any support
but the law, averted the mortifying disaster of a battle without
an enemy. As it was, the rural military, already melting away by
desertion, was disbanded, and the governor, unsupported by the
legislature and denounced on all sides as a tyrant, was compelled
to report a failure, amiably apologizing for the community at the
last, as being emphatically ready to "turn out in case of actual invasion." Fortunately, that actual invasion for which the strangely
but conscientiously lethargic city was willing to prepare, whenever
it should be obviously too late, did not come that spring, nor until
the events of the Creek war had brought to view the genius of Andrew Jackson.

Meantime affairs in New Orleans grew rather worse than better. In March it became necessary for the governor to suppress a
projected filibustering expedition to Texas. In April, although the
national government, too late for the act to afford relief, had raised
the embargo, the New Orleans banks suspended payment. The
same month brought word of the fall of Paris and of the abdication
of Napoleon, and of the consequent ability of England to throw
new vigor into the war with America, and to spare troops for the
conquest of Louisiana. The knowledge became painfully distinct,
too, that while the majority of the people were lamenting at once
the disasters of France and the fresh dangers of British invasion,
there were those in the city, Spaniards and Englishmen, to whom
the new face of affairs was entirely welcome.

However, the issue was fast approaching. In July the Creeks
sued for peace, and a treaty was made with them on the 9th of August. About the same time a number of British officers arrived at
Apalachicola, in Florida, forerunners of an expected military force.
They brought with them several pieces of artillery. To these some
still disaffected tribes of the Creek nation joined themselves, and
were by them armed and drilled.

But the point had at length been reached, when the United
States government—of which too little could hardly have been
expected since it has not yet protected its own capital—began to
take active measures for the preservation of its territory and the
defense of its citizens in the southwest. General Jackson was ap-

pointed to the work, and in August was expected soon to arrive in New Orleans to take command. Commodore [Daniel Thomas] Paterson received instructions from Washington to take the schooner Carolina, ordered to New Orleans for the purpose, and with the coöperation of Colonel [George] Ross, of the forty-fourth regiment, to make a descent on the Baratarians.*

The requisition for the state's quota of 1,000 militia was now made again, coming, this time, direct from the President, and Claiborne received the assurances of the officers of the city militia, including a corps of free men of color, that they would be ready when called upon to obey orders. Yet, certainly less ill-disposed than in the previous year, their attitude was still characterized by an entire lack of zeal. On the 15th of August Jackson wrote directing, through Claiborne, that they be ready to march to any point at a moment's warning; but the experienced governor did not issue his order calling them to rendezvous at New Orleans until the 5th of September, when Jackson had repaired to Mobile, where the invasion was about to take place.

A little after the landing of the British officers at Apalachicola, some companies of British infantry had arrived at Pensacola, in the sloops of war Hermes and Caron, coming from Bermuda via Havana, under command of [Lt.] Colonel [Edward] Nichols. He had landed and established his headquarters, unopposed by the nominally neutral Spanish authorities, and had soon been joined by the officers from Apalachicola, at the head of a considerable body of Indians. Toward the close of August he had issued a proclamation, appealing to native Louisianians to aid in liberating their paternal soil, and restoring it to its rightful Spanish master; and to Spaniards, Frenchmen, Italians, and Britons to lend their strength to abolish American usurpation; Kentuckians were promised money for supplies, and an open Mississippi in exchange for neutrality.

Claiborne applied to the governor of Kentucky to hasten forward the troops expected from that state. In a general order he warned his own people against the pretensions of the enemy, and exhorted them to an exercise of that spirit of zealous and united effort, the want of which was their greatest and most perilous deficiency.

The moment was certainly critical. The enemy was treating with the Baratarians, and endeavoring, by offers of commissions and rewards in the British service, to seduce them from their love

---

*I.e., Lafitte's privateers and smugglers on Grand Terre Island.

of country. One of the brothers Lafitte, who were the leaders of the band, had sent the British letter and laid it before Claiborne, with the offer of his services and that of his men in the American cause, on condition that their proscription be annulled. The governor called a council, comprising, with others, Commodore Paterson and Colonel Ross. The patriotism of the smugglers, displayed only when an expedition had been ordered and was almost ready to move for their destruction, was not highly esteemed. It was decided to have no communication with the pirates, and preparations were hurried forward to bring them to justice.

Under such portentous clouds as these the people could not but awake, at last, to the necessity of united effort, and, at a public meeting on the 15th of September, passed patriotic resolutions, and appointed six Creoles and three Americans a committee of safety. How soon afterward another was formed, with conflicting views and plans, is not plainly stated, but it is certain that on the very same day that the first public meeting was held, 700 British troops, 600 Indians, and 4 vessels of war, with 92 pieces of heavy artillery, attacked Fort Bowyer, the small but important fortification erected by Wilkinson to command the entrance to Mobile bay and Mississippi sound. The garrison of 130 men, with 20 guns, repulsed the attack, and the enemy retired again to Pensacola with the loss of 162 men killed and as many wounded; the sloop-of-war Hermes, which, having grounded, they were compelled, themselves, to burn.

Three days later the expedition of Paterson and Ross attacked and destroyed the piratical rendezvous at Barataria, taking vessels and some prisoners, and scattering those who succeeded in escaping. The brothers Lafitte fled up the Lafourche to the "German coast," a part of the Mississippi shore whence the Lafourche starts to empty into Barataria bay. Others by and by gathered upon Last island,* at the mouth of the Lafourche, and others found asylum in New Orleans, where they increased the fear of internal disorders.

The British, meanwhile, awaiting the arrival of troops that had sailed from Ireland early in September, to the number of 12,000 or more, were, with or without the consent of the Spaniards, occupying Pensacola, and even garrisoning its forts. General Jackson gathered 4,000 men on the Alabama river, regulars, Tennesseeans, and Mississippi dragoons, and on the 6th of November encamped

---

*Destroyed by a hurricane in 1856, the island was the subject of Lafcadio Hearn's novel *Chita: A Memory of Last Island.*

within three miles of Pensacola and demanded of the Spanish governor that American garrisons be received into the forts until Spaniards could be supplied. On the 7th, this proposition having been rejected, he entered the town and attacked and took the two forts, St. Michael and St. Charles. The British, with some Indians, retreated to the shipping in the bay and sailed away; the remainder of the Indians fled across the country, and Jackson returned to Mobile, and soon after called upon Claiborne to prepare the whole body of the Louisiana militia for service.

On the 10th Claiborne convened the legislature, and on the 15th, with great fear that that body "would not act with the promptitude and energy which the crisis demanded," laid General Jackson's letter before it.

The condition of affairs was indeed deserving of anxiety. The absence of a master spirit to command the confidence of a people accustomed to act only upon individual convictions and interests, caused a general state of discord, apprehension, and despondency. The two committees of safety were engaged in miserable disputes. Credit was destroyed. Money could be borrowed only at 3 or 4 per cent. per month. In the legislature, where time and means were being wasted in idle formalities, the Creole himself finally raised the voice of a noble impatience, and [Louis] Louallier, a member from Opelousas, asked: "Shall we always confine ourselves to addresses and proclamations?" It may be he distributed the blame more evenly than the governor had done: "Are we," continues his spirited report, "always to witness the several departments intrusted with our defense languishing in a state of inactivity, hardly to be excused even in the most peaceful times? No other evidence of patriotism is to be found, than a disposition to avoid every expense, every fatigue. Nothing, as yet, has been performed." For the defense of 600 miles of coast there were but one sloop-of-war and six gunboats, the feeble Fort St. Philip on the Mississippi, and the unfinished and but half defensible Fort Petites Coquilles on the Rigolets. The supply of ammunition, especially that for artillery, was totally inadequate, and the marching force in New Orleans numbered but 700 regulars, the 1,000 militia which it had required three imperative calls to bring into the field, and 150 sailors and marines. At Tchefuncta, on the farther side of lake Pontchartrain, lay a half-finished, flat-bottomed frigate, destined to carry 42 guns, work on which had been suspended and so remained, despite the appeals of Commodore Paterson and Governor Claiborne to the general government. "Our situation," says La Carrière Latour,* in his invaluable memoir, "seemed desperate."[3]

Suddenly confidence returned; enthusiasm sprang up; all, in a moment, was changed by the arrival, on the 1st of December, of General Jackson. On the day of his arrival he reviewed the uniformed city militia, a small, but well drilled and thoroughly equipped body of Creoles and French. The next day he went down the Mississippi, inspected Fort St. Philip, ordered its wooden barracks demolished and additional cannon mounted, a new battery of 24-pounders constructed opposite the fort, and another erected half a mile above St. Philip on the same bank. Returning to New Orleans, he visited the country northward and eastward behind the city, ordering the erection of a battery at the confluence of bayous Sauvage and Chef Menteur, and sending instructions to Governor Claiborne to obstruct all bayous on Orleans island leading to the Gulf; which instructions it was supposed by all in authority, until too late to repair the oversight, had been thoroughly carried out. The energy and activity of Jackson were imitated on all sides. Soon every able-bodied man in New Orleans and its environs was ready for the field, and the whole militia of the state was organizing and preparing to march.

But the new leader's example was not the only spring of this tardy alacrity. The enemy had hove in sight off Pensacola, a British fleet of 80 sail, under the dreaded [Vice Admiral Sir Alexander] Cochrane, so lately the ravager of the Atlantic coast and capturer of Washington city, and was bearing down toward Ship island; and when the legislature, on the 13th, appropriated some $30,000 for purposes of defense, a force of 45 barges, carrying 43 guns and 1,200 men, was at that moment eagerly endeavoring to join battle with the retiring American flotilla of five gunboats and a schooner, near the narrow passes of lake Borgne.

On the night of the 13th this little fleet took a defensive stand across the western passage of Malheureux island, and on the 14th, retreat being impossible by reason of a calm and a strong outward current, it fell, after a gallant resistance, into the hands of an enemy almost ten times its strength. The British were thus in complete possession of lake Borgne and its shores. Had this occurred before the arrival of Jackson in New Orleans, the British army would almost certainly have marched into the city without another battle.

*Arsène Lacarrière Latour, author of *Historical Memoir of the War in West Florida and Louisiana in 1814–15.*

On the next day Claiborne informed the legislature of the disaster, and on the 16th advised its adjournment. The matter was debated, and the legislature decided to remain in session, whereupon Jackson, displeased, took another step, which the same body had pronounced inexpedient, and himself proclaimed martial law, closing with the ringing announcement that, "the safety of the district intrusted to the protection of the general must and will be maintained with the best blood of the country; and he is confident . . . that unanimity will pervade the country generally; but should the general be disappointed in the expectation, he will separate our enemies from our friends. Those who are not for us are against us, and will be dealt with accordingly."

Measures of defense received a further acceleration. At the previous suggestion of the legislature slaves were furnished, by the planters of the neighboring parishes, for work on fortifications, in greater number than could be employed. Major [Pierre] Lacoste, with the battalion of free men of color, the Feliciana dragoons, and two pieces of artillery, was sent to the junction of bayous Sauvage and Chef Menteur, to erect and occupy a redoubt surrounded by a fosse. The garrison of the little post at the mouth of bayou St. John was re-enforced by a company of light artillery. Measures were taken to protect the unfinished frigate at Tchefuncta, and a passport system was established on lake Pontchartrain. The commander of Fort Petites Coquilles was ordered to defend it to the last extremity, and if not able to hold out, to spike his guns and fall back upon the post at Chef Menteur. Word was dispatched to the troops coming from the west to hasten their march. The commander at Mobile was warned to be on the alert against attempts of the enemy to disembark there. A second battalion of free men of color was raised, and the two bodies were put under Colonel Fortier,* an opulent white Creole merchant. A Captain Juzon was ordered to collect the Choctaw Indians about the city's outskirts and on the shores of lake Pontchartrain into companies. The inmates of the prisons were taken out of confinement and placed in the ranks. John Lafitte, upon action of the legislature and governor, intended to encourage the movement, again offered the services of himself and his men, bearing his overtures to Jackson in person. They were accepted, some of his band were sent to the forts Petites Coquilles, St. John and St. Philip. Others under Dominique* and

*Michel, or Miguel, Fortier.

[Renato] Beluche, private captains, were enrolled in a body as artillery, and all judicial proceedings against them were suspended. On the 18th Jackson reviewed and addressed his troops. Edward Livingston appeared as one of his aids. The same day Major [Jean Baptiste] Plauché was put in command at bayou St. John, with his battalion. The commanders of outposts and pickets received minute instructions. A guard consisting of firemen and men beyond military age, under General Labatut, policed the city, which was put under the strictest military rule. On the 19th General [William] Carroll arrived at the head of 2,500 Tennesseeans, and on the 20th General [John] Coffee came in with 1,200 riflemen from the same state.

The army of Jackson was thus increased to the number of about 6,000 men. Confidence, animation, concord, and even gaiety filled the hearts of the people. "The citizens," says Latour, "were preparing for battle as cheerfully as for a party of pleasure. The streets resounded with Yankee Doodle, *La Marseillaise, Le chant du Départ,* and other martial airs. The fair sex presented themselves at the windows and balconies to applaud the troops going through their evolutions, and to encourage their husbands, sons, fathers, and brothers to protect them from their enemies." That enemy numbered 14,450 men and a powerful fleet. Sir Edward Packenham commanded the land forces, with [Samuel] Gibbs, [John] Lambert, and Kane[†] for generals of divisions. The fleet was under Admirals Cochrane, [Edward] Codrington, and [Pultney] Malcolm.

The British, reconnoitering on lake Borgne, soon found at its extreme western end the mouth of a navigable stream, the bayou Bienvenue. It flowed into the lake directly from the west, the direction of New Orleans. There were six feet of water on the bar at the mouth, and more inside. It was more than a hundred yards wide. A mile and a half up the stream they found a village of Spanish and Italian fishermen, who used the bayou as a daily water route to the city market. These men were readily bribed, and under their guidance the whole surrounding country was soon explored. The bayou was found to rise close behind the lower suburb of New Orleans, whence it flowed eastward through a vast cypress swamp lying between bayou Sauvage on the north and the Mississippi river on the south, emerging by and by upon the broad quaking prairies bordering lake Borgne, and emptying into that water. Various

*Dominique You (half brother of Jean Lafitte).
†John Keane.

plantation draining-canals ran back from the cultivated borders of the Mississippi, and, connecting with the bayou, were found to afford on their margins firm standing ground and a fair highway to the open plains of the Mississippi river shore, immediately below New Orleans. By some oversight, which has never been explained, this easy route to the city's very outskirt had been left entirely unobstructed. On the 21st of December American scouts, penetrating to the mouth of the bayou, saw no enemy, and established themselves as a picket in the fishermen's village, which they had found deserted save by one man.

Meanwhile the enemy had been for some days disembarking on the *Isle aux Pois* (Pea island), at the mouth of Pearl river. On the morning of the 22d General Keane's division embarked from this point in barges, pushed up the lake, and some time before dawn of the following day surprised and overpowered the picket at the fishermen's village, passed on in their boats by way of bayou Bienvenue through the trembling prairie and into and through the swamp forest, disembarked at canal Villeré, and at half past eleven in the morning, the 23d, emerged, at the rear of General [Jacques] Villeré's plantation, upon the open plain, without a foot of fortification confronting them between their camping ground and New Orleans. Here, greatly fatigued, they halted until they should be joined by other divisions.

But General Jackson resolved to attack them without delay. At seven o'clock in the evening, the night being very dark, the American schooner Carolina dropped down the river to a point opposite the British camp, and anchoring close ashore suddenly opened her broadsides and a hot musketry fire at short range. At the same moment General Jackson, who, at the head of 1,200 men and two pieces of artillery, had marched upon the enemy from the direction of New Orleans, and had found them drawn up in echelons half a mile along the river bank, with their right wing extended toward the woods at right angles of the plain, fell upon them first with his right, close to the river shore, and was presently engaged with them along his whole line. The British right, unaware of the approach of General Coffee from the direction of the woods, with 600 men, under cover of the darkness, and attempting to flank Jackson's left, only escaped capture by an unfortunate order of the American colonel in command, restraining the Creoles, as they were about charging with the bayonet. The enemy gave way and succeeded in withdrawing under cover of the night, a rising fog, and the smoke, which was blown toward the American line. The engagement continued for a time with much energy on both sides, but with little system or order. On Jackson's right the British attempted the capture of the two guns, but their charge was repulsed. Companies and battalions on both sides, from time to time, got lost in the darkness and fog, sometimes firing into friendly lines, and sometimes meeting hostile opponents in hand to hand encounters. At the same time the second division of British troops were arriving at the fishermen's village, and hearing the firing, pushed forward in haste, some of them arriving on the field shortly before the state of the elements put a stop to the contest.

At four o'clock on the morning of the 24th Jackson fell back about two miles nearer to the city, and, behind a canal running from the river to and into the wooded swamp, and known as Rodriguez's canal, took up and began to fortify his permanent line, choosing this ground on account of the narrowness of the plain. This was only some four miles from the lower limits of the city.

Here from day to day the preparations for defense went rapidly on, while the British were diligently gathering their forces and laboriously, through much inclement weather and over miry ground, bringing up their heavy artillery. Skirmishing was frequent and of great value to Jackson's raw levies. On the 27th and 28th a brisk cannonade was interchanged from newly erected batteries on either side, resulting in the destruction of the Carolina with red-hot shot, leaving but a single American vessel, the Louisiana, in the river, but ending, on the other hand, in the demolition of the British batteries. On the 1st day of January, 1815, the enemy opened suddenly from three formidable batteries, driving Jackson from his headquarters, and riddling it with shot and shell. The Americans replied with vigor, opposing 10 guns to 28, and succeeded in dismounting several of the enemy's pieces. A few bales of cotton, forming part of the American fortifications, were scattered in all directions and set on fire. No further use was made of this material during the campaign. This artillery contest ceased at three in the afternoon, and during the night the British dismantled their batteries, abandoning five pieces of canon.

Thus they were, day by day, training their inexperienced foe, and while being augmented by the steady arrival of troops from their fleet in the Gulf, were allowing Jackson, also, to be materially re-enforced. Three hundred Acadians had joined him on the 30th of December. On the 1st of January 500 men arrived from Baton

Rouge, and on the 4th the expected Kentuckians, poorly clad and worse armed, but 2,250 in number, gave Jackson, after he had manned all strategic points, an effective force on his main line of 3,200 men. This line was half a mile of rude and extremely uneven earthworks, lying along the inner edge of Rodriguez's canal, across the plain, from the river bank to a point within the swamp forest on the left, and dwindling down after it entered the wood to a double row of logs laid over one another, with a space of two feet between the two rows filled with earth. The artillery defending this half mile of breastwork and ditch consisted of twelve pieces.

Winter rains had greatly impeded the British movements, but Lambert's division at length joined the others, and preparations were made for the decisive battle. On the 6th and 7th they were busy making ready to storm the American works, preparing fascines for filling the ditch and ladders for mounting the breastworks, and also getting boats through from Villeré's canal into the river, in order to cross and throw a force against Commodore Paterson's very effective marine battery on the farther side of the river, and some against extremely slender defenses beyond.

A little before daybreak on the 8th, the enemy moved out of their camp, and by daylight were plainly seen spread out upon the plain across two-thirds of its breadth, seemingly about 6,000 strong. The British plan was, at a given signal, to make four simultaneous demonstrations upon the American line, one to be made on the farther and three on the nearer side of the river.

About half past eight o'clock a rocket went up on the British side, near the woods, the Americans replied by a single cannon shot, and the attack began. On the American extreme left, inside the cypress forest, some black troops of the British force made a feeble onset—an evident feint—and were easily repulsed by Coffee's brigade. On the right, near the river, the enemy charged in solid column with impetuous vigor, and with such suddenness, that before the American battery stationed at that point could fire the third shot, the British were within the redoubt and had overpowered its occupant; but, in attempting to scale the breastworks behind, their leader, Colonel [Robert] Rennie, was killed, and the Americans presently retook the redoubt.

On the opposite side of the river, a column of the enemy had been expected to engage the Americans defending that quarter, and thus save the other attacking columns from the enfilading fire of the battery on that side. But this force had not been able to move with the celerity expected of it, and though it later reached its intended field of action, it easily driving the Americans, some 600 in number, from their indefensible line, and compelling the abandonment of the marine battery, this partial success was achieved only after the British had, everywhere else, lost the day.

The main attack was, meantime, made against that part of the American line in the plain, but near the edge of the swamp. At a ditch, some 400 yards in front of the American works, the main force of the enemy formed in close column of about 60 men front, and, burdened not only with heavy fascines made of ripe sugarcanes and with ladders, but with their weighty knapsacks also, they advanced, giving three cheers, literally led to the slaughter. Preceded by a shower of Congreve rockets, they moved forward in perfect order, covered for a time by a thick fog, but soon entirely exposed not only to the full storm of artillery and musketry from the American breastworks, but, upon their extended flank, to the more distant fire of Paterson's marine battery, not yet diverted by the forces sent against it, and manned by the trained gunners of the United States navy. The American fire was delivered with terrible precision, that of [Garrigues] Flaugeac's battery, against which the onset was principally directed, tearing out whole files of men. Yet, with intrepid gallantry, their brave enemy came on, still moving firmly and measuredly, and a few platoons had even reached the canal, when the column faltered, gave way, and fled precipitately back to the ditch where it had first formed. Here the troops rallied, laid aside their cumbersome knapsacks, were reinforced, and advanced again in the same fatal columnar form, though now at a more rapid gait and with less order. But the same deadly storm met them as before. The part of the line directly attacked was manned by Tennessee and Kentucky riflemen—Indianfighters, accustomed to firing only upon selected victims. This fact, with the unfortunate slowness of onset in the first attacking column, is probably the true explanation for the well-nigh unaccountable defeat of so fine an army by so ill-equipped a foe. First Sir Edward Packenham, then General Gibbs, then General Keane, the first two mortally and the last severely wounded, with many others of prominent rank, were borne from the field, the column again recoiled, and, falling back to its starting point, could not be induced to make a third attack. The British batteries, which had opened vigorously at the outset, continued to fire until two in the afternoon, and the British troops remained drawn up in their ditches to repel an American attack, if such should be made; but, from the first signal of the morning to the abandonment of all effort to storm the line was but one hour, and the battle of New Orleans was over at half-past nine.

On the 9th, two bomb-vessels, a sloop, a brig, and a schooner, a part of the British fleet, appeared in sight of Fort St. Philip, on the Mississippi, and, anchoring two and a quarter miles away, began a bombardment which continued until the 18th without result, whereupon they withdrew; and the same night General Lambert stealthily evacuated the British camp. On the 27th the last of his forces embarked from the shores of lake Borgne.

Even in the recital of history the scenes of triumphant rejoicing, the hastily erected arches, the symbolical impersonations, the myriads of banners and pennons, the columns of victorious troops, the crowded balconies, the rain of flowers, the huzzahs of the thronging populace, the salvos of artillery, the garland-crowned victor, and the ceremonies of thanksgiving in the solemn cathedral, form a part that may be left to the imagination. In New Orleans there was little of sorrow mingled with the joy of deliverance. Six of her defenders alone had fallen, and but seven were wounded. The office of healing was exercised principally on the discomfited enemy, whose dead and wounded were numbered by thousands.

On the 13th of February, Admiral Cochrane wrote to General Jackson: "I have exceeding satisfaction in sending to you a copy of a bulletin that I have this moment received from Jamaica, proclaiming that a treaty of peace was signed between our respective plenipotentiaries at Ghent, on the 24th of December, 1814, upon which I beg leave to offer you my sincere congratulations." It was not until the 17th of March that the American commander received official information of the same fact. On the day previous, Claiborne had written to Mr. [James] Monroe, Secretary of War: "Our harbor is again whitening with canvas; the levee is crowded with cotton, tobacco, and other articles for exportation. The merchant seems delighted with the prospect before him, and the agriculturist finds in the high price for his products new excitements to industry."

[15.] COMMERCIAL EXPANSION—1815 TO 1840

Now, at length, that era of great prosperity, so freely predicted, actually opened upon New Orleans. The whole Mississippi valley began to increase in population with wonderful rapidity. Its numbers in 1815 cannot be given with exactness, but the United States census shows the growth to have been from 1,078,000 in 1810, to 3,363,000 in 1830. These broadly scattered multitudes, applying themselves for a time almost solely to the development of their new country's vast agricultural resources, accepted for the fruits of their toil those broad avenues to the world's markets which nature afforded in the Mississippi and its immense tributaries; they used either the most primitive modes of transportation or only those improvements upon them furnished by distant enterprise.[1]

Steam navigation, which it has been seen made its first descent of the Mississippi in 1812, began in 1816, after a four years' struggle, successfully to ascend the powerful current of that stream. In 1817 the produce of the great valley came to New Orleans in 1,500 flatboats, and 500 barges. In 1821 the arrivals of laden river craft at the levee numbered 287 of steamboats, 174 of barges, and 441 of flatboats.[2]

This new and immeasurably superior mode of transportation was accepted, unquestioned, by the agricultural West. Not yet recognized as the stepping-stone from the old system of commerce by natural highways, to the new system by direct and artificial lines, it held out to the merchants of New Orleans, and the newcomers that daily poured into the town, not only present wealth, but the delusion of absolute and unlimited commercial empire inalienably bestowed by the laws of gravitation. It was hardly possible, but it would have been invaluable, to New Orleans to have discovered, thus early, the real truth unconsciously let slip by one of her citizens of that day, when, sharing, and intending to express, the popular conviction, he wrote: "No such position for the accumulation and perpetuity of wealth and power ever existed."[3]

But for a long series of years nothing transpired to force upon the notice of her merchants the change which lay, as yet, undeveloped in the future, and each year saw her expanding commerce choking her streets and landings, and her harbor front more and more crowded with river and ocean fleets. Her exports rose and sank on the wave of financial inflation and collapse that swept the country in 1815–19, and, with the clearing away of the wreck in 1820, showed a net increase from five million to seven and a half million dollars.[4]

Population pressed in "from all the states in the Union and from almost every kingdom in Europe.["][5] The people numbered 33,000 in 1815 and 41,000 in 1820.[6] New energies asserted themselves in every direction. The ancient parallelogram of ditch and palisades that had so long marked the city's ultimate bounds had disappeared in 1808, and the town was spreading far beyond it on every side. The hands of architect and builder were busy in the narrow streets of the old town, as well as in the broader ones of the suburbs; and halls, churches and schools, stores, warehouses, banks, hotels, and theaters went up in rapid succession. The old Charity hospital was built in Canal street in 1815.[7]

In the faubourg Ste. Marie the development outstripped that in all other quarters. The change in the nature of the city's commerce caused her trade to fall largely into new hands. The French and Creole merchants, looking to the West Indies, to France, and to Spain for a continuance of the old interchange of products and of merchandise, were forced to witness the growth of New Orleans outside the former boundaries and abreast the landing-place of the western and southern produce fleet. This landing-place, convenient to the flatboats because of its slack water, was the contested *batture,* large areas of which were, from 1817 to 1820, reclaimed and soon became the sites of well-compacted store buildings for the accommodation of the commercial Americans. Coffee, indigo, sugar, rice, foreign fruits, and wines the older town managed to retain;[8] but cotton, tobacco, pork, beef, corn, flour, and northern and British fabrics—in short, the lion's share, was intercepted in its descent of the river, or in ascending, was carried above and received at the faubourg Ste. Marie and fell into the hands of the swarming Americans, whose boastful anticipations of the city's future began to leave the Creole out of the account. These newcomers, still numerically in the minority, were seen on every side, looking about with the eye of the invading capitalist; but the faubourg Ste. Marie became distinctively the American quarters.

Here in 1817, in the face of much skepticism on account of the yielding nature of the soil, on Gravier street, between Tchoupitoulas and Magazine, the first square of cobblestone pavement was laid. In 1820 the wooden sidewalks and curbs on the main thoroughfares gave place to others of brick and stone, and in 1822, a general paving of the principal commercial streets, both in the old and the newer towns, was begun.[9]

It cannot seem strange, that among the Louisiana Creoles—a people not prepared by anything in their earlier career to welcome and appropriate the benefits of such a torrent of immigration—the feeling should have been hostile to it, or that they sought no farther in accounting for the lamentable condition of public order and morals. In December, 1816, Claiborne gave place in the gubernatorial office to General [Jacques] Villeré, a Creole, who, in a special message of March, 1818, called for by the "scandalous practices almost at every instant taking place in New Orleans and its suburbs," said, "indeed we should be cautious in receiving all foreigners."[10]

Yet steam navigation, and the enormous fruitfulness of the Mississippi valley, brought a prosperity wide enough to take in all, and the same governor, in the following year, not only congratulated the community on the suppression of disorder, through the establishment of an effective criminal court and the subsidence of party spirit and "idle prejudice," but persevered in an attitude of loyal affection to the American Union which had inspired him even earlier to say: "The Louisianian who retraces the condition of his country under the government of kings, can never cease to bless the day when the great American confederation received him into its bosom."[11]

In 1825 the exports of New Orleans were twelve and a half and her imports four and a half million dollars.[12] The earlier and extraordinary development, between 1810 and 1820, of a simple export and import trade to four times its original size, had caused the population of the city during that time, in the face of annual pestilence, repeated inundation, local disorders, a low state of morals, strangeness of manners and customs, and remoteness from the world's center, almost to double its numbers.

Yet these very figures, indicating an increase of trade twice as large as that of population, should have demonstrated to her citizens the insufficiency of mere commerce, without the aid of manufactures, to enhance the population or the wealth of their city in a proportion at all parallel to the growth of its opportunities. Between 1820 and 1830, the disproportion became still more evident. With an increase of 75 per cent. in the volume of its trade the numbers of the population advanced from 41,351 only to 49,826,[13] an increase of but 20 per cent. In truth, the influx of population in this period, seems to have consisted of only such limited numbers as the allurements of sudden fortune tempted to take the chances of a short sojourn amid many dangers and discomforts, with little idea of permanent residence.[14] In the same period the population of Baltimore increased 25 per cent., that of Philadelphia 39 per cent., and that of New York 67 per cent.[15]

Not only did the increase of numbers in New Orleans fall so

far below its increase of trade and the growth of population in the Atlantic cities, but it failed to keep pace with the numerical and commercial growth of that great valley of which it was supposed to be the sole entrepot. Between 1820 and 1830 the population of this immense region advanced 61 per cent., or three times as rapidly as that of New Orleans. As countries fill up with people the proportion of those who dwell in towns and cities steadily enlarges; but while New Orleans increased 20 per cent. the states of Louisiana, Arkansas, and Mississippi, entirely tributary to it, without developing any considerable town-life elsewhere, increased in population 57 per cent.[16]

The states farther up the Mississippi did not wait on New Orleans. Other towns and cities rose into importance and grew with astonishing speed. Cincinnati increased from 32,000 to 52,000;[17] Pittsburgh became "in the extent of its manufactures the only rival of Cincinnati in the West";[18] the embryo city of St. Louis added 41 per cent. to its single 10,000; while smaller, yet not exceeded in its significance by any, the town of Buffalo quadrupled its 2,100 inhabitants as the gateway of a new freight route to northern Atlantic tide-water many hundreds of leagues more direct than the long journey down the Mississippi to New Orleans and around the dangerous peninsula of Florida. For in 1825 the new principle of commercial transportation began to appear in the opening of the Erie canal. In the same year the Ohio canal was begun, and in 1832 connected the waters of the Ohio river with those of lake Erie, and in 1835 the state of Ohio alone sent through Buffalo to Atlantic ports 86,000 barrels of flour, 98,000 bushels of wheat, and 2,500,000 staves.

Thus early, while New Orleans was rejoicing yearly in an increase of population, commerce, and wealth, its comparative commercial importance was actually decreasing, and that sun of illimitable empire which had promised to shine forever upon her, was beginning to rise upon other cities and to send its rays eastward and even northward, away from and across those natural highways which had been fondly regarded as the only available outlets to the marts of the world. Even steam navigation, which had seemed at first the very pledge of supremacy to New Orleans, began on the great lakes to demonstrate that the golden tolls of the Mississippi were not all to be collected at one or even at two gates.[19]

The ability of New Orleans to arrest these escapes of a commerce that had promised at the opening of the century to be all her own, has been much overrated, as well by lethargic believers in the greatness of her destiny as by ungenerous critics, dazzled with the success of rival cities. The moment East and West recognized the practicability of taking straighter courses in the direction of the great commercial continent of Europe, the direct became the natural route, and the circuitous the unnatural. New Orleans might, it is true, have delayed the application of the new system by increasing the efficiency of the old, and thus have pushed forward into a more distant future facts which could never be pushed aside; but upon the establishment of east-and-west trade lines New Orleans stood at once and of necessity in a subordinate relation to the commerce of both continents, save in so far as she could continue to remain the most convenient port of the lower Mississippi valley, and until the growth of countries behind her in the Southwest should bring her upon the line of their commerce on its direct way to and across the Atlantic.

Moreover, the drawbacks that beset the city were many and great. Most of them have frequently been mentioned in these pages. Between 1810 and 1837 there were fifteen epidemics of yellow fever.[20] Small-pox was a frequent and deadly visitor, and, in 1832, while the city was still suffering from an epidemic of yellow fever, it was stricken with cholera, which alone destroyed one-sixth of the entire population. So great was the distress, that many of the dead were buried on the spot where they died, and many were thrown into the river.[21]

The danger of navigation on the Ohio and the Mississippi was another serious disadvantage. The losses of property on these two rivers alone, in the five years ending in 1827, were one and a third million dollars, or nearly 2 per cent. of the city's entire export and import trade. Through the offices of the federal government these losses, during the next five years to 1832, were greatly reduced, but in a third term, ending with 1837, the improvement was less obvious, and during a long subsequent period the ill-fame of steam navigation on the Mississippi was part of the count against New Orleans. In 1837 300 lives were lost on the Mississippi by the sinking of a single steamer, and 130 by the burning of another. In 1838 an explosion on the same river destroyed 130 lives, and another on the Ohio, 120 lives.[22] The cost of running a steamboat on these waters was six times as great as on the northern lakes.[23]

The low state of morals and of order continued to give the city an unfortunate character in the esteem of distant communities.[24]

In 1823 the legislature, seconded by the governor, who pronounced it "wonderful to have escaped for so long a time from serious internal commotion," urged that the number of United States troops in and near the city be not diminished.[25] The strife between American and Creole continued to call forth the exhortations of governors against jealousies and party spirit, with reference to the accidental circumstances of language or birthplace,[26] and in 1836 it culminated in the division of the city into three separate municipalities, under distinct governments and independent powers, with a mayor and a general council over the whole city.[27] The old town formed the first, the faubourg Ste. Marie the second, and the faubourg Marigny the third municipality. A "native American" party sprang up in 1837, founded on the fear, real or assumed, of the results to be apprehended from immense European immigration.[28] Accounts of travelers ascribed to the St. Domingan element a bad influence on the city's morals, in carrying the love of pleasure to licentiousness, giving themselves passionately to gambling, and resorting with great frequency to the field of honor. This latter practice was carried on in society to a fearful extent. During a visit of General Lafayette to New Orleans, which he made in 1825, a serious feud between officers of the militia, who were engaged in the ceremonies of his enthusiastic reception, was prevented from ending in a duel between the leaders only by Lafayette's personal intervention.[29] When, many years later, it was decided to disfranchise all persons engaging in affairs of honor and to disqualify them from holding office, a Mr. Garcia exclaimed, in the legislature: "It seems to me that there is a conspiracy against the chivalric portion of our population."[30] The legislature continued to make New Orleans the state capital throughout this period, except that from 1830 to 1832 it sat at Donaldsonville.[31] Whether this body and the managers of financial corporations were really open to the charges of bribery and corruption, so fiercely brought against them by a rampant city press, or not, the very recklessness of the accusations indicate a lowness of pitch in the public moral sentiment; and this is still more plainly evidenced in the long tolerance of such scenes as those open-air Sunday afternoon African dances, carousals, and debaucheries in the rear of the first municipality, which have left their monument in the name of "Congo" square. The city was a favorite rendezvous for filibusters. The year 1819 is marked by "General" [James] Long's naval expedition from New Orleans to Galveston bay, with men and supplies. In 1822 an expedition was fitted out to aid [Simon] Bolivar in his struggle against Spanish power in South America. One hundred and fifty men sailed in a sloop of war, the Eureka, for Porto Cabello in Venezuela, and joined in the naval demonstration to which the place, after a siege, surrendered.[32] The war of independence in Texas, in 1835 and later, produced much excitement in New Orleans, and many hastened to the standard of revolution there, though at that date it was totally discountenanced by both the state and the general government.[33]

Such are some of the impediments that partially obstructed this city's aggrandizement and progress. It may seem that the most of them might have been removed, but another existed which riveted these shackles upon every part: an invincible provincialism pervaded the entire mass of the heterogeneous population. Intensified by Creole influence, by remoteness from civilization, by a "peculiar institution" which doubled that remoteness, and by an enervating climate, it early asserted itself in the commercial and financial creeds of the New Orleans merchant, and in the general conduct of municipal affairs. From this radical misfortune resulted that apathetic disregard of obstacles, that surrender of advantages which need not have been parted with, at least for generations, and that long, boastful oblivion to the fact, that with all her increase in wealth and population, the true status of New Orleans was really slipping back upon the comparative scale of American cities.

The impulse toward municipal improvement that sprang up in 1822 soon subsided. Paving stones could be had in that alluvial region only by being brought from distant shores as ship's ballast, and up to 1835, although there had been another movement in the same direction in 1832–34,[34] only two streets in New Orleans had been paved in any considerable part of their length, notwithstanding pavements were found as useful and serviceable as elsewhere, and without them even carriages, in bad weather, sank to the axle in the mire.[35] But gas was brought into use for lighting the streets in 1834, and a supply of Mississippi water was furnished through mains under the principal thoroughfares in 1836.[36]

In the matter of sanitation, which so painfully called for attention, measures were well nigh as scarce as appropriations for their performance. Between 1825 and 1838 a natural drain in the rear of the second municipality was broadened and deepened into Melpomene canal. In 1836 a municipal draining company began operations with a draining machine on bayou St. John;[37] but such partial means were totally inadequate to effect a tithe of what the most urgent sanitary necessities of the city actually demanded. In 1821 a quarantine was established, continued until 1825, and then abandoned.[38] For the one item of generous and gratuitous care of the plague-stricken stranger, both in and out of its justly famed charity hospital, the city earned much well-deserved credit.[39] (This institution left its buildings on Canal street, to occupy its present quarters on Common street, in 1823. The old buildings became the state house.)[40] Beyond these efforts no notice was given the subject, except to make the perpetual assertion of the salubrity of the town, unsupported either by statistics or by the effort to obtain them.

The bar at the mouth of the Mississippi remained untouched until 1835, when an appropriation of $250,000 by the general government was so nearly exhausted upon a survey and the preparation of dredging apparatus, that nothing more was done for several years. "Northeast pass," then the deepest mouth of the river, gave 12 feet of water,[41] a depth whose inadequacy for the commercial needs of a near future was overlooked. At that time new vessels, built expressly for the carrying trade between New York and New Orleans, did not exceed 500 tons register. The steamboats on the Mississippi seem to have been about the same capacity, but in 1834 they numbered, on this river and its tributaries, 234.[42]

Indeed, when all is recounted to explain the partly unnecessary and partly inevitable failure of New Orleans to secure the unrivaled supremacy which had been too confidently waited for, it is nevertheless true that the city, in the less immeasurable sphere to which the improvements of the age had consigned her, increased rapidly in commerce and in wealth, and, in the decade between 1830 and 1840, more than doubled her population. The conviction forces its way, that could the people of New Orleans, as a whole, have been inspired with the enthusiasm and enterprise which their merchants expended upon the mere marketing of crops, and have turned those impulses to the removal of obstacles and the placing of their city in an advantageous light before the intelligent world, it would have been then, and for a long time might have remained, the boldest competitor of New York in population, wealth, and imports, as it already was in exports. In 1831 her total exports and imports were $26,000,000. In 1832 they were somewhat less. In 1833 they reached $28,500,000; in 1834 they rose suddenly to over $40,000,000, and in 1835 to $53,750,000.[43]

This sudden expansion is largely accounted for in the extraordinary rise in prices, which became in the whole country the leading feature of these two years. But there was beside, over and above the commerce indicated by these figures, another and a separate source of wealth to New Orleans. The enormous agricultural resources of Arkansas, Mississippi, and Louisiana, and especially the world's ever-increasing demand for cotton, offered the most tempting returns for the investment of even borrowed money. The credit system became universal among the planters of cotton, sugar, and tobacco in these regions, and New Orleans became not only the lender of millions in money at high rates of interest, but the depot of all manner of supplies, which it advanced in large quantities to the planters throughout that immense region. The whole agricultural community became, in a manner, the commercial slaves of the New Orleans factors, unable either to buy or sell save through these mortgagees. A common recklessness in borrower and lender kept the planters constantly immersed in debt, and the city drained of its capital almost the whole year round, to supply the extravagant wants of the planters and the needs of their armies of slaves. Much the larger portion of all the varied products of the West received in New Orleans was exported, not to sea, but to the plantations of the interior, often returning, along the same route, half the distance they had originally come. In this way not only was much of the capital of New Orleans diverted from channels which would have yielded ultimate results incalculably better, but it was converted into planters' paper, based on the value of slaves and the lands they tilled, a species of wealth unexchangeable in the great world of commerce, and, when measured by its results, as utterly fictitious as paper money itself, while even more illusory. But like the paper money which was then inundating the country, this system produced an immense volume of business, which, in turn, called in great numbers of immigrants to swell the ranks of manual labor. New Orleans once more surpassed Cincinnati in population. From 1830 to 1840 no other leading American city increased in such a ratio.[44]

And yet among all causes, there was probably none more potent in suppressing that industrial development, outside of mere commerce, which might so properly have taken place in New Orleans at this stage of her growth, than the all-prevailing blight which fell upon labor, and especially upon intelligent, trained labor, through this institution of African slavery, which seemed to assure untold wealth alike to town and country. A large share of capital was bound up in the labor itself, and that labor, from the necessities of the case, of a very inferior and really unremunerative sort. Hence, the city, though beset with opportunities and filling up daily with immigrants from the British isles and from Europe, failed either to evolve or to attract from abroad those classes of adepts in the mechanical and productive arts which most rapidly augment the common wealth. The gross increase in population between 1830 and 1840 was from 49,826, at the opening of the decade, to 102,193 at its close. One-third of this increase was composed of slaves and free persons of color, classes of population which, under the laws and conventionalities of the time and place, were to the higher orders of the community far more a burden than an advantage.[45] The remaining two-thirds, less so much as is to be accounted to natural increase, was an immense inpouring of Irish and Germans of the poorest classes.[46] The state of society, notwithstanding these reenforcements, which might so soon, in other regions, have yielded great numbers of the most valuable operatives, remained unattractive, repelled the prospecting manufacturer and his capital, and diverted them to newer towns where labor was uncontemned and skill and technical knowledge sprang forward at the call of enlightened enterprise.

The year 1837 will long be memorable in the history of the United States as the date of the calamitous crisis which followed the mad speculation in lands and the downfall of the United States Bank.* In those parts of the Union, especially, where large results had intoxicated enterprise, banks without number and often without foundation, strewed their notes among an infatuated people. In New Orleans, where enterprise had shown but little spirit of adventure outside the factorage of the staple crop, the number of banks was comparatively small, but the spirit of the day was evident in the fictitious character of much that pretended to be banking capital. In 1835–36 the banks of Louisiana (which may be read New Orleans), with but little over $2,500,000 specie in their vaults, and a circulation of $7,000,000, purported to have an aggregate capital of $34,000,000.[47]† One account of the following

---

*A reference to Andrew Jackson's veto of the bill rechartering the Second Bank of the United States, followed by a withdrawal of its federal deposits. The financial panic of 1837 is often attributed to the spread of "wildcat" banking, which grew unchecked after the demise of the United States Bank.

†For a more balanced account of banking in antebellum New Orleans, see George D. Green, *Finance and Economic Development in the Old South: Louisiana Banking, 1804–1861* (Stanford: Stanford University Press, 1972).

year, gives them at the time of their suspension $60,000,000 capital, $4,000,000 deposits, $1,200,000 specie, $1,800,000 real estate, and $72,000,000 receivables, mostly protested.[48]

The condition of affairs was described at that time as a "whirlwind of ruin which had prostrated the greater portion of the city."[49] So-called shinplasters became the currency of the day, driving out everything of intrinsic value. So great was the feeling against the banks and all banking schemes, and so general the ignorance of their true province, that a constitutional convention, sitting at the time, provided that no banking corporation should be established in the state,[50] thus unwittingly turning a banking monopoly into the hands of the few institutions that weathered the long financial stress, and that in 1843, having abandoned to shipwreck the weaker concerns, finally resumed the payment of specie with $4,500,000 in their vaults, and their circulation reduced to $1,250,000.[51]

The foreign commerce of New Orleans, at the date of this change, was $34,750,000, and for the first time in the city's history her exports of cotton exceeded 1,000,000 bales.[52]

[16.] POSITIVE GROWTH WITH COMPARATIVE DECLINE

The great inventions for the facilitation of commerce were each, as they came into the field, attended by a fresh discovery of the pecuniary value of time, which made the adoption of these facilities imperative on every city that sought to press its own aggrandizement or even to retain its commercial station. But even so, to seize these new advantages was practicable only to those cities that lay somewhere on right lines between the great centers of supply and demand, and it was the fate, not the fault, of New Orleans, that she was not found at either end or anywhere along the course of such a line. The case was more fortunate with St. Louis, Louisville, Cincinnati, Pittsburgh, Boston, New York, Philadelphia, Baltimore, while some cities owe their existence entirely to the requirements of these new conditions, as Cleveland, Buffalo, and Chicago.

The successful introduction of the locomotive engine into the United States as a commercial power, about the opening of the century's fourth decade, distinctly ordered what the projection and partial construction of great canals had previously threatened, the division of the commercial domain claimed by New Orleans in halves, and the apportionment of the best part of the commerce and trade beyond the mouth of the Ohio among her rivals.

It was pre-eminently the decade of development, of which the inflation of 1835, the collapse of 1836–37, and the prostration of 1838–40, with which it closed, were but symptoms, and when these had passed, the southern regions of the Mississippi valley had thrown their entire fortunes and energies into the "plantation idea." The more northern had at the same time filled up with farmers, towns had sprung up without number, and railroads and canals had started out eastward and westward from all the fortunately located cities, bearing immense burdens of freight and travel, and changing the measurement of distance from the scale of miles to that of hours.

Boston and New York had made what seemed, then, enormous outlays with an intrepidity sufficient in itself to assure the future, and had newly emphasized their union with the states along the northern banks of the Ohio by lines of direct transit. Pennsylvania had connected Philadelphia directly with the southern shore of the same river, laying out a larger capital in railroads and canals than any other state in the Union. Baltimore had pushed her Chesapeake and Ohio canal and railway well out toward the region of mines, with the resolution of ultimately piercing the great western valley. Ohio and Indiana had spent millions for canals by which to grasp hands with the East.[1]

It was while these rail and water ways were being constructed, and were only gradually and one by one reaching profitable stages of completion, that New Orleans, as already noticed, more than doubled the number of its inhabitants. At the close of the decade she was the fourth city of the United States in population, being exceeded only by New York, Philadelphia, and Baltimore. Boston was nearly as large, but beside these there was no American city of half its numbers.

Truly unfortunate was it for New Orleans, that this result had been rather thrust upon her than achieved by her enterprise, and so, instead of becoming a spur to future efforts, it bred nothing better than an overweening confidence in the ability of the city to become speedily and without exertion the metropolis of America, if not eventually of the world.[2]

That New Orleans was growing—that it was growing as the delta sands on which it stands had grown—by the compulsory tribute of the Mississippi, was the shining but illusory fact under whose beams the city entered, in 1841, upon the fifth decade of the century. Before that decade had advanced far the more reflec-

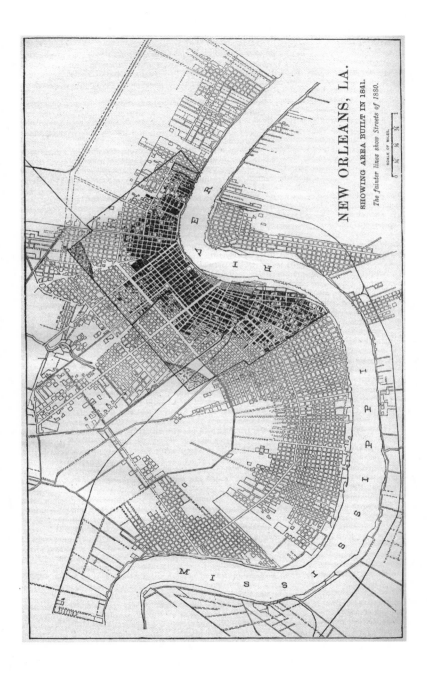

NEW ORLEANS, LA.

SHOWING AREA BUILT IN 1841.

The fainter lines show Streets of 1880.

SCALE OF MILES.

tive portion of the community began to perceive the less obtrusive though more important truth, that the rapid growth of the city was seriously slackening speed, and that the vast increase of production taking place in the upper and central parts of the Mississippi basin was being in great part poured into the laps of other cities.

The leading advantage lost being that of speedy transportation, the inroads upon the city's commerce were not yet seriously felt in the movement of those raw crops and milled breadstuffs, whose great bulk still demanded the cheapest rate of freights. The receipts of the great staples from the valley above kept steady pace with the immense increase in production, or seemed to do so. In 1842 these receipts from the interior amounted in value to more than $45,700,000; in 1843, to over $53,750,000; in 1844, to $60,000,000; in 1846, to more than $77,000,000; in 1847, to $90,000,000; and in 1850 they reached nearly the sum of $97,000,000.[3]

In 1840 the total production of corn in the eight states of Ohio, Indiana, Illinois, Missouri, Kentucky, Arkansas, Tennessee, and Louisiana was something over 210,500,000 bushels. In 1850 it was more than 350,000,000, an increase of over 66 per cent. In the same period the receipts of corn at New Orleans rose correspondingly from some 268,000 sacks and 168,000 barrels, to over 1,000,000 sacks and 42,000 barrels.[4]

In the same period the production of tobacco in these states diminished in those south, and more than correspondingly increased in those north, of the Ohio, yet the receipts in New Orleans rose in full proportion.[5]

As a palpable result the city expanded. Each year large numbers of new buildings were erected, while at the same time "rents continually rose." In 1845, in the second municipality alone—the American quarter—295 houses and stores were built, more than half the number being of brick and granite. It should be noted, however, that their average cost did not reach $3,500.[6] Thus, if the proportions of home consumption and marketable surplus in the agricultural movement of these states had remained the same, the relative importance of New Orleans would at least not have been retrograding, and her merchants might have repelled the charge brought by one, that they "sold the skin for a groat and bought the tail for a shilling." But improved transportation, denser population, and labor-saving machinery had almost indefinitely increased the individual producing power of the western man, and truly to have kept pace with it New Orleans should have been the receiver and exporter of a rapidly and steadily increasing fraction—in place of merely an increasing quantity—of the agricultural products of the country. Not perceiving, or unable to meet this necessity, she abandoned this magnificent surplus to the growing cities of the West and East.

Still more New Orleans failed to maintain a leading position in relation to the immense growth of western manufactures. It was the subject of much pardonable boasting that her commerce was so rapidly increasing, and during the decade it did expand in gross receipts, in exports, and, on a much lower scale, in imports, almost or quite 100 per cent. But meantime, and almost unnoticed by New Orleans, absorbed as she was in moving the crude products of the fields and supplying the wants of the producers, the manufactures of the eight states mentioned increased in value from about $50,000,000 to a little less than $164,000,000.[7]

Nor was any adequate compensation found in the city's import trade. In 1835 this had reached the amount of $17,000,000; but in the crash that followed it had shrunk to $8,000,000 in 1842, and in 1845 had risen only to $9,750,000. In 1847–48, while the city actually exceeded New York in exports of domestic produce, and in the total of exports was surpassed only by that city, her imports were less than a tenth of those of New York and not quite a third those of Boston. Coffee, iron, hardware, salt, and French fancy goods formed the chief items of this commerce.[8]

At the close of the decade that ended with 1850, New Orleans had fallen back from the fourth place to the fifth in the list of American cities. Boston had surpassed her in numbers, Brooklyn was four-fifths her size and St. Louis seven-eighths, Cincinnati lacked but one twenty-fifth of her numbers, and Louisville, Chicago, Buffalo, and Pittsburgh had populations ranging from 40,000 to 50,000.[9]

One or two considerations, however, somewhat modify the unfavorableness of these comparisons. During this time large numbers of Transatlantic immigrants made New Orleans their first landing-place on their way to the great West. Between 1845 and 1850 they numbered on an average 30,000 a year. Many stopped in the city and settled. As early as 1842 the population was reported "largely mixed with Germans." Before this sort of competition slave service gave ground, and the number of slaves in New Orleans was actually 5,330 less in 1850 than it had been in 1840.[10]

Again, no other part of the population in New Orleans was held in such total disesteem as the free mulatto class. This unenterprising, despised, and persecuted people had grown from an inconsiderable fraction of the whole in earlier years, to be in 1840 nearly one-third as numerous as the whites. The feeling which had always existed against them grew in intensity as the agitation concerning the abolition of slavery rose and increased.

They were looked upon as fit subjects of general suspicion, became the objects of grossly restrictive, unjust, and intolerant state legislation, and between 1840 and 1850 made such an exodus from the city that their numbers fell from over 19,000 to less than 10,000 souls. Allowing for natural increase, not less than 11,000 or 12,000 free persons must have left the city during this period, nor is there any evidence that they ever returned.

Under correct social conditions, such a loss of population could not rightly be counted a gain. If under all the circumstances there was in it an element of real advantage, it lay in the fact that the proportion was increased of that master class, whose strong hand and will ruled the fortunes of the community.

Furthermore, another town had sprung up immediately against the city's upper boundary. In 1833 three sparsely peopled suburbs, to wit, Lafayette, Livaudais, and Réligieuses, the last occupying lands that had belonged to and been bought from the Ursuline nuns, were consolidated into one and made a body politic, under the name of the City of Lafayette. In what was then considered the rear of this town many of the wealthy citizens of New Orleans began about 1840 to settle down in "large, commodious, one-story houses, full of windows on all sides, and surrounded by broad and shady gardens." Nearer the river front the immigrant Germans and Irish of the laboring class poured in abundantly, and by 1850 Lafayette, virtually a part of New Orleans, comprised a population of 12,319 white and 1,871 colored inhabitants.[11]

By these two movements of slave and mulatto exodus and European immigration, the proportion of whites to the whole population rose from 58 to 78 per cent., and the whole number of the one community which formed New Orleans and Lafayette was 133,650.

But now New Orleans began to take note of facts which ought long before to have been anticipated as possibilities. Her people began to perceive the losses she was sustaining, and to inquire with alarm into their causes. At one moment with admissions and the next with boastful denials of this or that unfavorable condition or relation, the progress of other cities at her expense was anxiously noted; much was remembered of those earlier times when New

Orleans was the commercial queen of her great valley, and merchants and property-holders exhorted each other to throw off their lethargy and establish their city in that universal supremacy for which her citizens were still confident that nature—that is, their river and their wish—had destined her.[12]

The city's curable ailments found many physicians and few nurses; while those difficulties of the situation which were really insuperable remained unmentioned by the more politic few, or were charged by sanguine commercial writers as the inexcusable sins of unprogressive financiers. It was confessed that New Orleans had depended too entirely upon the mere movement of crops; that there had long been a false pride among the cultivated classes of the South generally opposed to mercantile pursuits; that the sanitary condition of the city had been entirely overlooked; that no attempt had been made to cheapen the city's notorious port charges or to facilitate the safe and expeditious handling of freight. It was even boldly and ingeniously asserted by one, that the institution of slavery had much to do with the non-progressive attitude of New Orleans and her surrounding country; that that part of the community which mainly felt the inconvenience of antiquated methods was the voiceless slave class, and that the liberty which the northern workingman enjoyed, of thinking, speaking, and acting in his own interests, gave that section an immense preponderance through its multitude of practical thinkers. The absurd municipality system of city government, which virtually divided the city into three corporate communities beside that of Lafayette, was rightly blamed as the source of much confusion and non-progression.[13]

Such were some of the verdicts of those who spoke or wrote. Doubtless the quieter financiers and capitalists, who carefully studied the city's relative position and possible development, found other facts confronting them. The absence of railroads was not attributable only to the neglect to build them. Those laws of nature, upon which so much reliance was misplaced, included the nature and wants of mankind, and such observers could not but see that then, and for some time to come, capital—that winged and inexorable fate—could not swing out a railroad from New Orleans in any direction that had not better be stretched across from some point near the center of supply in the West, to some other point within the bounds of the manufacturing and consuming East. Or, to come to an underlying, fundamental fact, the peculiar and unfortunate labor system of the south had handed over the rich prize of European and New England immigration to the unmonopolized West, and the purely fortune-hunting canal-boat and locomotive pushed aside the slave and his owner and followed the free immigrant. In truth, it was not until some years later, when the outstretched iron arms of northern enterprise began to grasp at the products of the Southwest itself, that New Orleans capitalists, with more misgiving than enthusiasm, thrust out their first railroad worthy of the name through the great plantation state of Mississippi.

A lack of banking capital was attributed as a cause of decadence. But New Orleans bankers knew that New York, with a banking capital not three times as large as that of New Orleans, carried on a commerce three and a half times as great as hers, beside a large manufacturing interest.[14]

The absence of thousands of residents during the summer season was given as another drawback; but this, also, was true of the other great cities, of New York especially.

The want of common sentiment and impulse in a community made up from individuals of so many nationalities was much emphasized. This deficiency did not result merely—as often stated—from the large proportion of foreigners. When, by the census of 1860, this proportion came to be known, it was found to be but 44½ per cent. of the whole white population in New Orleans, against 42 in Cincinnati, 48 in New York, and 52 in St. Louis. But in these cities American thought prevailed and more or less inspired the foreign elements as they came in; hence a comparative unity of motive. In New Orleans, on the other hand, American thought was itself not only foreign, but unwelcome, disparaged by the unaspiring and satirical Creole, and often apologized for by the American, who found himself a minority in a combination of social forces, far more frequently in sympathy with European ideas than with the moral energies and the enthusiastic and venturesome enterprise of the New World. Added to this there were, in New Orleans, 28,000 persons—9 of whom out of every 14 were enslaved, and the other 5 practically expatriated—hampering, as by sheer dead weight, the progress of the community.

The languishing of the import trade was attributed to simple neglect to cultivate it. But among the vast plantations of the southern valley, where town life was comparatively unknown, where masters were few and spent the proceeds of their exports with their own hands in foreign cities, where the wants of slaves and of indigent whites were only the most primitive, and where a stupid and slovenly, unpaid laboring class made the introduction of labor-saving machines a farce, no stimulus to a large import trade could be hoped for. And as to the West, it was idle to think of competing with direct routes for the transportation of commodities which, unlike the bulkier articles of the export trade, could well afford to subordinate cheap freight rates to prompt delivery.

Much reproach was heaped upon the moneyed class for the non-development of manufactures; but nothing ought to have been plainer than the total irreconcilability of the whole southern industrial system with such establishments; a system employing one of the most unintelligent and uneconomical classes of laborers in the world, upon which it was useless to attempt to graft the higher-spirited operatives of other countries.

These conditions, then, recognized at that day only in their superficial aspect and assumed to be easily removable, were the causes of non-progression. Summed up in one, and this stripped of its disguise, it was a triumph of machinery over slave labor, unrecognized, however, or unconfessed, because if reparable at all, only so through a social revolution so great and apparently so ruinous that the mention of it kindled a white heat of public exasperation.

And yet, after this is said, something must still be allowed to a luxurious, enervating climate, under which all energies, Anglo-Saxon, Gallic, Celtic, Teutonic, in greater or less degree, surrendered; something to remoteness from competing cities; and something to the influence of that original people, a study of whose history and its resultant traits forms so much of the present work. For the Creoles, retaining much power as well by their natural force as by their extensive ownership of real estate and their easy coalition with foreign elements of like faith, caring little to understand and less to be understood, divided and paralyzed when they could no longer rule public sentiment, and often met the most imperative necessities for innovations with the most inflexible conservatism. Such causes kept the city comparatively unimproved, its municipal government in confusion, its harbor approaches and landings much neglected, and its morals and its health unestimated by careful statistics and a by-word in all lands.

Most of the improvements that had arisen during this long term of purely commercial development dated well back toward that era of inflation of which the crisis of 1837 has become the index, and were mainly confined to the American quarter. The parish prison, the same antique and gloomy pile of stuccoed brick that still stands on Orleans street just beyond Congo square, was built in 1830 at a cost of $200,000. Several market-houses were completed about this time, the French vegetable market in 1830, St. Mary's and Washington in 1836, and Poydras in 1837.[15] In 1834–35 the United States government, having six years before sold the old Spanish barracks in the heart of the French quarter, built the present Jackson barracks, then three miles below the city, now on its lower boundary. In 1832–34 the old Charity hospital in Canal street had become the state-house, and the present hospital was erected in Common street at an expense of $150,000. In 1832 and 1835 two extensive cotton-presses and warehouses had added an important feature to the commercial city. The Levee cotton-press cost $500,000, and the Orleans, in the lower part of the city, over $758,000. In 1835 the water-works, and in 1837 the gas-works, had come into operation. In the earlier year, also, the New Canal,* some seven miles in length, begun in 1832, had been finished. It brought the waters of lake Pontchartrain into an artificial basin deep enough for coasting schooners, situated immediately behind Rampart (then Hercules) street, between Julia and Delord.[16] In this year, too, the branch United States mint of New Orleans was founded on the small square bounded by Esplanade, Barracks, Decatur, and Peters streets, which had been the site of Fort St. Charles, and after the destruction of that fortification had been known as Jackson Square, a name afterward transferred to the ancient Place d'Armes. In 1833 had appeared that unique and still well-remembered structure, Banks' Arcade, a glass-roofed mercantile court in the midst of a large hotel in Magazine street, now long known as the St. James. In 1836 the Merchants' Exchange, just below Canal street, and extending through from Royal to Exchange alley, had been completed and had become the post-office. The first St. Charles hotel, called then the Exchange hotel, begun in 1835, had been completed three years later, at a cost of $600,000. The same year saw the completion, diagonally opposite on Common street, of the old Verandah hotel, with an outlay of $300,000. In 1834 the (second) First Presbyterian church, on Lafayette square, had been built. In 1837 the Carondelet Methodist church, on the corner of that street and Poydras, had followed, and in the same year the old Christ's church, on the corner of Bourbon and Canal

*Also known as the New Basin Canal. Interstate 10 and West End Boulevard track much of its now filled-in channel.

streets, had replaced the small octagonal predecessor, erected in 1809, and which the town wits had nicknamed "The Cockpit." In 1835 the St. Charles theater had been built, at a cost of $350,000. Between 1833 and 1839 several bank buildings of more or less pretensions had arisen; the Commercial, the Atchafalaya, the Orleans (later occupied by the Bank of America), the Canal, at the corner of Magazine and Gravier, the City, in Camp street near Canal, and that extremely picturesque ruin in Toulouse street of Grecian architecture, built for the Citizens' Bank and afterward occupied by the Consolidated. Many charitable associations and establishments— Poydras orphan asylum, the Female orphans asylum, the asylum for destitute boys, the Catholic male orphan asylum, the Fireman's charitable association, the Howard association, Stone's hospital, the Circus Street infirmary, and many others had their beginnings at various dates between 1830 and 1840.[17]

Such a list as this, extending over more than a decade, is probably doubtful evidence of that degree of progress which should have characterized a growing American city, or even of that degree of effort which would have excused some features of her decadence. Orphan asylums were indifferent substitutes for sanitation, and short-lived banks for improved harbor approaches. "Had a tithe of the exertion," writes one in New Orleans, in 1847, "been made to retain it, that has distinguished the efforts of the North to draw it off, we should not now be called to look with astonishment at beholding one-half in bulk and value of western produce seeking a market at the northern Atlantic cities, where twenty years ago not a dollar was sent through the channels now bearing it away from New Orleans."[18]

Yet it would have been unreasonable and unjust to assume that all deficiencies were due to lack of enterprise; and the fact that in the list of local movements and schemes, scarcely more than one or two bore any likeness to that bold outward reach which was making rival cities, through their more fortunate location, daily greater, should rather be taken as proof that the capitalists of New Orleans discerned and silently acknowledged the immovability of some of the fundamental difficulties that beset their town and port.

Two railroad enterprises alone, in this period, ventured to project their lines beyond the boundaries of Orleans island; but the "New Orleans and Nashville" scheme, ripening prematurely, fell to the ground, and the "Mexican Gulf" road, which it was hoped would develop the deep waters of Cat island into a harbor of easy access to large vessels, and greatly shorten the journey between New Orleans and New York, never got beyond the farther bounds of the adjoining parish, and is long since extinct.[19]

About the year 1840 or '41, there seems to have arisen in the room of that sort of public spirit, enterprising yet near-sighted, which had characterized the previous decade, a sentiment of more urgency, which began to contemplate relations beyond the boundaries of parish and state, and to realize the value and the necessity of public measures, addressed to higher and less strictly material wants, than could be supplied by gas- or water-works, banks, mints, or cotton-presses. An obvious subsidence of the tide of improvement which had made New Orleans at least a brisk laggard, united with this new feeling of exigency to produce inquiry, exhortation, and a general exchange of both deserved and undeserved reproach. Actual efforts presently followed, and steps were taken in the direction of popular education, culture, and social order, which, had they been taken when first proposed by a wise few in executive office, 25 or 30 years before, would have made New Orleans by that time, in fact and in spirit, as well as in name, an American, instead of a Franco-American city.

But the end contemplated in the earlier suggestions, wanted something of that popular and general benefit which has made the more modern idea of public education acceptable throughout America, not excepting Louisiana.

On the earnest recommendation of Governor Claiborne, in 1804, an act had been passed in April of the following year, by the legislative council, "to establish a university in the territory of Orleans." A primary object of this act had been the institution of the "College of New Orleans." Fifty thousand dollars were appropriated to carry out the provisions of the act; but the amount was to be raised by two lotteries. In 1811 nothing had yet been effected. Thirty-nine thousand dollars were then appropriated for state educational purposes, $15,000 of which were for the institution of a college in New Orleans, where, in addition to those who paid for their tuition, 50 children, selected from the poorest classes, were to be admitted without charge.[20] Under this stimulus New Orleans college was built and put in operation in 1812, at the corner of Bayou road and St. Claude street. Ten years later it was the only educational institution in New Orleans, of a public character, though some private or church schools accommodated a few charity scholars.[21]

In March, 1826, another legislative act established one central and two primary public schools in New Orleans. Ten thousand dollars a year were set apart for their support; they were duly established—the central and one primary in the old Ursuline convent, and the other primary in Tchoupitoulas near St. Joseph street—and "all the branches of a polite education" were taught. "Harby's public school," in the third municipality, finds mention in 1838, but New Orleans college seems to have disappeared.

At length, a convention called to frame a new state constitution, meeting in New Orleans, in January–April, 1845, again decreed the establishment of the University of Louisiana. It was intended to consist of four faculties, one each for law, medicine, natural science, and letters. The department of medicine was already in existence as the medical school of Louisiana, and this branch, and that of law, were in full operation in 1847, with 162 students in the former and 31 in the latter, and they have ever since continued to be a source of honor and pride to the city and the state.[22]

But the mass of educable youth had not been reached—had scarcely been sought—in these schemes. Another sentiment was lacking, a feeling of common interest in a common elevation. This feeling once aroused, men of public spirit were not wanting to give it guidance, and the names of such pioneers as Samuel J. Peters, Glendy Burke, Judah Touro, [François-Xavier] Martin, [Alexander] Dimitry, [James D. B.] De Bow, [Edmund Jean] Forstall, [Charles] Gayarré, and others, are gratefully remembered by a later generation for their labors in the cause of intellectual advancement. The year 1841 dates the establishment in New Orleans of the modern system of free public schools; for although they were not begun within the city's corporate limits until in the following year, when a single school was opened in the second municipality, "with some dozen scholars of both sexes," yet the adjoining city of Lafayette, always virtually a part of New Orleans, had founded the system in the earlier year.[23]

In the beginning of the year 1842 there were in the American quarter 300 children in private schools and 2,000 destitute of school advantages. By the end of that year there were 238 pupils in the public schools of Lafayette and 800 in those of the American quarter of New Orleans proper. In the next year the total attendance in the public schools of both sections was 1,314. In 1844 it was 1,798.[24]

Meanwhile there was a movement in the interest of adults. In 1842 Mr. B. F. French, having bought a collection of books known as the "Commercial Library," threw it open to the public. In 1846 it occupied two rooms in the Merchants' Exchange, on Royal street, and comprised almost 7,500 volumes.[25] About the same time the state library was formed with about 3,000 volumes, but was intended for the use of the legislature rather than for the general public. In this year, too, the New Orleans city library came into existence through the efforts of Samuel J. Peters and others, as an adjunct of the public-school enterprise in the second municipality. It numbered at first some 3,000 volumes, and in 1848 had been increased to over 7,500. It required, however, a yearly subscription of $5 to gain free access to this library. It was placed in the newly founded and unfinished municipal hall, the same whose classic Grecian architecture now adorns Lafayette square. The Young Men's Free Library Association, a body of commercial citizens, threw open a collection of some 2,000 well-selected volumes at the corner of Customhouse street* and Exchange place.[26]

In 1846 a course of public lectures by leading citizens was attended by a body of hearers which taxed the capacity of the city's largest hall. In the same year an historical society, originally founded in 1838, was revived with Judge Martin, the historian of Louisiana, as president. During a few years following, this body caused valuable researches to be made in the archives of the French and Spanish governments, in Paris and in Madrid through its zealous secretary, Mr. John Perkins, jr., and even began the transcription of important documents.[27] In 1847 Judge Charles Gayarré delivered before the Library and Lyceum Association the four lectures which afterward constituted the first four chapters of his history of Louisiana; and in the winter of 1848 J. D. B. De Bow delivered the initial lecture of a projected series on public economy, commerce, and statistics; but a terrible epidemic of cholera cut them short.[28]

About the latter date Alvarez Fisk, a merchant, bought Mr. French's library, and in order to carry out the designs of a deceased brother for the establishment of a public library in New Orleans, which should be free to strangers, offered the entire collection, then containing some 6,000 volumes, to the city, with a "building on Customhouse street for their reception."[29] But the late public enthusiasm had subsided. No adequate provisions was made by the city council or public for the acceptance of this gift,

*Now Iberville Street.

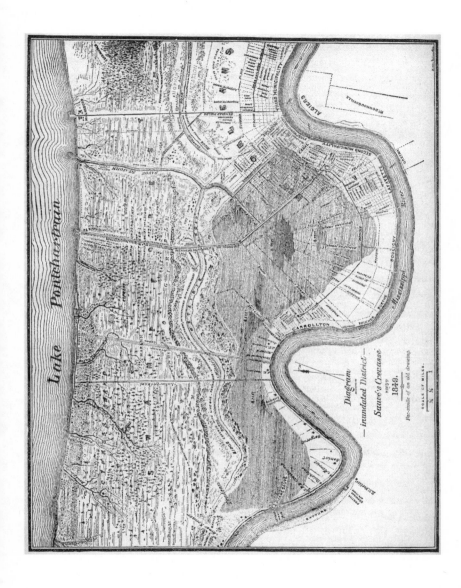

Lake Pontchartrain

ALGIERS

SECOND MUNICIPALITY

THIRD MUNICIPALITY

McDONOGHVILLE

Mississippi River

CARROLLTON

Diagram

— inundated District —

Sauve's Crevasse

MAY

1849.

Fac-simile of an old drawing.

SCALE OF MILES.

although under the generous zeal of Mr. French, its custodian, it grew considerably in extent. As late as 1854 it had not been put into efficient operation, and the city was still without a single entirely free library.[30]

A line or two may be proper here to afford a comparative view of library facilities in New Orleans and elsewhere at the time spoken of. In 1850 the public libraries of Louisiana numbered five and contained 9,800 volumes, and her school libraries two, with 12,000 volumes. Much the greater part of these were, doubtless, in New Orleans. However, taking the state at large, there was one school, Sunday school, or public library to each 73,966 persons, or 100 volumes to each 2,310 persons. In Delaware there were 100 volumes to each 707 persons; in Rhode Island there were 100 volumes to every 206 persons; in Massachusetts there were 100 volumes to each 188 persons. This disproportionate dearth of books in Louisiana might appear less by eliminating the numbers of the slave element; but even after thus omitting from the count what could not be omitted from the community, there would still appear but 100 volumes to each 1,218 free persons, while that could hardly be called a more favorable exhibit, which pointed out the fact of nearly 245,000 persons in the established population being without books, and legally incapacitated to receive them. In Michigan, a pioneer state without any large city there were 100 volumes to every 397 persons. Probably of the 22,400 volumes in Louisiana, all of those in public and half of those in school libraries, or 15,800, were in New Orleans, which would give 100 volumes to every 642 free persons in the city.[31]

Nothing else seems to have taken such hold upon the estimation of the whole body of citizens in New Orleans as did the public schools. These continued to grow rapidly in numbers and in efficiency, and it is pleasant to turn from the contrast just indicated, and find New Orleans in 1850 ranking well up among American cities in the advantages offered her youth, and received by them, in free schools maintained at the public charge. The pupils in the public schools of Boston numbered 16 per cent. of the whole population; in Philadelphia they were 11¾, and in New Orleans 7⅓ per cent. The character of the reports of New York, in the pages from which these facts are taken, makes the percentage there doubtful, but it seems not to have been greatly superior to New Orleans. St. Louis was slightly so; but those of Baltimore, Cincinnati, Charleston, and other towns, were more or less inferior. The total number of educable youth in New Orleans and Lafayette was over fourteen thousand, of which 6,700 attended public schools.[32] In 1858 these numbers had increased to 16,392.[33]

Few conspicuous improvements in real property, either public or private, appeared to view in this term. In the second municipality the massive and beautiful tower of St. Patrick's arose, and the city hall was pushed on toward completion. The first municipality ceded to the United States government the site of the present custom-house, and for many years the huge and lofty scaffolding of this still uncompleted pile of granite was one of the most prominent objects in a bird's-eye view of the city. The United States marine hospital, on the opposite side of the river, facing the second municipality, which had been commenced in 1834, but was unfinished and half in ruins, was taken under contract for its completion by James N. Caldwell, founder of theaters and gas-works, projector of the Nashville rail route, and, in short, the personal exponent of the material advance and enterprise of those times. This hospital, turned into a powder-house during the late war, met its end one day by being blown to atoms.

Yet the city was growing from year to year with greater or less rapidity, and in every direction. For some years the swamp lands in the rear had been in process of clearing and draining; and streets and houses appeared in the place of forest or marshy fields. Algiers, a suburb on the point of land opposite the river front of the old city, began to grow into notice through its marine workshops, though still but feeble in population. Lafayette, almost unknown to the "down-town Creole," reached, as has been seen, a population of 14,000 and upward, while the third municipality, almost as completely unobserved by the American as was Lafayette by the Creole, spread in unpretentious cottages down toward the near edge of Jackson's field of renown.[34]

This growth was effected in the face of many obstacles, chief among which was the still frequent mishap of inundation. This event in New Orleans must occur either by a crevasse—a giving way of the levee during a time of high water in the river—or by the rise of backwater from lake Pontchartrain, when long-prevailing southeast winds obstruct the outflow of the lake's waters through the narrow passes by which they commonly reach the Gulf of Mexico, or when a violent storm from the north more suddenly produces the same result. Against both these contingencies much vigilance has to be exercised at certain seasons.

The effects of these inundations, however, are easily overesti-
mated. Property within the boundary of their probable encroachment is desirable only to those who must seek the very fewest
advantages of location, and they have been a prime cause for the
inconvenient lengthening out of the city along the higher grounds
down, and especially up, the river shore. But the city is not en-
gulfed by the waters, life is not endangered, the business districts
and those occupied by highly improved houses are rarely or never
invaded, and the extent of the disaster is mainly confined to a distressing interruption in the daily affairs of the humbler classes,
the destruction of their market gardens and poultry, the damage
of household goods, and the injury to such public property as street
bridges and the like. The sickness which might be supposed to follow the subsidence of the waters has not been such, at least, as to
make inundations a subject of alarm on this account, and probably
no actual feature of these overflows does New Orleans as much
material injury as is done by their exaggerated bad fame.

Their frequency, also, is easily overrated. In the early history of
the town they occurred at first almost yearly, and for a long time
extremely often; but later they grew much more infrequent. The
moat and palisaded embankment which surrounded the Spanish
town seems not to have protected it from this enemy. A serious
overflow took place in 1780, another in 1785, another in 1791, another in 1799. All these resulted from crevasses in the river levee
above the town. The last of these occurred in the month of May,
in the "Macarty levee," near the site of the later town of Carrollton, now part of New Orleans. Subsequently putrid fevers were
ascribed to it, but the statement is made without proper investiga-
tion of the facts.[35]

Another inundation in 1813 was caused by a crevasse in the
levee of Kenner's plantation, a mile or two only above Macarty's.[36]

Next followed the noted overflow of 1816. On the 6th of May,
of that year, Macarty's levee, being undermined by the powerful current which there strikes the river bank, again broke, and
on the fourth day after, the rear parts of suburbs Montague, La
Course, St. Mary, and Marigny, and the whole of the suburbs behind them—Gravier, Trémé, and St. John—were under water to
the depth of from 3 to 5 feet. One could travel in a skiff from the
corner of Chartres and Canal streets to Dauphin, down Dauphin
to Bienville, down Bienville to Burgundy, thus to St. Louis street,
from St. Louis to Rampart, and so throughout the rear suburbs.

The waters found vent by way of Fisherman's and St. John's bayous to lake Pontchartrain, and in 25 days had subsided. The ensuing summer is stated, on the highest medical authority, to have been remarkably healthy.[37]

In 1831 the waters of an inundation reached the line of Dauphin street, the fifth from the river front—the result of a violent storm on lake Pontchartrain. A similar event occurred in October, 1837. In 1844 a storm backed the lake waters up to Burgundy street, sixth from the river front, and a similar disaster happened again in 1846.[38]

But probably the most serious overflow the city of New Orleans ever suffered was that of 1849. On the afternoon of the 3d of May, in that year, the waters of the Mississippi, being then at a higher stage than had been witnessed before for twenty-one years, broke through the levee in front of Sauvé's plantation, some 17 miles above New Orleans by the river's course, and at once defied all restraints. It was at first thought that they would not reach New Orleans, but would find their way into lake Pontchartrain by some route nearer at hand. But the swamp rapidly filled up behind the city, the opportunity for throwing up a levee along the rear of the town was let slip, and by the 15th of May Rampart street was under water.

The residents of the first municipality (French quarter) strengthened the small levee of Canal Carondelet on its lower side, and thus entirely shut out the advancing flood from the district beyond that canal; but the rears of Lafayette and of the second municipality were completely exposed. The water reached its highest stage on the 30th of May. Its line ran along behind Bacchus (Baronne) street, sometimes reaching to Carondelet, from the upper limits of Lafayette to Canal street, crossed that street between Carondelet and St. Charles streets, and thence stretched downward and backward to the old basin. "About 220 inhabited squares were flooded, more than 2,000 tenements surrounded by water, and a population of near 12,000 souls either driven from their homes or living an aquatic life of much privation and suffering."

All efforts to close the crevasse utterly failed until, on the 3d of June, Messrs. [George T.] Dunbar and [L.] Surgi, engineers, being allowed entire liberty as to ways and means, began work, and in seventeen days stopped the breach. On the 22d of June the water had virtually disappeared, heavy rains washed away its filthy deposits, and the people were able to begin the repair of their disasters. Public property, too, had suffered; pavements and gutters were much damaged and street bridges had been washed away. The second municipality in the following year (1850) levied $400,000 to cover "actual expenditures on streets, wharves, and crevasses," and built a levee in the rear of the municipality from the point where Claiborne street crosses the new canal up to Felicity road (street) and along this street to its intersection with Apollo (now Carondelet) street.[39]

Time showed these provisions to be entirely inadequate. The city continued at intervals to suffer from the same cause, the last occasion being no longer ago than February of the present year (1881). At such times the pecuniary and personal aid of her citizens is generously poured out to the unfortunate; but these admirable deeds are the fruits of emotional impulses, and, the distress passed, precautions against future calamity are omitted or soon fall into neglect. The last overflow simply overran the top of a neglected and decayed protection levee. The uneconomical habits of the South have not passed suddenly away with the change of its labor system. Private extravagance still makes public parsimony; public burdens are but feebly recognized, and New Orleans is not yet entirely protected from these pitiful disasters to her hard-working poor.

A number of other events require to be briefly summarized as making notable a short period between 1849 and 1852. It was in the first of these years that New Orleans ceased to be the capital, and the small Mississippi river town of Baton Rouge became the capital of the state.[40] Nor was this loss restored to New Orleans until after the destruction of the state-house in Baton Rouge by fire, and the occupation of New Orleans by United States forces, during the late war. In 1880 the seat of government was again removed to Baton Rouge, and the legislature, at its next regular session, will meet there.

As late as 1846 New Orleans was without telegraphic communication, but in 1847, and later, certain lines were taken under contract, and by 1850 the city was in telegraphic connection with St. Louis and other points.[41]

The first street pavement with square granite blocks was made in 1850.[42]

The project of a railroad across the isthmus of Tehuantepec received its first decided impulse in 1850, on the transfer by one [Peter A.] Hargous to Judah P. Benjamin, J. M. Lapeyre, Samuel J. Peters, and others, of extensive grants and privileges conveyed to him by José Garay, the original grantee of the Mexican government.[43] Surveys were begun by United States engineers, and by 1852 one route had been surveyed; but the Mexican government put a stop to the work, and the project, thus crippled, dragged feebly along. In 1853 a rival grantee, Mr. Thomas Sloo, appeared, and the state of Louisiana gave a charter to a new company, formed with $10,000,000 capital, of which Mr. Sloo was to receive half. To have realized so great a project would have redeemed New Orleans from the reproaches so freely bestowed upon her by her sister cities; but against the state of affairs existing in Mexico no headway could be made, though much effort was exhausted by the capitalists of the city, and the last year before the absorbing political campaign which preceded the outbreak of civil war, found their chamber of commerce recommending the enterprise with bare resolutions.[44] Meantime two other enterprises of more moderate scope, but of even greater urgency, met a better fate. In 1851 those two great works of internal improvement, which have proved, as they were intended to be, the commercial salvation of New Orleans, were set on foot, to wit, the two railroads that now respectively unite the city with the great central railroad system of the Union in the Mississippi valley, and with the vast southwest, still comprised within the outstretched boundaries of the state of Texas. The first of these roads was to stretch due north toward Jackson, the capital of Mississippi; the other was to strike westward toward the town of Opelousas, in Louisiana.* Both received state aid, and the first by the year 1855, the second by 1857, had reached a distance of over 80 miles from New Orleans, and on the northern road work was progressing rapidly in the direction of Jackson.[45]

Hardly of less importance to the city's future, was the consolidation of Lafayette and the three municipalities into one city government, on the 12th of April, 1852. Sixteen years of subdivision had demonstrated to Creole, to American, and to European immigrant the value of unity. Yet it was probably essential, that during just that term the progressive and the conservative elements of the city should have lived and worked apart, and thus their adverse ideas, operating side by side, be practically compared, and the superiority of the American principles of growth be plainly proven.

The first great step after the cession toward the *Americanization* of New Orleans, was the arbitrary establishment of the English

---

*The New Orleans, Jackson, and Great Northern Railroad and the New Orleans, Opelousas, and Great Western Railroad.

tongue. The second was the enforced one of its military defense against conquest in 1814–15. The third, a stage rather than a step, was the shifting of the port's commerce from the French and Spanish Americas on the south to the great valley on the north, and its consequent transfer into American hands and an American quarter. The division of the municipalities, in 1836, is of uncertain value; the next undoubtedly effective step was the establishment of the American public school system throughout the municipalities, a greater advance than its most sanguine advocates probably supposed could have been made at one stride. The fifth step was the consolidation. By this movement the second municipality, the American quarter, became the acknowledged center and core of the whole city. Its municipality hall became the municipal hall; its public grounds became the chosen rendezvous of all popular assemblies; its streets became the place of business domicile for all the main branches of trade; the rotunda of its palatial St. Charles, at whose memorable burning in 1850 the people wept, restored in 1852–53, usurped the early pre-eminence of the St. Louis *Bourse,* and became the unofficial guild-hall of all the more active elements—merchants, politicians, strangers from every quarter, and Cuban and Nicaraguan filibusters; and banks, whose charters still prevented their moving across the "neutral ground" of Canal street; moved close up toward it to catch a share of the financial breezes that blew so favorably upon its farther side.[46]

The consolidation did not come before a stern necessity called for it. The report of the "commissioners of the consolidated debt of New Orleans" in 1855, says:

"The commissioners . . . found the city without credit, confusion in most of its branches of government, and the people disheartened. To-day (January, 1855) its credit is above par." "The spirit of the people," they farther added, "has been awakened . . . and a brighter future is before us."

At the passage of the act of consolidation, the debts of Lafayette and the three municipalities aggregated $7,700,000, of which $2,000,000 were past due. Through the improved credit of the consolidated city, $5,000,000 of these debts were early extinguished, and the total debt of the city on the 1st of April, 1853, the greatest commercial year that thus far had ever risen upon New Orleans, was but little over $3,000,000.[47]

A small steel-engraved picture of New Orleans, made just before this period, is obviously the inspiration of the commercial and self-important American. The ancient plaza, the cathedral of St. Louis, the old hall of the cabildo, the calaboza, the remnant of Spanish barracks, the emptied convent of the Ursulines, the antiquated and decayed rue Toulouse—all that was time-honored and venerable are pushed out of view, and the lately humble faubourg Ste. Marie, grown to be the center of wealth and activity, fills the picture almost from side to side, with long ranks of huge Mississippi steamers smoking at the levee, and the majestic dome of the first St. Charles and the stately tower of St. Patrick's, rise high above the deep and solid phalanxes of brick and stone, in the midst of which they stood queen and bishop of the board.[48]

A little later a worse fate befell the group of ancient landmarks, than being left out of a picture. Renovation came in. In 1850 the cathedral was torn down to its foundations, and began to rise again with all its Spanish picturesqueness lost, and little or nothing gained in beauty. On its right and on its left absurd French roofs were clapped upon the cabildo and the court-house. The Baroness Pontalba, daughter of the benevolent Almonaster, replaced the plain, old-fashioned stone buildings on either side the square, with large, new rows of red brick. The city government laid off the Place d'Armes in blinding white shell-walks and dusty flower-beds, and later—in 1855—placed in its center the bronze equestrian figure of the deliverer of New Orleans, and called the classic spot Jackson square. Yet even so it remains to the present, the last lurking-place of the romance of early New Orleans.[49]

The commerce of the city waxed greater. That "forest of masts" of which she was so pardonably boastful, grew yearly longer and darker upon her splendid harbor front. In 1851 the receipts of cotton were greater than had ever before been handled. The total value of products from the interior was nearly $107,000,000. The mint coined $10,000,000 in silver and gold, the most of which had come from the new-found treasure-fields of California, wither large numbers of the more adventurous spirits of New Orleans had hastened. The tobacco trade, which for some years had languished, revived.[50]

The year 1853 brought still greater increase. The receipts of cotton alone reached the value of $68,250,000. The sugar crop was, by many tens of thousands of hogsheads, the largest ever known in Louisiana, and the total value of produce from the interior exceeded $134,000,000. Over 10 per cent. of all the arrivals from sea were steamships.[51]

But just here a symptom of decay, long overlooked, began to force itself upon public notice. The increase in size of sea-going vessels had been steady and rapid, and had not received the attention, in the port of New Orleans, which its importance merited, until the larger vessels had begun to shun the bars and mud-lumps of the Balize. In 1852 there had been, within a period of a few weeks, nearly 40 ships aground on the bar at the mouth of the Mississippi, suffering detentions ranging from two days to eight weeks. Some had been compelled to throw part of their cargoes overboard, and others to discharge into lighters, over 100 miles from their wharves in New Orleans.[52]

There had not been a total neglect, even in earlier years, to call the attention of government to the defects of this all-important entrance to the continent. Government, too, had responded; surveys and reports had been made as far back as 1829 and continuing through 1837, 1839, 1847, and 1851. Shortly after certain expensive surveys in 1837, Northeast pass, then the chosen channel, shoaled up; but Southwest pass was presently found to serve present purposes, being only less convenient of approach, and continued to be used with tolerable facility until about 1850. Then the increasing draught of ships brought a new difficulty, and "owing to pressing memorials of the citizens of New Orleans, Congress ordered an exploration of the region, and appropriated a large sum for the deepening of the channels of the river."[53] Neglect to pursue the matter to the point of consummating some permanent remedy, seems not more blamable upon government than upon the port itself. While various measures and half measures were timidly recommended in the reports of engineers—dredging, harrowing, jettying, the cutting of a canal to gulf waters several miles above the passes—vessels of less than 1,000 tons were grounding on the bar, and a committee of the New Orleans chamber of commerce, in petitioning Congress for the establishment of a navy-yard at New Orleans, was stating in its address that "formerly the bar at the mouth of the Mississippi presented a difficulty which is now obviated, for modern skill has applied to naval architecture the happy combination of increased capacity of hull, with diminution of draft," and so on.[54] Naturally the Balize remained unimproved,[55] and in 1853 vessels were again grounding on the bar and remaining, with valuable cargoes, for weeks, and even for months.[56]

But the year 1853 will always be more famed in the history of New Orleans for another calamity, so painful in its purely human aspect, that its commercial results, considerable as they were, are entirely obscured by its dark shadow. The yellow fever of that year gave New Orleans, for all time, a sad eminence in the list of plague-stricken towns, and must long continue to be a standard of comparison, for all pestilential visitations preceding or following it, in the annals of American cities.

From the beginning nothing could have been more obvious to the most superficial glance, than the insalubrity of the site chosen for New Orleans. But the almost total neglect of government and people to attempt its improvement, was hardly less so. Governor Perier, in 1726, did himself the credit to urge, in his dispatches, the necessity of sanitary measures, and the Baron Carondelet, toward the close of the last century, stood conspicuously apart from the long line of royal governors, in the attention he gave to the matter of public health, and for certain limited works, prosecuted with a view to decreasing the prevalence of malarial and putrid fevers.

Some beneficial changes came about gradually, without any intended reference to public sanitation. A certain defective surface-drainage, some paving, improved house-building, wiser domestic life, removal of much noxious forest and undergrowth, a better circulation of air, probably a slight reduction of temperature, and probably, too, what was more important, a reduction in humidity. But it was long before a system of public scavenging was adopted, and when it came it was only better than none. Later still open canals, intended for drainage, began to multiply, but they were ill-placed, poorly constructed, and entirely neglected.

Many features in the system of municipal cleansing were so far from being true sanitary measures, that a studied effort to make matters as bad as possible could hardly have been more vicious. Most of these, however, need no mention, being easily found in the contemporaneous history of almost any city. A singular effect of their combination in New Orleans, more amusing now than then, was that for a term of years—notably between 1837 and 1840—*rats* became a common and intolerable pest that defied extermination.[57]

The undrained state of the soil was the main source of many evils. Prominent among them was the custom of sepulture in tombs above ground, and the almost total interdiction of burial in the earth. A grave in the ground was lower than the water level. For a long time the tombs, later composed only of brick or stone, included wood in parts of their structure, and fell into decay so early as often to expose the bones of the dead.[58] As the town grew in age and in density of population it daily, and as unconcernedly as other towns, made the ground beneath it more and more poisonous, and spreading out upon the low ground behind it, actually began to occupy a district which had been used as a dumping-ground for its night-soil.

Meanwhile the town, expanding into a brisk commercial port, was yearly multiplying its communications with the West Indies, and a horrid and fatal disease began to make itself conspicuous, which in earlier days had visited the colony rarely if at all, and had been but vaguely recognized. In 1796, for the first time, a fatal epidemic disease was distinctly and popularly identified as the yellow fever. From that date its appearance was frequent, if not annual, and the medical records of the city enumerate, between that date and the present writing, 13 violent and 24 lighter epidemics of this dread visitant. It was present in 1799, in 1800, 1801, 1804, 1809, 1811, and 1812; was violent in 1817 and 1822, and from this time until the blockade of New Orleans by the United States fleet, in 1861, it made its appearance, sometimes in epidemics and sometimes only in sporadic form, every summer.

In 1832, when the first great cholera wave swept across the Atlantic, New Orleans suffered fearfully from its presence. It "made its appearance about the 25th of October, in the midst of an epidemic of yellow fever, and in . . . 20 days . . . killed about 6,000 people." The mortality amounted in some days to as high as 500, in a population which was estimated to have been reduced, by the flight of many, to at most 35,000.[59]

In 1839 over 1,300 persons died in New Orleans of yellow fever. In 1841 there were 1,800 victims. Between 1837 and 1843 some 5,500 deaths were from this cause. In the summer and fall of 1847 over 2,800 perished. In the second half of 1848, 872 died. It had barely disappeared when the cholera, which had again been ravaging Europe and the British isles, appeared and raged for eight months, carrying off 4,100 victims.[60] A month later, August, 1849, the yellow fever returned, and by the end of November had destroyed 744 persons. In this month the cholera again revived, and by the end of the year 1850 had added 1,851 to the long roll.[61]

It would seem, at first glance, that a city under such calamities would have been aroused to grapple with the facts of its condition, and at any cost to effect a sanitary revolution that would have presented to its own people and to the outer world the well-authenticated figures of a low death-rate. But sanitation could

scarcely make its way, where insalubrity was flatly denied or dis-
believed; and it probably requires a residence among a lethargic
and intensely provincial people, to understand with what honesty
of conviction such communities can assert and maintain the non-
existence of the most dreadful evils. "New Orleans, disguise the
fact as we may," writes De Bow in 1846, "has had abroad the repu-
tation of being a great charnel house. . . . We meet this *libel* with
facts"; and thereupon, though a professional statistician, he pres-
ents assertions, but no figures.[62] In January, 1851, at the close of
the frightful ills just recounted, the mayor officially pronounced
the city to have been "perfectly healthy during the past year and
free from all epidemic." The fact was omitted that the mortality
had been 62 per 1,000 of the population, and in the previous three
years respectively, 77, 66, and 84. The press was not behind the
public officials in a stout non-statement of facts, of which so purely
commercial a people supposed they had a right to require the with-
holding; and its persistent reiteration of the city's salubrity and of
the longevity of the native population, was oddly interwoven with
the assertion that the unacclimated absented themselves on the
approach of every summer by thousands.[63]

A few medical men, alone—Barton, Symonds, Fenner, Axson*—
about the year 1849, had begun to extricate from oblivion and
bring to light the city's vital statistics, and boldly and intelligently
to publish truths which should have alarmed any community. But
the disclosures that the mortality of New Orleans in 1849, even after deducting the deaths by cholera, had been about twice the common average of Boston, New York, Philadelphia, or Charleston,[64]
fell upon insensible ears. Doctor Barton's recommendation of un-
derground sewerage, urged in 1850,[65] was received in silence and
soon forgotten, to be revived and adopted in improved form thirty
years afterward.[66] A quarantine had been established in 1821, continued through 1824, withdrawn as useless in 1825, and has never
been re-established. Improved police measures were alluded to in
general terms as being in force,[67] but it is not clear what they could
have been intended to compass; a plan for daily flushing the open
street gutters, which are universal in New Orleans,[68] was proposed
to the city council and rejected, and the gutters left to present "a
most disgusting aspect."[69] Stagnant water stood under houses and

---

*Drs. Edward H. Barton, J. C. Simonds or Symonds, Erasmus Darwin Fenner,
and A. Forster Axson.

in vacant lots. The streets were proverbially muddy and filthy. A large portion of the dead were buried in thickly settled regions of the city.[70]

As the year 1853 drew near, all these unfortunate conditions seemed to approach a climax, under a contract scavenging system, and the "foul and nauseous steams arising from the street gutters and other depositories of decayed animal and vegetable matter" became the subject of public outcry.[71]

In the report of the board of health for the week ending the 28th of May, 1853, a death by yellow fever was announced, an exceptionally early commencement. The daily papers left it unpublished. Other reports in June were received in the same way. On the 2d of July, 25 deaths from yellow fever were reported for the closing week. A season of daily rains set in. At the end of the next week 59 deaths were reported. This was equivalent to not less than 300 cases, and the newspapers slowly and one by one began to admit the presence of danger.[72]

The disease now suddenly broke out like the flames of a conflagration. For the week ending July 16, 204 deaths were reported. The Howard Association* began active service. During the following week the admissions to the Charity hospital alone were from 60 to 100 a day, and its floors were covered with the sick. From the 16th to the 23d of July the deaths from the fever averaged 61 per day. Yet it was only in the preceding week that a city journal had professed its ignorance of the presence in New Orleans of any prevalent diseases, and in this week Dr. [J. S.] McFarlane, a noted physician of New Orleans, "supported by many others," advanced the theory that the accumulation of filth and offal in the yards, alleys, and streets of the city was calculated to retard the formation of a yellow-fever atmosphere. "It was ridiculed," says a medical writer in De Bow and an eye-witness of the great epidemic, "throughout the world outside of New Orleans." In that city some denounced the doctrine and others denied the filthiness of the streets. On the 25th of July the city council established a quarantine at Slaughter-house point, opposite the city.[73]

The interments of fever victims for the week ending July 30, averaged 79 a day. The rains continued and the weather became unseasonably cool. The usual summer custom of the municipal

*Formed by young businessmen to care for the sick following the 1837 yellow fever epidemic.

authorities of ordering the poisoning of vagrant dogs, had not been suspended, and their bloated carcasses lay in abundance, exposed in the streets and floated by dozens in the eddies among the wharves. Gormley's basin, a small artificial harbor at the intersection of Dryades walk and Felicity road, for the accommodation of cord-wood and shingle cutters, was termed "a pestilential muck-and-mire pool of dead animals and filth of every kind."[74] The fever raged with special violence in the fourth district (Lafayette), where German immigrants abounded.

The month of August set in. The weekly report of the 6th showed 187 deaths from other diseases, an enormous death-rate, to which was added 947 victims of the fever. The deaths throughout the week, in the Charity hospital solely, had averaged night and day 1 every half hour. As the 7th of August drew to a close, 71 bodies, in a single cemetery in an inhabited district, were left unburied, "piled on the ground, swollen and bursting their coffins, and enveloped in swarms of flies."[75] In the twenty-four hours of the 8th of August the deaths were 228. Of these deaths 198 were reported as the result of yellow fever; but such an appalling mortality, as this would leave to be attributed to other diseases, is incredible, and the true explanation must be found in the infatuation with which many professional men will at such times cling to theories concerning the name of a prevailing pestilence.

Such a state of affairs now existed, that the city was well described as a "theater of horrors," and the results of the plague were turned into fresh causes. "Alas," cried the editor of one of the daily papers, giving utterance to a literal fact, "we have not even grave-diggers." Sufficient numbers of these could not be hired at five dollars an hour. While some of the dead were buried with pomp and martial honors, the drivers of dead-carts went knocking from door to door, asking at each if there were any dead to be buried. Long rows of coffins were laid in furrows of scarce two feet depth and hastily covered with a few shovelfuls of earth, which the heavy rains falling daily washed away, and the whole mass was left "filling the air far and near with the most intolerable pestilential odors."[76] In the neighborhood of the graveyards funeral trains jostled each other and quarreled for place, in an air reeking with the effluvia of the earlier dead. Many "fell to work and buried their own dead." Many sick died in carriages and carts on their way to the hospitals. Many were found dead in their beds, in stores, in the streets, and in other places. The lengthened police reports indicated one of the natural results of a common mortal jeopardy. But heroism, too, was witnessed on every hand. The "Howards" won a fame as wide and lasting as the unhappy renown of their city, while hundreds of others displayed an equal, though often unrecorded, self-abnegation. Forty-five distant cities and towns sent pecuniary relief.

On the 11th of August 203 persons died of the fever, and in the week ending two days later, the total deaths were 1,494. Rain fell every day for two months, and it became almost impossible for the hearses to reach some of the cemeteries. On the 20th of August the week's mortality was 1,534. On the 18th 400 discharges of cannon were made and large quantities of tar burned, in the forlorn hope of purifying the air. The noise of the cannon threw many sick into convulsions, and was promptly discontinued. In the little town of Algiers, on the river shore opposite the city, there died in this week one thirty-sixth part of the whole population. On the 21st, in New Orleans, there were 269 deaths.

At last, on the 22d day of August, the maximum was reached when death struck a fresh victim every five minutes, and 283 deaths summed up the confessedly incomplete official record of the day. The next day there were 25 less. The next there was a further reduction of 36. Each day following the number diminished, and by the 1st of September was reduced to 119. By the 10th it was 80, by the 20th 49, and by the 30th 16. The total interments in the cemeteries of New Orleans, between the 1st of June and the 1st of October, was but a few short of 11,000.[77]

But this number does not include the many buried without certificate, nor the hundreds who perished in their flight from the city, nor those who fell victims to the fever brought into their towns by refugees. On the 7th of September the mail-bill was returned to New Orleans from the little town of Thibodeauxville, with the indorsement, "Stores closed; town abandoned; 151 cases of fever; 22 deaths; postmaster absent; clerks all down with the fever." It raged in these interior towns with the most terrible virulence until the middle of October.[78]

In New Orleans it lingered through the autumn, and disappeared only in December. In the next two summers, 1854 and 1855, it returned and destroyed more than 5,000 persons; to which number cholera added 1,750. The rate of mortality for these two years exceeded, respectively, 72 and 73 per 1,000. That of 1853 was 111, or one-ninth of the whole population.[79]

Thus closed the darkest period in the history of New Orleans. In three years more than 35,000 people had died, in a population reduced by flight to about 145,000.[80]

In the twenty-eight years since, only one mild and three severe epidemics of yellow fever have fallen upon the city. In 1858 the total deaths from all causes was 11,720; in 1867 they were 10,096; in 1873 they were a few less than 8,000, and in 1878 a few over 10,700. The epidemic of 1878 is the last in the city's history, and the only severe one in fourteen years.[81]

The rate of mortality since the "great epidemic" of 1853, has been steadily and greatly reduced. That visitation awakened New Orleans to the necessity of measures heretofore neglected, and even while the fever was still epidemic, a sanitary commission was formed with comprehensive instructions and powers to investigate the nature of the disease, to pronounce upon the adaptability of a sewerage system to the needs of New Orleans, to inquire into the real value of quarantine, and to recommend rules of general sanitation.[82]

Of the sewerage scheme nothing came; but in March, 1855, the legislature re-established quarantine,[83] and the efficiency of that branch of sanitation and the enforcement of health laws have ever since, with little or no interruption, improved. The average annual death rate, which in the five years ending with 1855 was 70, fell in the next five to 45; in the next to 40; in the next to 39; in the next to 34½, and in that which closed with 1880, notwithstanding the terrible epidemic of 1878, the rate sank to 33½. The mortality of 1879 was under 24, and that of 1880 under 25 per 1,000.[84]

It has already been intimated that the effect of the great epidemic upon the commerce of New Orleans was great. It may be too much to say that the whole reduction in its volume, which so promptly followed that calamity, was due to it alone; yet a careful search among contemporaneous authorities fails to reveal any other cause, and the coincidence, otherwise, remains unexplained.

In 1853 the aggregate value of exports, imports, and domestic receipts in New Orleans, exceeded $236,000,000. In 1854 it fell below $213,500,000. In 1855 it slightly recovered, and in 1856 the lost ground was much more than retaken.[85]

This year marked the beginning of another era of inflation, and the numbers which are being used in these pages to indicate the amount of the city's business—but which, it will be noticed, do not include the immense, unascertained amounts of shipments *into* the interior—rose to the unprecedented total of $271,750,000.[86] Yet the movement of 1857 cast this in the shade and reached an aggregate of $302,000,000.

In this year, nevertheless, came the crash, a crisis grievously felt throughout the entire country. In New Orleans 58 mercantile houses were wrecked before the opening of the next year, and in 1858, 45 others followed. This result, bad as it was, compared most favorably with that in other cities, New York chronicling 1,321 and Boston 376 failures.[87] In 1858 another epidemic of fever visited New Orleans, but it was undoubtedly the effect of the crisis, not of the epidemic—whose commercial results would not be seen until the following year—that the year's total of exports and imports declined in value more than $36,000,000.

The year 1860 must close this record. Much, even, that belongs to earlier years has already been passed by almost or quite unmentioned,—the city's political attitude toward, and relations with, American and Central American states, and her internal agitations, the growth and the decline of filibustering schemes which divided the public attention with the Know-nothing disorders in 1853–58, the history of her slave system and of her free people of color, the gradual though still partial amalgamation of Creole, American, and immigrant, the story of her world-renowned carnival, and the development of the fierce "abolition" question. This question in its growth, stifled for a time that love of the American union which had come to be, and is again to-day, a characteristic of all classes of her people. In that year New Orleans rose to the proudest commercial exaltation she has ever enjoyed, and at its close began that sudden and swift descent, which is not the least pathetic episode of our unfortunate civil war, whose events do not as yet bear cold discussion. In 1860 the city that one hundred and forty years before had consisted of one hundred palmetto-thatched huts in a noisome swamp, counted as the fraction of its commerce, comprised in its exports, imports, and domestic receipts, the value of $324,000,000.[88]

CABLE'S NOTES TO
"HISTORICAL SKETCH"

NOTES TO "SITE AND ORIGIN" (CHAPTER 1)

1. Hardee.
2. Stone of U.S. Coast & Geodetic Survey, Lafayette Square, New Orleans.
3. Official Memorandum, St. Louis Board of Underwriters.
4. *Traveler's Official Railway Guide.*
5. Route of Cromwell Line, N.Y., and N.O. steamers.
6. Piedmont Airline [railway].
7. Average voyage.
8. Bénard de La Harpe, 142.
9. "M. de Bienville etant [resur] des Natchez à la Moubile . . . dit qu'il avoit remarqué sur le bord du fleuve un endroit très propre," etc. Charlevoix, 4:10 [?—corner of MS page torn].
10. Bénard de La Harpe, 142.
11. Dumont de Montigny, 2:47.

NOTES TO "POPULATION AND SOCIAL ORDER" (CHAPTER 2)

1. Gayarré, *History of Louisiana,* 1:253. [Cable generally did not specify the English edition of Gayarré, but it is assumed that is intended except where he specified the "French edition" (indicated herein as *Histoire de la Louisiane*). Occasionally he did indicate "Gayarré's *Louisiana,*" and in a few places here the English title has been added silently for clarification.]
2. Bénard de La Harpe, 219.
3. Ibid., 224.
4. Ibid., 238.
5. "—de choisir dans ce petit canton un emplacement propre à bâtir une Ville digne de devenir la Capitale," etc. Dumont de Montigny, 2:46.
6. Ibid., 2:47, 48.
7. Bénard de La Harpe, 293, 294.
8. Gayarré, 1:272.
9. Ibid., [1:]303.
10. Charlevoix, 4:229; Dumont de Montigny, 2:49.
11. Ibid., 334. [Cable's "Id., 334" here. He probably meant Gayarré.]
12. Martin, quoting Charlevoix, makes the year 1723 and others repeat the error. Charlevoix arrived in New Orleans from Canada Jan. 31, 1722, sailed for France at the end of March of the same year, suffered shipwreck, returned to Louisiana June 4, and departed finally on the 16th. See Bénard de La Harpe, 285, 287, 325, 328. Confirmed also by Le Page du Pratz in his notice of a similar storm at Natchez six months before (1:173–76).

13. Bénard de La Harpe, 339. This much mentioned storm seems to have been from the first the subject of many errors. Charlevoix dates it the evening of the twelfth, and gives its duration as scarcely one day. Dumont de Montigny says three days. Martin dates it a year ahead, an error which has misled Monette and many others. Bénard de La Harpe gives its duration as six days—the eleventh to the sixteenth. He was an eye-witness, but his second date is probably a typographical error. It was probably three days in sweeping the whole coast.

14. Martin, 1:256.

15. Gayarré, 1:383.

16. Martin, 1:256–58.

17. Gayarré, 1:366.

18. Dumont de Montigny, 2:30, 36; Bénard de La Harpe 239; Gayarré, 1:126, 133, 392; Martin 1:264; Monette, 1:254.

19. "—sans religion, sans justice, sans discipline, sans ordre et sans police." Gayarré, *Histoire de la Louisiane,* 1:228, quoting Drouot de Valdeterre.

20. Gayarré, 1:376.

21. Charlevoix, vol. 4, map facing p. 196, copied from original in Department of Marine, Paris.

22. Dumont de Montigny, 2:82.

23. Martin, 1:264; Gayarré, 1:381.

24. Martin, 1:262.

25. Ibid.

26. Charlevoix, vol. 4, map [facing?] p. 196; Martin, 1:263; Gayarré, etc.

27. Martin, 1:263; Gayarré 1:378, 379; *New Orleans Directory for 1842,* 2:50.

28. Ibid., 1:264. [Martin?]

29. Plan of Official Survey made in 1763 for the purpose of partition and sale of confiscated estate of the Jesuit fathers.

30. Martin, 1:263.

31. Ibid., 1:320; Gayarré, 2:63.

32. Martin, 1:264.

33. Gayarré, 1:382.

34. Ibid., [1:]432.

35. See Charlevoix's copy in his *Nouvelle France,* 4:196.

36. Dumont de Montigny, 2:50.

37. Dumont de Montigny says there were at his time of writing (1753) houses in New Orleans four and five stories high (2:52). In reality the first four-story house in New Orleans was built about 1806. Dumont de Montigny's map ([2]:51) abounds in inaccuracies and is not true to its own scale.

38. Acknowledgement [*sic*] is here due to Mr. A. J. Villeré of New Orleans for access to an official copy of the map in the French archives.

39. "—une petite caffette de linge & d' habits, [coresime?], coëffes, chemises, bas, &c." Dumont de Montigny, 2:50.

40. Martin, 1:264; Gayarré, 1:390.

NOTES TO "INDIAN WARS" (CHAPTER 3)

1. Charlevoix, 4:243; Martin 1:269, 270.

2. Dumont de Montigny, 2:170. [Insertion point estimated.]

3. Le Page du Pratz, 3:230.

4. Charlevoix, Martin, Gayarré, etc.

5. Périer's dispatches, quoted in Gayarré, *Histoire de la Louisiane*, 1:246, 251 . . . ; Martin, 1:276; Charlevoix, 4:261.

6. Ibid. [Insertion point estimated.]

7. Gayarré, Martin, etc.

8. Martin, 1:281; Gayarré, *Histoire de la Louisiane*, 1:245. Dumont de Montigny's account (2:203) is manifestly erroneous. Compare it with Périer's own dispatches.

9. Martin, 1:282.

10. Le Page du Pratz, 3:304–17; Martin, 1:294–96; Charlevoix, 4:294; Gayarré, 1:440. The account of Le Page du Pratz is that of an eye-witness and one of the discoverers of the plot. Martin mi[s]states the year.

11. Martin, 1:279; Le Page du Pratz, 3:296 ("les veuves ne le furent pas long-tems").

12. Dumont de Montigny, 2:210; Le Page du Pratz, 3:403.

13. Dumont de Montigny, 2:211; Le Page du Pratz, 3:403.

14. Martin, 1:300; Gayarré, 1:471.

15. Martin, 2:303; Gayarré, 1:484.

16. Martin, 1:306–9; Gayarré, 1:503–10.

17. Gayarré, 1:519.

18. Ibid. [Insertion point estimated.]

19. Gayarré, 1:452; Martin 1:287.

20. Martin, Gayarré, etc.

NOTES TO "THE FIRST CREOLES" (CHAPTER 4)

1. "Les habitants en general, et les creoles en particulier, se sont bravements conduits partout." Périer's dispatch, April 10, 1730. Gayarré, *Histoire de la Louisiane*, 1:265. This was previous to any Spanish immigration.

2. Gayarré, 1:458, 469, etc. Bienville's dispatches [in?] Gayarré, 1:392.

3. Gayarré, 1:377.

4. Bénard de La Harpe, 148, etc.

5. Gayarré, 1:457; dispatches of [Bernard Diron] D'Artaguette, April 23, 1733.

6. Gayarré, 1:498.

7. Martin, 1:312, 316.

8. Ibid., 1:305.

9. Ibid., 1:316.

10. Gayarré, 1:523.

11. Ibid., 2:18.

12. Ibid., 1:470.

13. Ibid., 1:499.

14. Ibid., 2:28, 56, 66.

15. Ibid., 2:48; Martin, 1:319, 320.

16. Martin, 1:321.

17. Gayarré, 2:65.

18. Martin, 1:333.

19. Gayarré, 2:87.

20. Plan of New Orleans in 1770, by Captain Pittman of the British army.

21. Gayarré, 2:84, 88.

22. Martin, 1:352.

23. Gayarré, 2:82.

24. Ibid., [2:]88.

25. Martin, 2:318.

26. Gayarré 2:65, Report of Michel de la Rouivillière.

27. Gayarré, 2:105.

28. "Art. 23.—'Any Negro who shall be met in the streets or public roads, carrying a cane, a rod, or a stick, shall be chastised by the first white man who shall meet him, with the very same instrument found in the possession of said Negro; and should said Negro be daring enough to defend himself or run away, it shall be the duty of the white man to denounce the fact, in order that the black man be punished according to the exigencies of the case. . . .'" Regulations of Police decreed by de Vaudreuil. Gayarré, vol. 2, appendix, p. 365.

29. Gayarré, 2:105, 106, 375, etc.

30. Ibid., 2:57, Dispatch of Michel de la Rouvillière, May 15, 1751.

31. Ibid., [2:]66, etc., etc. [Emphasis should be placed on the *etceteras.* There is no reference to education on p. 66 in Gayarré.]

32. *Vue du Mississippi,* Berquin-Duvallon (1802), 206, 309, etc. (This valuable work by a resident of New Orleans in 1802, is consulted repeatedly in a succeeding chapter. [GWC])

33. Gayarré, 2:66.

34. Ibid., 2:28.

35. Ibid., [2]:355.

36. Ibid., 2:355; Bayou St. John & Gentilly show population of 307.

37. Some of these establishments have not yet disappeared.

38. Ibid. [Gayarré], [2:]354.

39. Gayarré, 2:23–107—numerous decrees and reports.

40. Ibid., 2:108, etc.

41. Ibid., [2:]105.

42. Ibid., [2:]36, 105, 106.

43. Ibid., [2:]79–81.

44. *American State Papers: Public Lands,* 2:17, 41.

45. Gayarré, 1:521; Bienville and Salmon to the French government, June 15, 1742.

46. Martin, 2:30.

47. Gayarré, 2:92, 93.

48. Martin, 1:345, 346; Gayarré, 2:115–25.

49. Martin, 1:343. Gayarré (2:101) quotes, from official report, "a number of officers, with 320 soldiers, 20 women and 17 children."

50. Martin, 1:339.

51. Ibid., 1:343; Gayarré, 2:94.

52. Martin, 1:343.

53. Ibid.

54. Gayarré, 2:112, 113, 110.

NOTES TO "THE INSURRECTION OF 1768" (CHAPTER 5)

1. Gayarré, 2:106.

2. Ibid., 107.

3. Gayarré, *Histoire de la Louisiane,* 2:119.
4. Gayarré, *History of Louisiana,* 2:109–12.
5. Martin, 1:348, 349; Gayarré, 2:127.
6. Gayarré, 2:127–29.
7. Ibid., [2:]129, 130.
8. Martin, 1:355.
9. Gayarré, 2:115, 123, 166, 161, 88, 179.
10. Ibid., [2:]88, 147, 143, etc. Gayarré, *Histoire de la Louisiane,* 2:136, 137.
11. Gayarré, 2:131.
12. Ibid., [2:]131, 132.
13. Gayarré, *Histoire de la Louisiane,* 2:141–43.
14. Ibid., 2:241, 242.
15. Ibid., 2:139.
16. Ibid., [2:]141, 142; Gayarré, *History of Louisiana,* [2:]161.
17. Gayarré, *History of Louisiana,* 2:167.
18. Martin, 1:355.
19. Gayarré, 2:185.
20. Ibid., 2:167.
21. Gayarré, *Histoire de la Louisiane,* 2:146–52.
22. Gayarré, *History of Louisiana,* 2:181, 248, etc.
23. Ibid., 2:180.
24. Ibid., 2:185, 186.
25. Ibid., [2:]226, 227.
26. Ibid., 2:187, 303.
27. Ibid., 2:188, 189.
28. Ibid.
29. Ibid., 2:109–213. A minute account with translations of dispatches, etc. Also Martin, 1:359.
30. Gayarré, 2:210, 225, 229.
31. Gayarré, *History of Louisiana,* 2:219; Gayarré, *Histoire de la Louisiane,* [2:]174, 198, 212, 213, 216, 217, 222.
32. Gayarré, *History of Louisiana,* 2:232; Gayarré, *Histoire de la Louisiane,* 2:242; Martin, 1:357.
33. Gayarré, *Histoire de la Louisiane,* 2:227.
34. Gayarré, 2:211.
35. Gayarré, *History of Louisiana,* 2:275; Martin, 1:360.
36. Gayarré, 2:276–78.
37. Ibid., 2:278, 279.
38. Ibid. [2:]281, 282.
39. Ibid., 2:282.
40. Ibid. [2:]295–300
41. Ibid. [2:]303–5.
42. Ibid. [2:]291–95.
43. Ibid. [2:]309.
44. Ibid., 2:308.
45. Ibid., [2:]309, 313.
46. Ibid., [2:]313.
47. Ibid., [2:]306.

48. Martin, 2:4.
49. Gayarré, 2:336–43.
50. Ibid.
51. Ibid., 2:211.
52. Ibid., 2:336–43.
53. *American State Papers,* 1:363.
54. Gayarré, 2:344.

NOTES TO "THE SUPERIOR COUNCIL AND THE CABILDO" (CHAPTER 6)

1. Charlevoix, 4:169, 170. "Il avoit neanmoius [sp?] juge à propos d'y établir pour trois ans un Conseil Supérieur, qui juegât toutes les affaires, taut civiles que Criminelles; . . . & que suivant l'usage qu'ils ferout de l'Administrations de la justice, qui leur etoit confiée, il se determineroit a continuer, & même à augmenter l'Etablissement de Conseil, on a l'abgandonner."
2. Martin, 1:180.
3. Charlevoix, 4:170 (footnote); Martin, 1:193, 182.
4. Martin, 1:193, 194.
5. Ibid.
6. Charlevoix, 4:193; Martin, 1:196.
7. Martin, 1:215.
8. Ibid.
9. Ibid.
10. Bénard de La Harpe, 334.
11. Gayarré, 1:362, 366.
12. Ibid., [1:]371.
13. Ibid., [1:]391.
14. Martin, 1:260.
15. Ibid., 1:292; Gayarré, 1:455.
16. Martin, 1:313.
17. Ibid., [1:]307.
18. Gayarré, 1:362.
19. Gayarré, vol. 1, appendix.
20. Gayarré, 2:80.
21. *American State Papers: Public Lands,* 2:17, 41.
22. Gayarré, 2:85–90.
23. Ibid., [2:]106.
24. Gayarré, *Histoire de la Louisiane,* 2:338 (appendix).
25. Ibid.
26. Ibid. In this appendix the proclamation is given entire.
27. Gayarré, *Histoire de la Louisiane,* vol. 2, appendix.
28. Ibid.
29. Ibid.
30. Martin's misstatement on this point (2:10) must have been a mere slip of the pen.
31. Gayarré, *Histoire de la Louisiane,* vol. 2, appendix.
32. Martin, 2:13.
33. Gayarré, *Histoire de la Louisiane,* vol. 2, appendix.

34. Martin, 2:16.

35. Ibid., [2:]14.

36. Leovy, 22; "The Laws of Louisiana and Their Sources," a paper read before the N.O. Academy of Sciences, January 23, 1871, by Hon. E. T. Merrick, late Chief Justice Sup. Ct. of La. [Insertion point estimated.]

37. Chief Justice Merrick's "The Laws of Louisiana."

38. Gayarré, 3:372.

39. Ibid.

40. Ibid.

41. Ibid., 3:27–29.

NOTES TO "SPANISH CONCILIATION" (CHAPTER 7)

1. Gayarré, 3:28.

2. Gayarré, *Histoire de la Louisiane,* 2:147.

3. Ibid., 2:185, etc.

4. Ibid.; Martin, 2:26.

5. Gayarré, *Histoire de la Louisiane,* 2:185, etc. The original text of the memorial on the events of Oct. 29th, 1788.

6. Martin, 1:196.

7. Ibid., 2:25.

8. Gayarré, 3:26, 27.

9. Martin, 2:25, 26.

10. Ibid., [2:]27.

11. Ibid., 2:26, 28.

12. Ibid., [2:]31.

13. Gayarré, 3:49.

14. Unzaga's letters to the bishop of Cuba and the Marquis de la Torre, Captain-General of Cuba and Louisiana. Gayarré, 3:85–97, etc.

15. Martin, 2:22.

16. See Monette, 1:453. His impression of a Spanish and Spanish American immigration seems to want foundation.

17. Gayarré, 3:30.

18. Martin, 2:13, 16, 25, 30, 32, etc.

19. Gayarré, 3:105.

20. Martin, 2:31.

21. Gayarré, 3:105–7.

22. Gayarré (3:115) says earlier.

23. Martin, 2:40, 44; Gayarré, 3:108.

24. Ibid. [Gayarré?], [3?:]121.

25. Gayarré, 3:110, 111.

26. Ibid., [3:]31; Martin, 2:12.

27. Gayarré, 3:100, 109, 113.

28. Ibid., 3:117; Martin, 2:44, 45.

29. Gayarré, 3:100.

30. Martin, 2:27.

31. Ibid., 1:329, 2:18.

32. Ibid., 2:43.

33. Ibid., [2:]211.
34. Gayarré, 3:121.
35. Ibid., 3:122–24.
36. Ibid., [3:]125, 126.
37. Ibid., [3:]126–31.
38. Ibid., 3:135, 136.
39. Ibid., 3:137–47.
40. Martin, 2:24.
41. Gayarré, 3:156, 157.
42. Ibid., 3:153.
43. Ibid., [3:]156.
44. Martin, 2:68–71.
45. Ibid., [2:]72.

NOTES TO "THE CREOLES STILL FRENCH" (CHAPTER 8)

1. See the citizens' reply to Navarro's address on the disasters of 1779–80: "But we shall endeavor to conform, as much as may be permitted by the frailties of human nature, to your pressing exhortations to patience." Translated by Gayarré, 3:153.
2. Gayarré, 3:91.
3. Martin, 2:209, 210.
4. Ibid., 2:26.
5. Ibid., [2:]125; Gayarré, 3:346.
6. Martin, 1:174, 210, 221.
7. Monette, 1:297. Dr. Monette does not give his authorities, but the probabilities attaching to the statements are very strong.
8. *DeBow's Review* 1:300, quoting a paper in the French Archives.
9. Gayarré, vol. 2, appendix, 370.
10. *DeBow's Review* 1:302, quoting [Whitemarsh Benjamin] Seabrook's *Memoir on the Origin, Cultivation and Uses of Cotton* (1843).
11. Martin, 2:234, 236.
12. Ibid., 1:320.
13. Ibid., 2:125.
14. Monette's contrary statement, unsupported by authority (1:297), is at odds with Martin. Le Page du Pratz, in 1758, treating the productions of Louisiana at length, does not mention sugar or sugarcane.
15. Martin, 1:334.
16. Monette, 1:298. Dr. Monette, who most probably had good authority for this interesting statement, erroniously [sic] attributes it to Martin—who does not mention it.
17. Martin, 2:109.
18. Ibid., [2:]125; *DeBow's Review* 1:54.
19. Ibid.; Martin, 2:125, 126, 131.
20. Ibid.
21. Martin, 2:234.
22. Ibid., [2:]3. [Insertion point estimated.]
23. Gayarré, 3:203 (Miró's dispatch of April first, 1788).

24. Ibid.; Martin, 2:97. See map.
25. Gayarré, 3:335, 336; Berquin-Duvallon, 27.
26. Gayarré, 3:336.
27. Berquin-Duvallon, 26.
28. Ibid.; *Voyage à la Louisiane,* par Bxxx Dxxx [*sic*; probably Baudry des Lozières], Paris (1802), 162.
29. Martin, 2:18, 19.
30. Ibid.
31. Norman, 98. Quoting from inscription of tablet in the façade of the chapel.
32. *Report of Board of Administrators of the Charity Hospital,* 1877 (Dr. Jas. Burns), 31.
33. Martin, 2:122, 126.
34. Berquin-Duvallon, 27.
35. Ibid.
36. Martin, 2:204.
37. Map of N.O., 1813.
38. Gayarré, 3:582.
39. Martin, 2:111, 112.
40. Gayarré, 3:374.
41. Martin, 2:137.
42. Ibid., [2:]124, 125, 128, 131.
43. See Schedule.
44. Martin, 2:137.
45. Ibid., 2:176.
46. Gayarré, 3:336; Martin, 2:124
47. Gayarré, 3:378, Bishop Peñalvert's letter [of November 1, 1795, reporting on the moral, religious, and sanitary conditions of the town and its inhabitants].
48. Gayarré, 3:311.
49. Berquin-Duvallon, 34, etc.
50. Gayarré, 3:310, 327.
51. Ibid., 3:309–10.
52. Ibid., [3:]327, 328.
53. Martin, 2:117.
54. See maps. [The Census Office publication includes maps showing the "Plan" of the city in 1763 and 1770 and "New Orleans in 1798" as well as later maps of the city.]
55. Martin, 2:123.
56. "In front of the principal street of the city,"—General Collet's dispatch. Gayarré, 3:381.
57. Ibid.
58. Ibid., [3:]329, 330.
59. Ibid., [3:]340–42.
60. Ibid., 3:96.
61. Ibid., [3:]377.

NOTES TO "THE AMERICAN GRASP" (CHAPTER 9)

1. Martin, 2:50, 53.
2. Ibid., 2:72.

3. Gayarré, 3:181.

4. Martin, 2:89, 91.

5. Gayarré, 3:182.

6. "se prepara contra esta provincia un nublado que descargara algun dia, y seria mucho mas el perjuicio, so por desgracia inundase las tierras de Nueva Espana." Navarro's letter of twelfth of February 1787. Gayarré, 3:183, 184, footnote. [This page is smudged in Cable's manuscript; the quotation is copied from Gayarré's note.]

7. Ibid., [3:]183 and footnote.

8. Ibid., 3:189.

9. Ibid., [3:]192, 193.

10. Ibid., [3:]192. [Part of this note is water-smudged and illegible.]

11. Ibid., [3:]194, etc.

12. Ibid., [3:]219.

13. Wilkinson's letter to Miró, Gardoqui, Navarro, the King of Spain, etc. Gayarré, 3:[247–51].

14. Martin, 2:94, 94 [probably 95].

15. Ibid., [2:]98.

16. Gayarré, 3:204.

17. Martin, 2:98.

18. Gayarré, 3:219.

19. Ibid., [3:]297.

20. Gayarré, 3:293.

21. Martin, 2:105, 106.

22. Ibid.

23. Gayarré, 3:294.

24. Ibid., [3:]314.

25. Ibid., [3:]309.

26. Martin, 2:108.

27. Ibid., [2:]115.

28. Gayarré, 3:190, translating from Navarro's letter.

29. Ibid., [3:]332, 333.

30. Martin, 2:128; Gayarré, 3:337, 353. [Martin at this point has several pages numbered in duplicate.] See also *History of Louisiana* by Barbé-Marbois, American translation (1830), 156, etc.

31. Gayarré, 3:344, etc., and 365.

32. *American State Papers: Foreign Relations,* 1:547–49.

33. Gayarré, 3:373.

34. Monette, 1:520, etc., quoting [U.S. commissioner Andrew] Ellicott's journal.

35. Gayarré, 3:372, quoting Intendant [Francisco] Rendon's dispatch.

36. Monette, 1:525, etc.

37. Gayarré, 3:366.

38. Ibid., [3:]397.

39. Pontalba's memoir [Joseph Xavier de Pontalba, "Memoirs on Louisiana," to the French minister of the navy, September 15, 1801, in Martin, 2:186–215]; see Gayarré, 3:443.

40. Gayarré, 3:397, 443, 444; Berquin-Duvallon, 156.

41. Monette, 1:539.

42. Rendon: see Gayarré, 3:373.
43. Monette, 1:539.
44. Gayarré, 3:386.
45. Ellicott's journal. See Monette, 1:532.
46. Gayarré, 3:398, 399.
47. Ibid., [3:]409
48. Martin, 2:175, 176.
49. Gayarré, 3:409, 410.
50. Ibid., [3:]451, 452.
51. Ibid., [3:]470.
52. Martin, 3 [probably 2]:182.
53. Gayarré, 3:405, 406, 447.
54. Ibid., [3:]456, etc.
55. Ibid., [3:]456, 483, 592; Martin, 2:181.
56. Gayarré, 3:591, 589, 524, 599, etc.
57. Martin, 2:193, 194.
58. Ibid., 2:199.

NOTES TO "A FRANCO-SPANISH AMERICAN CITY" (CHAPTER 10)

1. From 1769, when O'Reilly landed in N. Orleans, to 1803, when Laussat received the province.
2. Gayarré, 3:87.
3. Martin, 2:76.
4. Ibid., [2:]99.
5. Ibid., [2:]43, 46, 84.
6. Ibid., 2:45, 46.
7. Berquin-Duvallon, 249.
8. Martin, 2:85.
9. Gayarré, 3:353; Berquin-Duvallon, 248.
10. Berquin-Duvallon, 201, 252.
11. Gayarré, 3:309, 310.
12. Ibid., 3:314, 325; Berquin-Duvallon, 234–36.
13. Gayarré, 3:407, 456; Barbé-Marbois, 138.
14. Berquin-Duvallon, 41, 249; Gayarré, 3:432 (Pontalba's memoir); *American State Papers: Miscellaneous,* 1, 347, 348, 384, footnote to census table. "It is asserted by the best informed on the subject that there are not a hundred Spanish families in all Louisiana and West Florida. The bulk of inhabitants are French people . . . and emigrants from the United States, and a few English, Scots, Dutch and Irish" (Winterbotham).
15. *American State Papers: Miscellaneous,* 1:354–56; Gayarré, 3:443 (Pontalba's memoir); Martin, 2:236.
16. *DeBow's Review* 6:156 (letter of Maunsel White).
17. Berquin-Duvallon, 24, 60; "Louisiana and West Florida," by T. Hutchins, geographer to the United States, appended to *A Topographical Description of the Western Territory of North America,* by [Gilbert] Imlay (London, 1795) [probably the 1797 3rd ed. of this work, listed in the bibliography], 414.
18. (Including the ground floor.)

19. Such a house is being torn down in New Orleans at the present writing.

20. *American State Papers: Miscellaneous,* 1:348; Imlay (Hutchins), 413; Berquin-Duvallon, 26.

21. Norman, 93, 94.

22. Berquin-Duvallon, 40, etc.

23. Ibid., 26, 27, 40, 90, etc.

24. Ibid., 249, 185, 248–52. [Insertion point estimated.]

25. Ibid., 33, 159, 218, 280; Perrin du Lac, 395.

26. Official certified copy of original plan, certified by Trudeau, Surveyor General; now in hands of J. Q. A. Fellows, Esq., New Orleans.

27. Official map, now in possession of J. Q. A. Fellows, Esq., New Orleans.

28. *DeBow's Review* 6:157.

29. Official maps.

30. *American State Papers: Miscellaneous,* 1:348.

31. Berquin-Duvallon, 40.

32. Hutchins and Perrin du Lac give the population of New Orleans at this time at about 7,000.

33. Gayarré, 3:204–6 (Miró's dispatch of April 1, 1788).

34. Gayarré, 3:179, 180, 351; *DeBow's Review* 6:157; Berquin-Duvallon, 184, 185, 314.

35. Berquin-Duvallon, 206, 207, 238, 31–37, 286, 185, 186; Gayarré, 3:376, 377, 408, 4:408.

36. Perrin du Lac, 394; Berquin-Duvallon, 285; Gayarré, 3:377.

37. Berquin-Duvallon.

38. Ibid.

39. Ibid., 201–29, 243–47, 276–315. [Insertion point estimated.]

NOTES TO "FROM SUBJECTS TO CITIZENS" (CHAPTER 11)

1. Gayarré, 4:46 (Mr. Lucas, in Congress).

2. Ibid., 4:99.

3. Ibid.

4. Martin, 2:245; Laussat's dispatch.

5. Gayarré, 4:12; Laussat's dispatch.

6. Gayarré, 4:24, 26.

7. Ibid., [4:]9–15, 27.

8. Ibid., 4:4–16, etc.; *American State Papers,* vol xx, p. [probably *Miscellaneous,* class 10 of *American State Papers,* which Cable elsewhere referred to as "vol xx"; apparently he neglected to fill in the page number in this instance].

9. Ibid., 4:26, 27.

10. Ibid., 4:5, 17.

11. Martin, 2:251; Gayarré, 4:19.

12. Ibid. [Gayarré?], [4?:]19–21.

13. Ibid. [Gayarré?], [4?:]21 (footnote).

14. Ibid. [Gayarré?], [4?:]16.

15. Ibid. [Gayarré?], [4?:]6, 7.

16. Gayarré, 4:26.

17. *American State Papers[: Miscellaneous?],* vol xx, 399.

18. Gayarré, 4:33.
19. Ibid., 4:23, 106. Dr. James's pamphlet.
20. Ibid., 4:38.
21. Ibid., 4:66.
22. Ibid., [4:]76.
23. Ibid., 4:84, 90, 91, 103, 106, 107, 115, 131, 132.
24. Ibid., 4:159, quoting Executive Journal, 2:340.

NOTES TO "BURR'S CONSPIRACY" (CHAPTER 12)

1. Gayarré, 4:80, 81.
2. Ibid., 4:81, 129, 130, 134.
3. Ibid., 4:131–55.
4. Ibid., [4:]152; dispatch of 9th September.
5. Ibid., 4:157.
6. Ibid., [4:]158.
7. Ibid., [4:]153, 160; Martin, 2:271.
8. Gayarré, 4:160, 161; Martin, 2:272.
9. Martin, 2:273–76.
10. Ibid.
11. Gayarré, 4:165.
12. Ibid., [4:]166–69.
13. Ibid.
14. Ibid., [4:]164.
15. Ibid., 4:170–73.
16. Ibid., 4:174, 175; Martin, 2:284.
17. Gayarré, 4:176.
18. Ibid., 4:174, 177, 178.
19. Ibid., 4:179, 182; Martin, 2:285, 286.
20. Ibid. [Martin?], [2?:]287.

NOTES TO "THE WEST INDIAN IMMIGRATION" (CHAPTER 13)

1. Gayarré, 4:212. Claiborne [in a letter to Madison, May 18, 1809, quoted by Gayarré] estimates but 2,000 to 2,700 American immigrants for the whole territory between the years 1806 and 1809.
2. Gayarré, 4:123, 212; Martin, 2:205. Berquin-Duvallon, p. 46, estimates the population of New Orleans at 10,000 as early as 1802.
3. Martin, 2:297.
4. Ibid., [2:]294; Gayarré, 4:218.
5. *DeBow's Review* 7:420, quoting Paxton.
6. Gayarré, 4:218.
7. Ibid., [4:]217.
8. Ibid., 4:123.
9. Ibid., [4:]125, 126.
10. Ibid., 4:197, 198.
11. Ibid., [4:]127, 197, 212.
12. Ibid., 4:143, 144, 147, 155, 185.

13. Ibid., 4:185–90.
14. Ibid., [4:]197.
15. Ibid., 4:204, 205.
16. Ibid., [4:]209.
17. Ibid., [4:]214–20; Paxton.
18. Gayarré, 4:268, 274, 280.
19. Martin, 2:311, 312; *DeBow's Review* 11:496.

NOTES TO "THE WAR OF 1812–15" (CHAPTER 14)

1. Bryant, 4:184.
2. The authorities for the statements contained in this chapter are, almost solely, Gayarré, 4:276–510, and Martin, 2:311–79.
3. Quoted repeatedly by Gayarré. [Latour's memoir is *Historical Memoir of the War in West Florida and Louisiana in 1814–1815* (Philadelphia: John Conrad and Co., 1816).]

NOTES TO "COMMERCIAL EXPANSION—1815 TO 1840" (CHAPTER 15)

1. Monette, 2:519, etc.
2. *DeBow's Review* 1:48, 7:415, 416.
3. Paxton.
4. *DeBow's Review* 4:61. Paxton gives larger figures which probably include shipments into the interior.
5. Paxton.
6. *DeBow's Review* 1:48.
7. Paxton.
8. *DeBow's Review* 11:451.
9. Bernhard, 2:56; *DeBow's Review* 11:481; Paxton.
10. Gayarré, 4:634, 635.
11. Ibid., [4:]634 –36.
12. *DeBow's Review* 4:61.
13. U.S. Census.
14. Bernhard, 2:84. *DeBow's Review* 11:78.
15. U.S. Census.
16. Ibid.
17. Ibid.
18. *Encyclopedia Britannica,* 7th ed., 17:224.
19. Monette, 2:533.
20. *New Orleans Medical and Surgical Journal,* 15:817.
21. *DeBow's Review* 15:635.
22. *DeBow's Review* 4:83.
23. Ibid. [4:]84.
24. Paxton, quoted in *DeBow's Review* 7:420.
25. Gayarré, 4:644.
26. Ibid., [4:]646, 647.
27. *DeBow's Review* 1:420.
28. *New Orleans Picayune,* Sep. 31, 1837.

29. Levasseur, 2:110, 94.

30. *DeBow's Review* 1:428.

31. Ibid. [1:]439.

32. *DeBow's Review* 15:580.

33. *DeBow's Review* 26:595; Gayarré, 4:657, etc.

34. *DeBow's Review* 11:481.

35. Bernhard, 2:56; Levasseur, 2:109.

36. *New Orleans Directory for 1842,* 2:13, 42.

37. Dr. E. H. Barton, in *DeBow's Review* 11:481.

38. *New Orleans Medical and Surgical Journal,* 15:817.

39. See especially Harriet Martineau's *Retrospect of Western Travel,* 2:256, 257.

40. Report of the Board of Administrators of the Charity Hospital (1877).

41. Official Report, *DeBow's Review* 17:15.

42. *True Republican* (newspaper) (1837), advertising columns; *DeBow's Review* 1:73.

43. *DeBow's Review* 4:61.

44. U.S. Census.

45. Ibid.

46. *DeBow's Review* 4:555; Bernhard, 2:84.

47. *DeBow's Review* 23:656.

48. *True Republican* (newspaper), July 4, 1837.

49. Ibid.

50. *DeBow's Review* 10:587, 11:78.

51. Gayarré, 4:661.

52. *DeBow's Review* 4:61, 1:48.

NOTES TO "POSITIVE GROWTH WITH COMPARATIVE DECLINE" (CHAPTER 16)

1. *DeBow's Review* 3:98, 132, 178.

2. *DeBow's Review* 3:107.

3. *DeBow's Review* 1:50, 4:394, 9:456.

4. *DeBow's Review* 1:50, 4:394, 9:456.

5. Ibid. These figures are quoted by DeBow from the *New Orleans Price-Current.* Though not absolutely complete, they are sufficiently correct to make any error in *proportions* trivial.

6. *DeBow's Review* 8:37, 1:174.

7. *DeBow's Review* 4:68–72, 3:392; U.S. Census, 1870.

8. *DeBow's Review* 2:423.

9. U.S. Census.

10. Dr. E. H. Barton, in *DeBow's Review* 11:481; *New Orleans Directory for 1842,* 13.

11. *DeBow's Review* 4:262; U.S. Census.

12. *DeBow's Review* 2:59, 3:107, 4:77, 5:173, 7:269, 9:120, 529, 13:89, etc.

13. *DeBow's Review* 3:44–46, 4:209, 10:586–88, 13:89, etc.

14. *DeBow's Review* 10:587, 15:297.

15. These markets had been commenced gradually during a period of eight to fifteen years.

16. *DeBow's Review* 11:481.

17. Acknowledgement [sic] is due for this long series of details to the publisher of Soards' *New Orleans City Directory,* whose file of early directories was kindly placed by him at the disposal of the writer.

18. *DeBow's Review* 3:100.

19. *DeBow's Review* 1:84, 85, 3:146.

20. *DeBow's Review* 18:555–58.

21. *DeBow's Review* 7:412, etc., quoting Paxton.

22. *DeBow's Review* 1:73, 422, 430, 5:236.

23. *DeBow's Review* 1:83, 3:277.

24. *DeBow's Review* 1:83, 3:277.

25. Another account gives a lesser number.

26. *DeBow's Review* 1:381, 382, 2:350, 351, 5:539.

27. *DeBow's Review* 2:351, 8:97, 432.

28. Gayarré, 2:13; *DeBow's Review* 3:449, 19:432, 433.

29. *DeBow's Review* 5:241, 242.

30. Ibid., 17:218.

31. Ibid., 16:92; U.S. Census.

32. *DeBow's Review* 9:240.

33. Ibid., 26:355, quoting Report of Superintendent of Public Education.

34. *DeBow's Review* 5:98; Norman, 125; Fenner, 1:27.

35. Gayarré, 3:153; Fenner, 1:56; *DeBow's Review* 11:481; Berquin-Duvallon, 152, 153.

36. Gayarré, 3:153. [Insertion point estimated.]

37. Fenner, 1:59–62.

38. *DeBow's Review* 11:481; Fenner 1:19.

39. Fenner, 1:18, 39, 65–71.

40. *DeBow's Review* 19:429.

41. Ibid., 1:139, 4:138.

42. Fenner, 1:22.

43. *DeBow's Review* 8:589, 10:94–76.

44. *DeBow's Review* 13:48, 15:216, 25:232, 26:340.

45. *DeBow's Review* 11:322, 329, 15:209, 19:88, 22:432.

46. *DeBow's Review* 10:365.

47. *DeBow's Review* 15:304; see also *DeBow's Review* 3:346, for the municipality debts of 1847.

48. Norman, frontispiece (1845); *DeBow's Review,* vol. 1, frontispiece (1846).

49. *DeBow's Review* 10:365–66.

50. *DeBow's Review* 11: 494, 495, 489.

51. *DeBow's Review* 15:525, 526, 528; New Orleans Board of Aldermen, 13.

52. *DeBow's Review* 13:104, 7:269.

53. *DeBow's Review* 17:15.

54. *DeBow's Review* 13:534.

55. A Balize towboat company contracted with the government to open a channel by harrowing and did open one; but it soon was as bad as ever. *DeBow's Review* 26:432.

56. *DeBow's Review* 17:15–25.

57. *True Republican,* July 17, 1837; *Picayune,* Aug. 7, 1840; ibid., Aug 16, 1840, etc.

58. *DeBow's Review* 13:33.

59. *DeBow's Review* 15:635; Fenner, 1:134.

60. Chaillé, table 3.

61. Ibid., tables 2 and 3.

62. *DeBow's Review* 2:349. Three years later this truly invaluable chronicler abandoned so untenable a ground and became one of the earliest advocates of sanitary reform in New Orleans.

63. *DeBow's Review* 11:487, 8:500, 15:598; Chaillé, table 1.

64. Dr. Symonds in *DeBow's Review* 9:460.

65. Fenner, 1:22; *DeBow's Review* 9:228.

66. Projected and contracted for work to commence before the end of 1881.

67. *DeBow's Review* 2:73.

68. Put into satisfactory operation in 1880–81 by the N.O. Auxilliary [*sic*] Sanitary Association.

69. Fenner, 1:23.

70. *DeBow's Review* 13:312.

71. *DeBow's Review* 15:599.

72. Ibid., 15:599, 603.

73. Ibid., 15:602, 603.

74. Ibid., [15:]608, quoting newspapers.

75. Ibid., 15:619, quoting daily papers of New Orleans.

76. Ibid., 15:620, 621, 622.

77. The unreasonableness of attributing only 8,200 of this number to the epidemic is manifest.

78. *DeBow's Review* 15:595–635.

79. Chaillé's *Vital Statistics,* table 1. This admirable report of the Louisiana state board of health for 1880 gives 102 as the death rate of 1853; but if allowance be made for the large exodus that occurred long before the fever had reached its worst, the true rate will be higher than that given by either of these authorities.

80. Louisiana State Board of Health (1880, Dr. Jos. Jones, president), mortality table facing p. 226. [In Cable's manuscript the population figure is 156,000 instead of 145,000.]

81. Ibid.

82. New Orleans Sanitary Commission.

83. *New Orleans Medical and Surgical Journal,* 15:817.

84. Louisiana State Board of Health (1880), tables facing p. 226.

85. *DeBow's Review* 17:530, 23:372, 21:511, 23:364, 365, 369; New Orleans Board of Aldermen.

86. New Orleans Board of Aldermen. [Though the footnote number is inserted in the text, Cable provides no citation. I've assumed this is the correct source, based on penciled-out deletions.]

87. *DeBow's Review* 25:559, 26:24, 325, 25:469, 564, 27:478, 29:662.

88. *[New Orleans] Price-Current,* Annual Statement, Sep. 1, 1860.

/

WORKS CITED BY CABLE

American State Papers. *Documents, Legislative and Executive, of the Congress of the United States.* Selected and edited under the authority of Congress. 38 vols. Washington, DC: Gales and Seaton, 1832–61.

Barbé-Marbois, François. *The History of Louisiana, Particularly of the Cession of That Colony to the United States of America, With an Introductory Essay on the Constitution and Government of the United States.* Philadelphia: Carey & Lea, 1830. Reprint, edited with an introduction by E. Wilson Lyon, Baton Rouge: Louisiana State University Press for American Revolution Bicentennial Commission, 1977.

Baudry des Lozières, Louis Narcisse. *Voyage à la Louisiane, et sur le continent de l'Amérique Septentrionale, fait dans les années 1794 à 1798; contenant un tableau historique de la Louisiane.* . . . Paris: Dentu, 1802.

Bénard de La Harpe, Jean-Baptiste. *Journal historique de l' établissment des Français à la Louisiane.* New Orleans: A. L. Boimare, 1831.

Bernhard, Duke of Saxe-Weimar-Eisenach. *Travels through North America, during the Years 1825 and 1826.* 2 vols. Philadelphia: Carey, Lea & Carey, 1828.

Berquin-Duvallon, Pierre-Louis. *Vue de la colonie espagnole du Mississipi, ou des provinces de Louisiane et Floride occidentale en l'année 1802.* Paris: Imprimerie expéditive, 1803.

Bryant, William Cullen. *A Popular Bryant's History of the United States: From the First Discovery of the Western Hemisphere by the Northmen, to the End of the First Century of the Union of These States.* 4 vols. New York: Scribner, Armstrong, and Company, 1876–81.

Chaillé, Stanford Emerson. *Vital Statistics of New Orleans: From 1769 to 1874.* [New Orleans:] Jas. A Gresham, 1874.

Charlevoix, Pierre-François-Xavier de. *Histoire et description generale de la Nouvelle France, avec le Journal historique d'un voyage fait par ordre du roi dans l'Amérique Septentrionnale.* 6 vols. Paris: Chez Rollin fils, 1744.

DeBow's Review (and *DeBow's Commercial Review of the South & West*). Vols. 1–27. New Orleans: J. D. B. DeBow , 1846–57.

Dumont de Montigny, François-Benjamin. *Mémoires historique sur la Louisiane contenant ce qui y est arrivé de plus mémorable depuis l'année 1687: jusqu'à présent.* . . . 2 vols. Paris: C. J. B. Bauche, 1753.

Encyclopedia Britannica. 7th edition. Edinburgh: A. & E. Clark, 1830–42.

Fenner, Erasmus Darwin. *Southern Medical Reports.* 2 vols. New Orleans: B. M. Norman, 1849–50.

Gayarré, Charles. *Histoire de la Louisiane*. 2 vols. New Orleans: Magne & Weisse, 1846–47.

––––––. *History of Louisiana*. 4 vols. New Orleans: Redfield, 1854–66.

Hardee, Thomas S. [?] *Official Maps of Louisiana and Mississippi*. 1871, 1872.

Hutchins, Thomas. "Louisiana and West Florida." In *A Topographical Description of the Western Territory of North America; Containing a Succinct Account of Its Soil, Climate, Natural History, Population, Agriculture, Manners & Customs . . .* , by Gilbert Imlay, 3rd ed. London: J. Debrett, 1797.

Latour, A. Lacarrière. *Historical Memoir of the War in West Florida and Louisiana in 1814–15*. Translated for the author from French by H. P. Nugent. Philadelphia: John Conrad and Company, 1816.

Leovy, Henry J. *The Laws and General Ordinances of the City of New Orleans, Together with the Acts of the Legislature, Decisions of the Supreme Court, and Constitutional Provisions Relating to the City Government*. New Orleans: Simmons & Co., 1870.

Le Page du Pratz, Antoine Simon. *Histoire de la Louisiane, contenant la découverte de ce vaste pays; sa description géographique; un voyage dans les terres; l'histoire naturelle, les moeurs coûtumes & religion des naturels, avec leurs origines; deux voyages dans le nord du nouveau Mexique, dont un jusqu'à la Mer du Sud; ornée de deux cartes & de 40 planches en taille douce*. 3 vols. Paris: De Bure, l'aîné, 1758.

Levasseur, Auguste. *Lafayette in America in 1824 and 1825; or, Journal of a Voyage to the United States*. 2 vols. Philadelphia: Carey & Lea, 1829.

Louisiana State Board of Health. *Report of the Louisiana State Board of Health*. Baton Rouge, 1880.

Martin, François-Xavier. *The History of Louisiana, from the Earliest Period*. 2 vols. New Orleans: Lyman and Beardslee, 1827–29.

Martineau, Harriet. *Retrospect of Western Travel*. 2 vols. London: Saunders and Otley, 1838.

Merrick, E. T. "The Laws of Louisiana and Their Sources. Read before the New Orleans Academy of Sciences in 1871." *American Law Register* 38, no. 1, new series, vol. 29 (second series, vol. 3) (Jan. 1890): 1–21.

Monette, John Wesley. *History of the Discovery and Settlement of the Valley of the Mississippi, by the Three Great European Powers, Spain, France, and Great Britain, and the Subsequent Occupation, Settlement and Extension of Civil Government by the United States until the Year 1846*. 2 vols. New York: Harper & Brothers, 1846.

New Orleans Board of Aldermen. Finance Committee. *Report upon the Wealth, Internal Resources and Commercial Prosperity of the City of New Orleans*. New Orleans: Bulletin Book and Job Office, 1855.

New Orleans Daily Picayune.

New Orleans Directory for 1842: Comprising the Names, Residences and Occupations of the Merchants . . . and Citizens of New Orleans, Lafayette, Algiers and Gretna. Together with Historical Notices of the State of Louisiana, the City of New Orleans . . . A Record of the Victims of the Epidemic

of 1841, and the Details of the General Business of the City of New Orleans. 2 vols. New Orleans: Pitts & Clarke, 1842.

New Orleans Medical and Surgical Journal. New Orleans: Louisiana State
Medical Society, 1844–73.

*New Orleans Price-Current, Commercial Intelligencer, and Merchants' Tran-
script.*

New Orleans Sanitary Commission. *Report of the Sanitary Commission of
New Orleans on the Epidemic Yellow Fever, of 1853.* Published by au-
thority of the New Orleans City Council. New Orleans: printed at the
Picayune office, 1854.

Norman, Benjamin Moore. *Norman's New Orleans and Environs.* New Orleans: B. M. Norman, 1845.

Paxton, John A. *Paxton's New Orleans Directory of 1822.* New Orleans: John
A. Paxton, 1822.

Perrin du Lac, [François] M[arie]. *Voyage dans les deux Louisiane . . . et
chez les nations sauvages du Missouri, par les Etats-Unis, l'Ohio et les
provinces qui le bordent, en 1801, 1802 et 1803.* Lyons: Bruysset aîné et
Buynand, 1805.

*Report of the Board of Administrators of the Charity Hospital to the General
Assembly of the State of Louisiana.* New Orleans: The Hospital, 1842–77.

True Republican, and Newbern Weekly Advertiser. New Bern, NC, 1810–37.

U.S. Census Office. First through tenth decennial censuses. Washington,
DC: U.S. Census Office, 1790–1880.

Winterbotham William. *An Historical, Geographical, Commercial, and Philosophical View of the United States of America, and of the European Settlements in America and the West-Indies.* 4 vols. New York: Tiebout and
O'Brien, 1796.

INDEX

Adair, John, 119
Adams, 100
Afro-Creoles. *See also* Creoles, black
Almonsester y Roxas, Andrés, 90–91,
    109, 171
Aragon, Pedro, 109
Armesto, Andreas Lopez de, 109
Aubry, Charles-Phillipe, 62, 64, 65,
    66–67, 70
Axson, A. Forster, 175

Baker, Marion, 7, 19, 23
Baker, Page, 7, 18
Bancroft, George, 6, 9, 14, 23, 25
Baratarians: at Battle of New Orleans,
    132–33; mentioned, 128, 129
Barton, Edward H., 175
Batture riots, 123
Bassett, John Spencer, 25
Beauregard, P. G. T., 18
Beluche, Renato, 133
Benjamin, Judah P., 168
Bienville, Jean-Baptiste Le Moyne
    Sieur de: founds New Orleans, 39–40;
    death of, 68; Indian campaigns of, 44;
    removed from command, 44
Black, William, 6
Bolivar, Simon, 145
Bollman, Erick, 119
Bonaparte, Napoleon, 101, 112, 123,
    127
Boston Transcript, 29
Bradford, William, 119
Bras Coupé, 7, 17
Braud, Denis, 69, 70
Burke, Glendy, 161
Burr, Aaron, 116, 118, 119, 120

Cabildo, 73–75. *See also* New Orleans:
    municipal government in

Cable, George Washington: Civil War
    service of, 3; family and professional
    background of, 3–4, 6; religiosity of,
    3–4; as historian, 2, 6–7, 8–9, 22,
    25–26; lectures with Mark Twain, 1;
    literary career and legacy of, 1–2, 30;
    as journalist, 4; on mixed schools, 5,
    7; on "public rights," 8; racial views
    of, 5, 15–16; as reformer, 4–5, 9,
    28–29; relationship with Gayarré,
    15–21; relations with social elite, 6,
    17–18; relations with white Creoles,
    9–10; reliance on Gayarré's history,
    22–23, 25; relocates to Massachu-
    setts, 8, 28–29; views on black Cre-
    oles, 7, 9; views on white Creoles,
    9–10, 27
Cajuns (Acadians), 51, 66, 81
Calena, Francisco de la, 109
Canary Islanders (Isleños), 81–82
Canonge, Placide, 10, 12
Caresse, Pierre, 66, 69, 70
Carondelet, Francisco Louis Hector de,
    88, 91, 93, 94, 97, 98, 99, 100, 107,
    173
Carroll, William, 133
Casket girls, 47, 54
Caso Calvo, Sebastien Marqués de,
    101, 115, 117
Censuses, 87
Century magazine, 16, 19, 25
Charity Hospital, 90, 158, 176, 177
Charles III, 77
Choiseul, Duc du, 61, 68
Claiborne, William Charles Cole, 102,
    112, 113, 114, 115, 118, 119, 120,
    122–23, 124, 126, 127, 128, 130, 131,
    138, 141, 160
Clark, Daniel, 115, 116
Clark, George Rogers, 94, 98